Society and Homicide in
Thirteenth-Century England

Society and Homicide in Thirteenth-Century England

JAMES BUCHANAN GIVEN

Stanford University Press, Stanford, California 1977

Stanford University Press
Stanford, California
© 1977 by the Board of Trustees of the
Leland Stanford Junior University
Printed in the United States of America
ISBN 0-8047-0939-4
LC 76-23372

Published with the assistance of
The Andrew W. Mellon Foundation

In memory of my father, Ivan A. Given

Preface

It can be argued that in order to be a pacifist one must be fascinated by violence. Whether or not this is so, I began research on this book during the Vietnam War while I was working as a conscientious objector at a state mental hospital in New York. Most of the hospital's patients came from a slum in New York City, from strata of American society where violence is far more common and far more acceptable than it is among the wealthy suburban and academic circles in which I have passed most of my life. While working at the hospital I knew on intimate terms for the first time homicides, rapists, and arsonists. And a few of the people whom I had come to know well in the hospital died violently—whether as suicides or as the victims of murderous assaults—after being discharged. As a result of these experiences, understanding the roots of violence, both in others and in myself, became an important question for me. In this book I hope that through a study of homicide in a medieval society I have contributed something to a formulation of answers to these questions.

In preparing this work, which was originally submitted to the Department of History at Stanford University as a doctoral dissertation, I have accumulated many debts. Grants from the Mabelle McLeod Lewis Memorial Fund and the James Birdsall

Weter Fund allowed me to do archival research in England in 1973 and 1974. The staff of the Public Record Office, especially Mr. C. A. F. Meekings and Mr. R. F. Hunnisett, and the staffs of the British Museum, the Corporation of London Records Office, and the Institute of Historical Research of the University of London were unfailingly courteous and helpful to me, often no mean achievement in light of the economic difficulties that Britain experienced in the winter of 1973–74.

I also wish to thank the staff of the Stanford Center for Information Processing for their aid in mastering the mysteries of their computers. James Inverarity, now of the Department of Sociology at the University of California, Los Angeles, helped me in designing the schema by which the information I had gathered in the English archives was translated into a form that could be fed into a computer and, together with Gloria Guth, one of my fellow history graduate students, held my hand while I took my first tottering steps in the field of cybernetics.

Alan Bernstein and Paul Seaver of the Stanford History Department read this work in its initial stages with a care unusual among second and third readers of a doctoral thesis and made many valuable suggestions. Ruth Kittel of the Mills College History Department, Jane Collier of the Stanford Anthropology Department, and Paul Hyams of Pembroke College, Oxford, also read this work in manuscript, and made many valuable criticisms and suggestions. Although Barbara Hanawalt of the University of Indiana History Department has not read any of this work, I have benefited from a number of conversations with her.

George Behlmer, Genevieve Steele Edwards, James Robertson, Cheryl Sullivan, Timothy Tackett, and Ruth Shepard—my fellow students in either history or medieval studies—contributed encouragement and aid in the writing of this work and I am indebted to all of them. Mrs. Loraine Sinclair, the graduate secretary of the Stanford History Department, throughout the course of my graduate career has been a good friend and unfailing champion. And the editors and others at Stanford University Press, while holding me to their usual high standards, have been a delight to work with.

My principal debt of gratitude, however, is owed to Gavin Langmuir, my adviser as a graduate student. Not only did he originally formulate this project, provide guidance and encouragement, and allow me to use his office to write the first draft; his skillful and incisive editing produced a second draft far superior to the first in organization. More important, he has provided a model for me of what a scholar and a historian should be. Much of whatever merit this book may have is attributable to Professor Langmuir.

ERRATA

On p. 30, line 16, the author's estimate of the population of the county of Warwick, as calculated on the basis of Domesday Book, is incorrectly given as 31,900. The correct figure is 78,500.

The following changes in homicide rates for Warwick should be made: p. 36, Table 2, column 4, rows 21–24: "16, 26, 19, 19" for "38, 64, 48, 47"; p. 107, Table 15, column 4, rows 16–18: "0.5, 1.6, 1.3" for "1.2, 3.9, 3.2"; p. 136, Table 17, column 3, rows 11–12: "15.3, 3.3" for "38.2, 8.3"; p. 35, line 33: "26/100,000" for "64/ 100,000"; p. 35, line 36, p. 157, line 1, and p. 170, line 11: "19/ 100,000" for "47/100,000"; p. 55, line 25: "0.8/100,000" for "2.1/ 100,000"; p. 168, line 3 of notes: "3.3" for "8.3." The following changes should also be made: p. 56, lines 8–9: delete "Warwick" after "Kent" and insert after "Bedford"; p. 108, line 2: "five" for "seven"; p. 155, bottom line: delete "exceedingly."

The corrected Warwickshire homicide rates are considerably lower than those given in the text and make Warwick only the third most violent county. Statements in the text, especially those on pp. 35, 151–52, 155–57, and 170, concerning Warwick's high homicide rates, should therefore be treated with caution.

James Buchanan Given,
Society and Homicide in Thirteenth-Century England

Contents

Tables

Society and Homicide in
Thirteenth-Century England

Introduction

Homicide is a social relationship. For a killing to take place, at least two people must interact, if only for a single moment. To onlookers, and to those who later attempt to reconstruct the circumstances surrounding a slaying, a murder may at first seem to be a senseless, irrational event, the product of unfathomable psychological processes. Yet even the most bizarre and apparently unmotivated murder is not without social meaning. Like every other form of human behavior, murder is patterned by the prevailing relationships—affective, economic, political— that exist within a society. Each society therefore has its own specific patterns of violent behavior, patterns that are as characteristic of it and as unique to it as the way in which its members secure their food, raise their children, and choose their leaders.

The study of the patterns of violence and murder in a given society dramatically reveals the web of interrelationships that unite its members, and the tensions and conflicts that these relationships engender. A study of homicide is therefore of value to anyone interested in the dynamics of social interaction. It is of even greater interest and value for a medieval historian. Despite the excellent work done on the social history of medieval Europe in this century, the image of medieval society it has presented to us is full of lacunae. Much is known of the structure of society—

the ranks and orders of men and their legal obligations to one another, the distribution of wealth and power, and the means by which men gained their living. But this image is largely static. The groups that composed society may be well known in outline, but the ways in which these groups, or individuals, interacted remain largely unexplored. This is especially true of the peasantry, the shadowy mass that made up the bulk of the population. Rarely do medieval records allow the peasants to be seen as anything other than ciphers, a wealth-producing resource that owed to its rulers labor, money, respect, and deference. A study of the patterns of homicide in one medieval society, thirteenth-century England, however, provides a means by which we can penetrate beyond this static façade and grasp some of the dynamics of life in medieval Europe.

In analyzing these patterns of homicide, I have relied primarily on court records. This has made this study primarily a quantitative one. No other approach to the laconic court records upon which it has been based would have yielded readily usable results. My method has been to discern what patterns emerge from a quantitative analysis of jurors' verdicts and then to search for corroborative or illustrative material in other sources—chronicles, letters, didactic works, and so forth. In many instances, I failed to find such corroborative material. In such cases the reader should bear in mind that my hypotheses about the patterns I have found are even more than normally conjectural.

Although this study bristles with what I hope the reader will find impressive and persuasive tables and statistics, he should beware of ascribing to them more validity than they possess. The court rolls that have been analyzed in this study are indeed a mirror for their society, but a mirror in which the outlines of many things only appear darkly. For the purposes of analysis I have been forced to accept the jurors' verdicts at face value and to proceed on the assumption that the killings the jurors report took place essentially as they describe them. Most important, I have had to assume that all those accused of having committed a murder probably did so. In addition, some distortions and biases have undoubtedly crept into the analysis by virtue of the fact that the events described in the rolls have been filtered through many minds and many different languages. Much of the business transacted in the courts must have been in various dialects of thirteenth-century English. These discussions were in turn recorded by clerks, who probably spoke Anglo-Norman as their first language, in yet another language, the Latin of the English administrative machine. This has in turn been filtered through my mind, which thinks in American English, and translated by it into a language comprehensible to a computer. The figures that ultimately emerged from the computer are thus at many removes from the actual events that occurred 700 years ago in England. However, I hope that the large size of the sample with which I have worked has offset these biases and distortions, and that the patterns I have discovered existed not only in thirteenth-century court rolls but in thirteenth-century society. The rolls may be a dark and obscure mirror, but I believe that they still reveal the outlines of medieval English violence with fidelity.

1. The Records and the Societies

Thirteenth-century England is probably the only region of northern Europe for which a systematic study of homicide can be made. Some Italian city-states in the fourteenth century may have kept records that could be used for such a study. But north of the Alps no country other than England produced records at such an early date which deal so thoroughly with homicidal activity. Not only did England produce large numbers of chronicles, legal treatises, letters, and didactic works which at times deal with homicide; it has also left behind massive legal records which permit a statistical analysis of the phenomenon of medieval murder. The most important of these records are the rolls that recorded the sessions of the eyres *ad omnia placita*.

The eyres, whose origins lay in the twelfth century, were one of the chief means by which the Angevin kings of England welded their realm into a unified political entity. Not only did they bring the king's justices into the counties on a periodic basis; they generated a large amount of revenue and provided a means of controlling the conduct of sheriffs, bailiffs, coroners, and the host of other administrative figures with which England abounded in the Middle Ages.

An eyre was a visitation of a county, made every few years, by a panel of royal justices empowered to hear and determine every type of action that could be heard in a royal court. The justices in eyre could try all civil actions, all crimes, and inquire into the conduct of any authorities charged with maintaining the king's peace or his rights.[1] The moment the justices formally opened their session, their jurisdiction superseded that of the local courts and of all other judicial commissions within the county. The central court at Westminster would thenceforth refuse to hear any cases originating in the county and would send them down to be tried at the eyre.[2]

The justices transacted a great deal of civil business, but what is of interest for this study is the criminal side of their jurisdiction. By the thirteenth century the English kings had managed to establish a virtual monopoly of the right to judge crimes that involved the possible loss of life or limb as a punishment. Since the only penalty that medieval English law knew for criminally culpable homicide was death, this made the judgment of homicide an exclusively royal matter. Therefore the justices in eyre were required to inquire into all homicides that had occurred since the last eyre. To do this, they had recourse to that all-purpose instrument of medieval English law, the jury. In thirteenth-century England, shires were subdivided into smaller territorial units, known as hundreds or wapentakes, each with its own court. In addition, each county contained a number of towns with the privileged legal status of boroughs. When the shire was informed that it would undergo a visitation by the justices in eyre, each hundred and each borough were required to produce a jury of twelve men. The bailiff of each district chose two men as electors. They in turn chose ten others to serve with them as jurors.[3] When the justices opened their session, each jury was presented with a list of questions, known as the articles of the eyre, which they had to answer. Among other matters, the articles required them to report on "all deaths from violence (including accidents) and suspicious causes, all capital executions by judgment of the courts in the county or on persons from the hundred in courts elsewhere, all abjurations of the realm by self-confessed felons, and all appeals."[4] Having received a copy of the articles, the jurors retired to draw up their reply. This document was known as their *veredictum.*[5] When the various juries had handed in their veredicta, the process of hearing the pleas began. The justices proceeded hundred by hundred and borough by borough through the veredicta.

This is an important point, for it means that in the rolls that were handed in at Westminster after the eyre, the homicide cases were arranged by hundreds and boroughs. This makes possible a more sophisticated analysis than would otherwise be possible. First of all, the distinction between boroughs and hundreds makes it possible to see how patterns of homicide differed in urban and rural areas. Second, from other sources it is possible to learn a fair amount about individual hundreds and boroughs. The great inquests carried out at the end of the thirteenth century and the tax lists that began to proliferate at the beginning of the fourteenth century provide information about the distribution of wealth and the structure of lordship within individual hundreds. All this information can be used to illuminate the phenomenon of homicide in medieval England.

The nature of the information found in the surviving eyre rolls themselves is illustrated by the following example, taken from the presentment made by the jurors of Barlichway Hundred during the 1221 eyre of Warwickshire: [6]

Nicholas Hawene of Bidford appealed Peter son of Livitha, Sandulf his brother, and Roger son of Cecily of the death of William his son. All have fled and are outlawed by Nicholas' suit, and they were in the frankpledge of Brian of Bidford in Bidford, which is therefore in mercy. Peter's chattels, 2 shillings and 6 pence, whence let the sheriff answer. No Englishry, and therefore murder.

This entry provides information about both the victim and his killers. That relating to the victim is rather less full than that dealing with his alleged killers. For the victim usually little more than his or her name is given. At times not even this is listed, the victim being described simply as an *ignotus* or an *extraneus.* Yet even if the victim is not identified, his or her sex is almost invariably specified. Very small infants, on the other hand, seem to

have been described simply as *pueri,* and unless they are specifically named there often is some ambiguity about their sex. The
entry will also on occasion give an occupational surname. By the
thirteenth century the surnames of the upper classes had largely
become fixed. For the lower classes this process had not yet been
completed, and it is very possible that someone called a *car-
bonarius* in the records was at least some time in his life engaged
in the manufacture of charcoal, although this might not have
been his only trade.[7] Occasionally the records will tell, although
they do not do so in this case, where the victim was killed and
with what kind of weapon.

If the death resulted in an appeal, the eyre rolls invariably
record this fact. An appeal was a highly formal and formalistic
accusation, which in the case of a homicide could only be made
by a blood relative of the deceased, or by someone bound to him
by ties of homage or lordship.[8] The appellor was supposed to
make his appeal at the first meeting of the county court after the
commission of the homicide. If the person making the appeal
was a man and was neither maimed nor too old to fight, he had
to be willing to prove his appeal by offering to fight a duel. If the
accused was present when the appeal was made, he was to be arrested immediately and kept in custody until the coming of the
king's justices, before whom he would be tried. If the accused
was not present, the process of outlawry was begun. At the next
meeting of the county court the appellor repeated his appeal. If
the accused was still not present, he was "exacted," i.e. formally
summoned to attend the county court. If, after the fourth exac-
tion, the accused had still not appeared, he was outlawed.[9] Outlawry was a grave matter. It involved the immediate escheat and
forfeiture of the outlaw's property. And if the outlaw was captured and brought before the justices, he could be hanged on
the mere proof of the fact of his outlawry. Once a person had
begun an appeal, he was expected to see it through to the end,
which meant ultimately appearing before the justices in eyre.
Should he fail to do so, he was liable to imprisonment and
amercement.[10]

The eyre rolls often state that the accused were persons unknown. But, when their identities are known, the rolls contain fuller information about them than they do about their victims. In addition to name, sex, and on occasion occupation, the rolls detail what disposition was made of them in court. If they appeared before the justices, it is stated whether they were acquitted, executed, pardoned, or claimed clerical privilege and were transferred to an ecclesiastical court where they were allowed to purge themselves with the aid of oath-helpers. If they did not appear in court, the rolls state whether they had been or were to be outlawed, whether they had abjured the realm, or had in some other fashion slipped through the net of medieval English justice.

Medieval English law distinguished between principals and accomplices in homicide cases. Accomplices suffered the same penalty as principals, death by hanging, whether they had held a man while his throat was cut or had only counseled or advised the homicide.[11] But since there were procedural differences in the way principals and accomplices were treated in court (e.g. if the principal was acquitted, his accused accomplices were *ipso facto* acquitted without the need of separate trial), they were specified as such in the records.

The chattels, or movable property, of convicted felons, outlaws, and those who had abjured the realm were forfeit to the king. Their value was therefore recorded in the rolls. Undoubtedly, the value placed on a felon's chattels must often have been inaccurate. The exact amount of chattels that a felon or an outlaw possessed may have been underestimated out of feelings of pity for his wife and children. Also, according to English law, the chattels of a married woman were technically the property of her husband, and thus did not find their way into the records. Similarly, the possessions of a son living in his father's household might be construed as belonging to his father. For these reasons the rolls undoubtedly tend to underestimate the true value of a felon's chattels. And just as the king had a right to seize the chattels of a felon, he also had a right to exploit any freehold property he might have had for a year and a day. Therefore, a felon's freehold land was also specified in the rolls.

If an accused killer failed to appear in court, the eyre rolls noted whether or not he belonged to a frankpledge or mainpast. Although frankpledges, also known as tithings, did not exist everywhere in England, they did exist in the counties that will be considered here. The frankpledge essentially functioned as a substitute for a police force. Every male over the age of twelve, free or unfree, was required to be a member of a tithing, with the exceptions of vagabonds, magnates, lords in general, knights, holders of free tenements or of real property in boroughs, and the physically and mentally incapable. Twice a year frankpledges were inspected, at what was known as a "view of frankpledge," to ensure that they were full and that everyone who ought to be in one was. The size of tithings varied from ten men to a number that embraced every adult male in a village. If a member of a frankpledge was accused of having committed a felony, his fellow members were to see to it that he appeared in court to answer to the king's justices. If he failed to appear, they were amerced for this dereliction in their duties. In addition to this system, every man was responsible for the members of his household, his servingmen and on occasion his guests, who were said to be in his "mainpast." In the thirteenth century family members were also at times regarded as members of a man's mainpast. If a member of a man's mainpast committed a felony and did not appear in court, this man was also liable to an amercement. When outsiders moved into a village, they were not immediately admitted to a frankpledge. They had to live in the village for a year and a day before being enrolled, but whoever in the village received them had to answer for them if they committed any crimes.[12]

The eyre rolls also contain various other types of information. The clerks at times noted who first discovered the victim's body, and listed the names of those people who had been present at the killing. Whenever anyone discovered a felony being committed, he was supposed to raise the hue and cry. The neighboring villages were required to turn out to pursue the felon. If they did not, they were liable to an amercement. Consequently, the clerks often recorded which villages failed to fulfill this duty. Similarly, the body of a murder victim was not supposed to be buried until it had been viewed by a coroner. Villages that buried a body before the coroner had held his inquest were subject to an amercement, and this fact is often found in the rolls. But information of this kind is not invariably included, since the practice of the clerks in regard to enrollment of this sort of matter varied from one eyre to another.

One piece of information invariably included in the rolls, the presentment of Englishry and the *murdrum* fine, will not be of any concern in this essay. The murdrum fine, an invention of William the Conqueror, was levied on an entire hundred whenever a dead body was discovered and it could not be proved that the deceased was of Anglo-Saxon as opposed to Norman ancestry. By the thirteenth century what tensions had existed between the Norman conquerors and the Anglo-Saxon conquered had disappeared, and the murdrum fine had simply become a means of extorting money from the countryside. As such, it throws no light on the problem of homicide and will not be discussed here.

The eyre rolls provide a surprising amount of information about thousands of otherwise anonymous medieval English men and women. They make possible a large-scale statistical analysis of the phenomenon of homicide and violent conflict, one that could not be undertaken for any other region in Europe at such an early period. But before the rolls can be exploited in this fashion, the question of their completeness must be addressed. For if any particular type of homicide were systematically omitted from the records, the results of a statistical analysis might be biased and misleading.

Fortunately, and to a degree that is truly amazing in a nonindustrial society where people were not habituated to thinking in terms of numbers and percentages, the records appear to be remarkably complete. This is undoubtedly due in large part to the fact that the king stood to make money out of everyone who died violently in thirteenth-century England. A murder inevitably meant some sort of profit for the king's treasury, whether in the form of a *murdrum* fine, confiscated chattels, the waste of a felon's lands, amercements of appellors who failed to prosecute their appeals, or of juries, coroners, frankpledges, and villages that had somehow failed to fulfill their obligations in the investigation of a homicide and apprehension of the accused.

It might be thought that jurors would have tried to conceal some homicides out of fear or favoritism when a powerful man was involved. Similarly, if the killing had been the work of unknown culprits who had gotten away scot-free, juries might have tried to cover it up out of a desire to protect their communities from the rapacity of royal justices ever on the lookout for the opportunity to amerce someone. Since eyres often took place at rather long intervals, it is also possible that the jurors might simply have forgotten a number of deaths that had occurred many years before. However, the underreporting of violent deaths by juries was kept to a minimum by the coroners' rolls, which provided the justices with a means of checking on the jurors' veredicta. From the end of the twelfth century each county, and many boroughs and liberties, were required to have coroners. The office of coroner, or keeper of the pleas of the crown, had been created in 1194, when the justices in eyre were required to see to it that three knights and one clerk were elected to that office in each county.[13] However, it rapidly became common practice for each county to have only two coroners.

The coroners were expected to perform a great variety of duties, such as receiving the abjurations of felons who had taken refuge in churches, hearing the appeals of approvers, and investigating the discovery of treasure trove. But of greater importance is the fact that they were required to investigate the deaths of all people who died violently, whether by accident, as the result of homicide, or under suspicious circumstances. Upon the discovery of a body, the coroner was supposed to be summoned immediately to hold an inquest. But getting the coroner to appear was not often easy. Coroners were notorious for expecting to be bribed before they would perform their duties.[14] Yet once the sufficiently bribed coroner arrived on the scene, he summoned an inquest jury, which in the thirteenth century consisted of men from four or more of the townships adjacent to the place where the killing had taken place or the body had been discovered. At the inquest the coroner and the jury examined the body and measured any wounds on it. They were also required to determine whether the victim had been killed where he had been found. If he had been killed elsewhere, they had to attempt to locate the exact place of his death. The first finder of the body, anyone who had been present at the killing, and the four nearest neighbors of the victim were required to find pledges to guarantee their appearance before the king's justices. If anyone had been arrested for the deed, the coroner sent that person to the local jail. If no one had been arrested but the jury suspected someone, the coroner ordered that person's arrest. If the accused had any movable property, the coroner and the jury valued it.[15] If anyone related to the victim wished to make an appeal, the coroner also had to note it and its subsequent course in the county court. All these proceedings were recorded on loose pieces of parchment by the coroner's clerk.

When the justices in eyre opened their session, the coroners, or their heirs if they had died since the justices last visited the county, were required to surrender their records. The coroners assembled their files of inquests and appeals. Their clerks then made a fair copy of them onto a continuous roll. On the first day of the eyre, these rolls were given to the justices and kept in sealed pouches until the pleas were heard. The members of the presenting juries thus had no access to them when drawing up their veredicta. As the cases were heard, the jurors' veredicta were checked against the coroners' rolls and the veredicta annotated by the justices' clerks. Any discrepancy resulted in the amercement of either coroner or jury.[16]

This system of double-checking the veredicta against the coroners' rolls and the coroners' rolls against the veredicta produced remarkably complete records. There are, nonetheless, some errors and omissions in them. The rolls provide a much fuller list of victims than of accused. Although dead bodies could not usually be disposed of discreetly, it is possible that both juries and coroners may on occasion have doctored the records to protect powerful men or because they felt that a particular homicide had either been justified or excusable and they wished to protect the culprit from the rigors of the law.[17] It also appears that information may have been left out or distorted as the result of purely clerical errors. Coroners' clerks, in making fair copies from the original files, may have made mistakes in the process of transcription. The clerks of the justices may have made further slips in the process of drawing up the final rolls using the annotated veredicta. A few veredicta have survived from the thirteenth century and can be compared with the entries found on the corresponding eyre rolls. The veredictum delivered by the jurors of the Wiltshire hundred of Chippenham in 1281 reported eleven homicides committed by unknown assailants. One of these cases was not copied onto the eyre roll. Similarly, of 21 homicides where the identity of the killer was known to the jurors, one case was also omitted from the final roll.[18]

Despite these errors of omission, the eyre rolls portray violent conflict in medieval England with a completeness that is unmatched by the records of any other country in northern Europe in the Middle Ages. In England itself, such thorough records were not kept again after the beginning of the fourteenth century until the nineteenth, when professional police forces were organized. The eyre rolls thus afford a unique glimpse into the lives of thousands of thirteenth-century Europeans.

The very completeness of the eyre rolls, of which there are over 100 in the Public Record Office in London, raises certain methodological problems. The rolls contain more information than can be dealt with by the traditional techniques of the historian. Therefore, in this study I have limited myself to an analysis

Table 1. *List of Eyres Analyzed*

County	Date	Document no.	Approximate no. of months since last eyre
Bedford	1202	J.I.1/1	47
	1227	J.I.1/2	104
	1247	J.I.1/4	83
	1276	J.I.1/10	172
Bristol	1221	J.I.1/271, 272	212
	1248	J.I.1/274	83
Kent	1227	J.I.1/358	99
	1241	J.I.1/359	61
	1255	J.I.1/361	83
Norfolk	1250	J.I.1/565	62
	1257	J.I.1/568	78
	1268–69	J.I.1/569a	130
Oxford	1241	J.I.1/695, 696	69
	1247	J.I.1/700	78
	1261	J.I.1/701	99
Warwick	1221–22	J.I.1/950	155
	1232	J.I.1/951a	67
	1247	J.I.1/952	82
London	1244	Corp. of London Rec. Office, Misc. Roll AA	216
	1276	British Museum, Add. Ch. 5153	290

SOURCE : Except where otherwise noted, all documents are from the London PRO. The Bristol pleas are taken from the eyre rolls for the county of Gloucester. The information in the last column is based on material kindly supplied me by Mr. C. A. F. Meekings, formerly of the Public Record Office, and Mr. Martin Weinbaum.

Of the above rolls, the following have been published.

Bedford: G. H. Fowler, *Roll of the Justices in Eyre at Bedford, 1202* (the roll of the sessions held at Dunstable has been lost), *Roll of the Justices in Eyre at Bedford, 1227,* and *Calendar of the Roll of the Justices in Eyre, 1247.*

Bristol: F. W. Maitland, *Pleas of the Crown for the County of Gloucestershire . . . in . . . the Year of Grace 1221.*

Warwick: D. M. Stenton, *Rolls of the Justices in Eyre . . . for . . . Warwickshire . . . 1221, 1222.*

London: H. M. Chew and Martin Weinbaum, *The London Eyre of 1244,* and Martin Weinbaum, *The London Eyre of 1276.* This latter edition appeared too late for me to make use of it. However, Mr. William Kellaway, the honorary general editor of the London Record Society publications, kindly allowed me to consult a manuscript version.

of only twenty rolls, drawn from the counties of Bedford, Kent, Norfolk, Oxford and Warwick and the cities of London and Bristol. See Table 1.

With two exceptions, the originals of all these rolls are today in the Public Record Office in London. The original roll for the

1244 London eyre has not survived. Sometime around 1276, however, the now lost original was copied for the City of London and this roll is now among the City's archives. It appears that the original roll for the 1276 London eyre came into the City of London's possession in the late fourteenth century. It is last mentioned as forming part of the city archives in the fifteenth century. Thereafter it was lost sight of until 1841, when the British Museum acquired it. The roll was apparently annotated by London clerks in the late fourteenth century, and the consequent strange appearance of the roll has led some historians to regard the surviving roll as a copy. Even this relatively small sample of eyre rolls provides information on 2,434 victims and 3,492 accused killers.* To cope with this large number of people, it has been found necessary to utilize a computer.

THE SOCIETIES

In the thirteenth century, England was a far from socially homogeneous country. The way of life of the people who dwelt in the high mountain valleys of Cumberland and Westmoreland was very different from that of those who lived in the open plains of the Midlands or in the scattered hamlets of Kent. Language, settlement patterns, personal status, the impress of lords on villagers, and the ways of winning a living from the land differed substantially from one region of England to another. From isolated crofts to large nucleated villages, England was a microcosm of the diversity of social organization to be found throughout northwestern Europe. Coupled with the unparalleled richness of the English archives, this regional diversity gives the historian a nearly unique opportunity to study the ways in which the members of the different subcultures of which medieval Europe was composed organized themselves and dealt with the problems of living together. In an effort to include as

* Two types of homicide found in the rolls have been systematically excluded from the analysis: (1) those committed outside the county but reported at the eyre; (2) those in which someone was accused solely of unspecified "robberies, burglaries, and homicides."

many of these different types of groupings as possible in this study, five counties—Oxford, Bedford, Kent, Norfolk, and Warwick—together with the cities of London and Bristol, have been selected as the foci for this study. These particular regions were chosen for two reasons. First, there are several surviving eyre rolls for each of these areas; second, the social structure of these regions has been studied in some detail, and we are therefore in a better position to understand the patterns of homicide that emerge from the records. Some areas of England have regrettably been omitted from this study, notably the counties in southwestern England and along the Scottish border. In most cases few or no thirteenth-century eyre rolls survive for these counties. And, in the case of northern England, there has as yet been little investigation of the forms of social organization that existed in the Middle Ages. Despite the fact that the areas included in this study are all in the south and east of England, the diversity of social organization found in them provides us with ample opportunity to see how different social, political, and economic structures affected the patterns of homicidal behavior. Before the patterns of homicide found in the eyre rolls are analyzed, these different types of social organization will be sketched briefly in the following pages.

The common-field regions: the Oxford plains and Bedfordshire. Within the borders of Oxfordshire and Bedfordshire prevailed the system of agriculture known as common-field,* or champion, husbandry. This system of social organization has been de-

---

* The reader may find this terminology strange, for what earlier historians, such as the Orwins, referred to as "open-field" husbandry is now referred to by many historians as "common-field" husbandry. The practice followed by recent writers such as Joan Thirsk, A. R. H. Baker, and R. H. Butlin has been to use the term "open field" to refer to fields composed of unenclosed parcels that are not definitely known to have been cultivated or grazed in common and to reserve the term "common field" for fields over which common rules of cultivation and grazing are known to have operated. I have followed this usage throughout this essay. (See Joan Thirsk, "The Common Fields," *Past and Present,* 29 (1964): 3; A. R. H. Baker, "Some Terminological Problems in Studies of British Field Systems," *Agricultural History Review,* 17 (1969): 136–40; and Baker and Butlin, p. 385, note 5.) For detailed studies of two common-field village communities, see Hoskins, *The Midland Peasant,* and P. D. A. Harvey, *Cuxham.*

scribed in many works, and here it will be sketched in only the briefest terms.[19] The plains of northern Oxford especially were the home of the classic common-field system. Here men lived together in large, compact, "nucleated" villages, surrounded by the great open fields. The holdings of those peasants who possessed land were scattered through the fields in strips. The exploitation of the arable, meadows, and wastes was regulated by the village community as a whole. An individual was not free to sow what he wanted in his strips whenever he wished. The crops to be planted and the times at which they were to be sown and reaped were regulated by the village as a whole. Here also the pressure of lords on the peasants was the most intense and continuous. In his analysis of the Hundred Rolls of 1279, E. A. Kosminsky found that in Oxford, and in Stodden and Willey Hundreds of Bedfordshire, fully one-third of all the land under cultivation was held in demesne by manorial lords.[20] Not only did the lords hold in subjection much of the land; they possessed many of the peasants as their naifs, their serfs. Of 1,071 households recorded in Bampton Hundred in Oxford in 1279, 736 (68.7 percent) were villein households. The figures for Chadlington Hundred were 700 of 1,090 households (64.2 percent), and for Ploughley Hundred 1,081 of 1,321 (81.8 percent).[21] In the county as a whole, almost twice as much land was held in villein tenure as in free tenure, 4,043½ virgates as opposed to 2,485½.[22] Here, as perhaps nowhere else in medieval England, manor and village tended to coincide. The Hundred Rolls show that in 191 Oxfordshire villages (63.2 percent) manor and village were coterminous, whereas in only 111 villages they were not.[23] In those villages where village and manor coincided, the unity of the village community was reinforced by the unity of lordship.

Bedford was, like Oxford, an area of common-field husbandry. Although the survival of the Hundred Roll inquest for only Willey Hundred and a portion of Stodden Hundred makes it impossible to know Bedfordshire as well as Oxfordshire, this county, which had anciently been part of the southern Danelaw, manifested some differences from Oxford. The settlement pattern tended to be more scattered.[24] The chief distinguishing characteristic, however, was the fact that lords did not control the peasants as closely as they did in Oxfordshire.[25] Although Bedfordshire lords held in demesne as much of the land as their Oxford counterparts (about one-third of the total),[26] their control of the villagers was not as thorough. In contrast to the situation in Oxfordshire, where many manors engulfed entire villages or parishes and lords were thus able to control the life of an entire community, in Bedfordshire the manors rarely embraced an entire village. Kosminsky found that, in 1279 in the two northern hundreds of Willey and Stodden, in only seven of the 25 recorded villages were manor and village coterminous.[27] Since lordship was more attenuated in this county, personal freedom was more widespread than in Oxfordshire. Of 1,435 households recorded in the Hundred Rolls, 930 (64.8 percent) were free, whereas only 505 (35.2 percent) were servile.[28]

Little is as yet known of family structure in Oxfordshire and Bedfordshire. Virtually all that is known for certain are the rules that governed the descent of land. In the common-field regions of England a regime of impartible inheritance prevailed.[29] A tenement, when the current holder died, descended undivided to a single heir. The widow was allowed to exploit one-third to one-half of her deceased husband's property as her "widow's bench." The heir's siblings, especially brothers, had either to leave the village if they wished to rise in the world or to resign themselves to a life of dependence on the inheriting brother if they remained.

A hill community: the Chilterns. Although Oxfordshire was in large part a common-field region, this form of social organization did not prevail everywhere in the county. The scheme of large common-field villages tightly controlled by lords was largely confined to the plains in the north of the county. In the Chiltern Hills in the south, a somewhat different system existed. Here the settlement pattern was far more diverse. In the valleys there were small nucleated villages, whereas on the ridge-tops and on the plateau small hamlets and isolated farmsteads existed.[30] Even the largest of the common fields were small compared with those that lay in the plains to the north.[31] As opposed to the system of two great common fields that prevailed there, some Hill villages had up to 30 common fields.[32] The ordinary peasant was also less subject to the communal regulations of the village. Large amounts of the arable were not included in the common fields, but were worked separately by individual cultivators.[33] Indeed, the typical peasant held land both in the common fields and in severalty.[34] Although primogeniture was the rule here as in the plains, succession to land was, in effect, more flexible because most tenants had the right to transfer their land during their lifetime,[35] and parents frequently made gifts of a few acres to their noninheriting children.[36] In addition, there was an active land market in the Chilterns, with peasants freely alienating and leasing parcels of land to nonfamily members.[37] The pressure of lords on the peasants was also less intense here than elsewhere in the county. The services that peasants owed their lords were not very heavy,[38] and the Hundred Rolls reveal that there were large numbers of freeholders in the Chilterns in the late thirteenth century. In Pirton, Ewelme, and Langtree Hundreds the percentage of land held freely hovered around 45 percent, as contrasted with figures of 17 percent for Bullingdon Hundred and 20 percent for Ploughley Hundred in the plains.[39]

A region of hamlets and free peasants: Kent. To the south and east of Oxfordshire and Bedfordshire, on the far side of the Chilterns, lay Kent, a county that in the thirteenth century had a unique social structure. In contrast to the Midlands, where men lived in large villages surrounded by the great common fields, in Kent they lived not only in nucleated villages but also in scattered hamlets and isolated farms.[40] Open fields did exist, but they were small and numerous and were based as much on dispersed farms and hamlets as on nucleated villages. And these fields, although open, were not "common" fields. The plots within them were not worked communally, but in severalty by individual peasants.[41]

In this county the peasants were perhaps freer of the constraints of lordship and the village community than anywhere else in England outside the highland and mountainous regions. In an area where settlement was so scattered, it was difficult for lords to maintain tight control over the inhabitants. Manors sprawled disjointedly over the countryside. At Wingham in east Kent, a manor belonging to the archbishop of Canterbury, the tenants were scattered among 34 different hamlets and farmsteads.[42] As a result, it appears that by the thirteenth century the legal freedom of the Kentish peasants had been fairly well established. Gavilkind, Kent's distinctive form of land tenure, was regarded as a free tenure and as such was protected in the royal courts.[43] Indeed, it was a peculiarly privileged form of free tenure. If the gavilkinder defaulted in his service, the lord of the tenement could not immediately distrain upon it, but had to go through a lengthy judicial process involving a delay of at least a year before he could lay hands on the land,[44] and at any time during this process the defaulting tenant could preserve his holding by making amends.[45] The rents that Kentish tenants paid were also small, and they performed few, if any, labor services.[46]

Just as the Kentish peasants were free of constraints imposed by lords, so they were largely free of any restrictions imposed by their fellow villagers. Peasants held and worked their land in severalty. The cultivation of a tenant's land was a private, individualistic affair. The village, in the form of the manorial court, did not intervene to regulate the individual's agrarian activities.[47] Peasants did band together to cooperate in the laborious and all-important task of plowing, but this was "a venture in agricultural cooperation by individuals, by friends, neighbours and relations on an ad hoc basis, rather than a collective enterprise by a manorial community." [48]

With neither lordship nor the village community important as a focus of social integration, the family undoubtedly played a far more important role in social life here than in the Midlands.[49] Although almost as little is known of the nature of Kentish families as is known of their Midland counterparts, it is known that Kentish families differed from Midland ones in one very important respect: whereas in the Midlands the villein's tenement descended intact to a single heir, in Kent gavilkind land descended equally to all a man's male heirs or, in the lack of these, to female heirs.[50] Although groups of brothers or sisters may have maintained the unity of the tenement and worked it jointly in some cases, the physical partition of the estate among the heirs seems to have been more common in the thirteenth century.[51] Not only was gavilkind land divisible among heirs; the holder could freely alienate it during his lifetime.

Some of the Kentish towns—Beksbourne, Grange, New and Old Romney, Lydd, Hythe, Dover, Faversham, Folkestone, Margate, Sandwich, Fordwich, Stonor, and Sarre—were members of the confederation of the Cinque Ports.* The study of the patterns of homicide in these towns that existed principally on sea-borne commerce would have been very interesting. Unfortunately, however, the "barons of the Cinque Ports," as they were called, had the privilege of being tried only in a special court which sat at Shepway and over which the warden of the Cinque Ports presided. The records of these proceedings do not seem to have survived.

An East Anglian community: Norfolk. On the east coast of England, the county of Norfolk had a social system in many ways like that of Kent. Like their confreres in Kent, the East Anglian peasants were largely free of seigneurial control. The extremely small size of manors made it almost impossible for lords to effec-

---

* According to the report made in 1293 by Stephen of Pencester, constable of Dover and warden of the Cinque Ports, the complete confederation then consisted of Hastings with its members Winchelsea, Rye, Pevensey, and Bulvarhythe in Sussex, and Beksbourne and Grange in Kent; Hythe in Kent; New Romney with its members Old Romney and Lydd, all in Kent; Dover with its members Faversham, Folkestone, and Margate; and Sandwich with its members Fordwich, Stonor, and Sarre. (Murray, pp. 241–42.)

tively control the peasants. The Nomina Villarum of 1316 lists 695 villages in the county. In only 163 of these was there one lord. The other 532 villages had more than one lord, usually two or three. In some cases the fragmentation of seigneurial power attained an almost absurd level, as at Wymondham, which was shared among no fewer than thirteen lords.[52] In such a confused situation, it was inevitable that personal freedom should be widespread. Indeed, in the eleventh and twelfth centuries East Anglia, with its history of intensive settlement by Danish peasants, had been unique in England for its large number of freemen and socmen, who frequently had the right to go with their "soke," or right to jurisdiction, where they would.[53] From the end of the twelfth century, the lords, especially the great ecclesiastics, managed to depress the status of these free tenants and bring them more under their control.[54] But the number of freemen remained large, often embracing more than half the population of a township. Even where the lords managed to turn the peasants into villeins, the services that they required of them were much lighter than those imposed on peasants in the Midlands. And the commutation of these light services was very widespread. To draw an example, not from Norfolk itself but from another East Anglian region, in the Cambridgeshire hundred of Chilford in 1279 as much as 48 percent of the land was held in demesne, but only 15 percent was held in villein tenure, whereas more than twice as much, 37 percent, was held freely.[55]

Norfolk peasant families also displayed analogies with Kentish ones, for Norfolk was another area where partible inheritance was widespread, though not universal.[56] In the thirteenth century only land that had anciently been partible, whether villein or socage, was allowed to descend in this fashion. Thus in the same village partible and impartible inheritance existed side by side.[57]

Although the Norfolk peasant was similar to the Kentish one in that he was largely free of seigneurial control and his land in large part descended in partible inheritance, his life, especially his economic life, was much more closely controlled by the village community. In East Anglia people did not live in dispersed hamlets and farmsteads as in Kent, but in large villages.[58] And these villages appear to have had a strong sense of corporate unity. In the twelfth century, East Anglian villages collectively witnessed charters.[59] These tightly knit village communities did not allow an individualistic agrarian regime to exist. In contrast to the situation in Kent, individuals could not sow as they pleased. Instead, the management of the village arable was regulated by the village community.[60]

The forest regions: Arden and the Weald. In contrast to Bedford, Oxford, Kent, and Norfolk, which for the most part had been thoroughly settled by the Anglo-Saxons, most of the county of Warwick was an area of late colonization. The area to the south of the Avon River, later known as Felden Warwickshire, which roughly corresponded to Kineton Hundred, was settled at an early date. As in the plains of neighboring Oxfordshire, large, nucleated villages practicing common-field husbandry prevailed here. But the power of the lords over the peasants was probably not as great as in the common-field regions of Oxford. More than two-thirds of the manors in Kineton Hundred were very small, consisting of less than 500 acres of arable, including both demesne and tenancies. Personal servitude was not as universal as in Oxford. R. H. Hilton has classified the tenants listed in the 1279 Hundred Roll inquest into the categories of free tenants, villeins, and small holders, many of whom were personally free. In Kineton 30 percent of the population was free, 24 percent small holders, and 46 percent villeins.[61] Labor services were also light. Of 48 hamlets and villages in the hundred, no labor services at all were owed in ten. In eight, what Hilton classifies as "light" services were owed. In 22 villages only seasonal services were required of the tenants, and in only eight were the heavier week-works exacted.[62]

On the far side of the Avon River, in the Forest of Arden, the peasant's condition was even freer. The Forest of Arden had not been settled by the Anglo-Saxons. But from the twelfth century there had been rapid colonization in the forest. The colonists had not settled in large nucleated villages, but in scattered farms, cottages, and hamlets.[63] The control that lords exercised over this dispersed peasantry was not very great. The 1279 Hundred Roll inquest for the Stoneleigh division of Knightlow Hundred shows that 50 percent of the land-holding population was free. Another 23 percent was made up of small holders. Only 27 percent of the population was servile.[64] The labor services that these peasants owed were extremely light. In eighteen of the 45 villages and hamlets no labor services at all were owed; light services were owed in twelve; seasonal works were required in thirteen; and the more onerous week-works were required in only two.[65]

The Weald of Kent, which had been almost devoid of inhabitants in the late eleventh century, was also an area of late medieval colonization where people lived in scattered hamlets. However, by the thirteenth century the process of colonization had proceeded further than in the Forest of Arden, and the Weald was a much less wild region.

To summarize the chief aspects of the social structure of these different regions, Bedfordshire, Kineton Hundred in Warwickshire, and the plains of northern Oxfordshire were regions of common-field husbandry, where people lived in large villages, agrarian practices were regulated by the village community, impartible inheritance prevailed, lords exerted strong control over the villagers, and personal servitude was common. In Kent, the Chiltern Hills, and Norfolk, however, lords exerted less control over the populace, personal freedom was common, and partible inheritance was practiced. In Norfolk people tended to live in large villages which controlled the agrarian practices of their residents. But in Kent and the Chiltern Hills settlement was more scattered and people were freer from interference by their neighbors. The Weald of Kent and the Forest of Arden were areas of late medieval colonization. Here settlement was very scattered, the power of the lords over the peasants negligible, and personal freedom widespread.

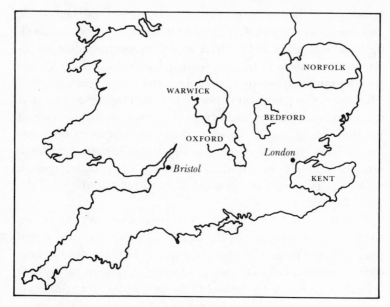

Map of England Showing Areas Studied

The urban areas. Although England in the thirteenth century was not as urbanized as Flanders or northern Italy, it still contained numerous towns and a few large cities. Most "towns" were small, regional markets. Indeed, some were so small that it is at times difficult to tell if they were true "towns" or only villages with a special juridical status. Thirty-one of these regional centers have been included in this study: four from Bedford, four from Kent, two from Norfolk, nine from Oxford, and twelve from Warwick.* In addition, four cities—London, Bristol, Norwich and Great Yarmouth—have been studied. Although these cities were modest in size compared with those of northern Italy, they, especially London, were truly urban areas.

* These towns are as follows: *Bedford:* Bedford, Dunstable, Leighton Buzzard, and Luton; *Kent:* Canterbury, Rochester, Newenden, and Tonbridge; *Norfolk:* Thetford and King's Lynn; *Oxford:* Banbury, Burford, Chipping Norton, Eynsham, Henley-on-Thames, Oxford, Thame, Witney, and Woodstock; *Warwick:* Alcester, Atherstone, Birmingham, Bretford, Brinklow, Coventry, Henley-in-Arden, Kenilworth, Kineton, Stratford-on-Avon, Tamworth, and Warwick.

London and Bristol in particular were specialized mercantile and manufacturing centers. At least in London there was developing a large, unskilled proletariat. As in most preindustrial cities, the birthrate in thirteenth-century London and the other cities was not high enough to replace the losses from death.[66] Therefore, this population deficit had to be made good by a constant stream of immigrants from the countryside. At least in London this influx of outsiders seems to have been of major proportions. Indeed, in the mid-fourteenth century the large number of immigrants resulted in a change of the dialect spoken in the city from that of the southeast of England to that of the East Midlands.[67]

The new urban societies of which these cities were examples were in a constant state of flux. Lines of power, authority, and prestige were matters of chronic dispute. Throughout the thirteenth century, for example, the wealthier citizens of London fought one another for control of the city. These struggles easily became involved in the wider politics of the realm as a whole, and royal intervention in London affairs was frequent and far-reaching.[68]

Just as the distribution of power was fluid and changing, so was the distribution of wealth. Although money was no stranger to the peasant economy, peasants finding themselves compelled to secure a certain amount of coin every year to pay seigneurial dues and to buy what goods and services were not produced by the peasant household, it did not play a predominant role in the peasants' life. Medieval English peasants produced only secondarily for the market. Instead they organized the exploitation of their homesteads primarily with an eye to providing employment and sustenance for their family. The consumer demands of the peasant family therefore determined both the quantity and the quality of what the peasants produced, and their economy remained for the most part on the margin of the new market and money-oriented economy that was developing in the towns in this period.[69] The primary source of wealth was therefore the land, which produced the goods needed for consumption and provided labor for the family. Despite the existence of an active land market, the primary means by which land was obtained in thirteenth-century English society was by inheritance. Therefore the hierarchy of wealth in peasant society, especially in those areas where impartible inheritance was practiced, tended to remain stable from one generation to the next.[70] In urban areas, however, almost all inhabitants were tightly linked to a money economy, and their livelihood depended on producing commodities for the market, whether those commodities took the form of the finished goods of the artisan or the brute force of the unskilled laborer. The great patricians in cities like London invested some of their capital in lands and rents,[71] but for most urban dwellers what wealth they had was in the fluid and unstable form of money. Unlike the landed patrimony of the peasant, the integrity of which was guarded by family law, the wealth of the urban dweller was subject in large part not only to the capriciousness of the market but also to the untrammeled will of the individual. Therefore a city dweller's wealth was more likely than a peasant's to be dissipated by bad luck, poor business sense, or gifts to the church and other charities.[72]

Assessing the relative wealth or prosperity of these regions, especially the rural ones, is difficult. From the end of the thirteenth and the beginning of the fourteenth centuries, several tax lists survive. But they must be used with caution. Not only are there lacunae in the surviving lists; evasion and bribery of the assessors were also common. Bearing these caveats in mind, we can turn to the evidence provided by the 1334 lay subsidy role. The assessed movable wealth on which the tax was levied was £50,827 8s. 9d. in the county of Norfolk, £27,803 14s. ¾d. in Kent, £20,119 17s. 1d. in Oxfordshire, £12,244 4s. 8¼d. in Warwick, and £10,019 19s. ¼d. in Bedford.[73] These raw totals, however, are misleading, giving as they do only the total assessment of each of the counties. Therefore, the 1334 assessments reveal their prosperity only indirectly.[74] Although Norfolk and Kent had the highest assessments, it is very probable that there were large numbers of impoverished peasants in each of these areas.[75] Land was the basis of most wealth in medieval Europe. In general, the more land a man possessed, the wealthier he was. In Kent and Norfolk peasant holdings could be fragmented by the practice of partible inheritance and by the play of market forces. Despite the appearance of general prosperity that the tax records initially seem to suggest, the interplay of these two factors may have reduced many peasants to a level but little removed from that of poverty. For example, when a tax of a fifteenth of movable goods was levied by the king in 1301, 102 residents of the Kentish town of Bexley were assessed. Of these, three had chattels in the form of corn, livestock, and some household goods worth more than £10. Three had goods worth £5 to £10, 15 worth £2 to £5, 27 worth £1 to £2, and 54 (i.e. 53 percent) less than £1. In addition, there may well have been a hundred other people in the village who were tenants or heads of families but who were not rich enough to be assessed.[76] The same may have been true of the inhabitants of the Chiltern Hills, where partible inheritance and free alienation *inter vivos* were also common. Conversely, in Oxford and Bedford, with, respectively, only the third and fifth largest assessments, peasant prosperity may have been greater. Restrictions on alienation of land and the practice of impartible inheritance preserved the integrity of many farmsteads and may have contributed to the creation of a reasonably well off middling class of peasants. Yet at the same time, since many of the peasants in these areas were unfree, their lords were in a position to siphon off a large part of whatever surplus they accumulated. And the lot of the landless or nearly landless cottars must have been truly desperate. Although Warwick received the next to lowest assessment in 1334, the inhabitants of the Forest of Arden may have been very well off, largely free of seigneurial exploitation and in a position to utilize the natural resources of a relatively untouched region.

If it is difficult to assess the general prosperity of these five counties at the end of the thirteenth and the beginning of the fourteenth centuries, it is even more difficult to know anything of the distribution of wealth among the different groups within them. This will become an important question when the social status of accused killers is discussed. Often the only reliable indication of their status is the value of their confiscated chattels. But it is difficult to evaluate what any given amount meant in terms of real wealth. It is possible that men with exactly the same amount of movable property, but from different areas, may have occupied different positions within their respective communities. A man with 20s. from Kent, Norfolk, or the Chiltern Hills, areas where there may have been many impoverished peasants, may have occupied a position of much greater authority and prestige than a man with 20s. from the plains of northern Oxford, Bedford, or the Forest of Arden. But in face of the lack of any comparative studies of the distribution of wealth in the different regions of England, this must remain only speculation.

Estimating the population of these regions presents difficulties as great, if not greater, than those found in gauging their relative prosperity. But this is a task that must be undertaken if any idea of the relative frequency of homicide in these different areas is to be arrived at. Even determining the number of settlements in a given county in the thirteenth century is difficult. The royal surveys made late in the thirteenth and early in the fourteenth centuries do, however, provide a guide. In 1316 the government carried out a survey of all the villages and towns in England and their lords. The returns are known as the Nomina Villarum. The survey is complete for Bedford, Norfolk, Oxford, and Warwick. Unfortunately, for Kent it is fragmentary.[77] Therefore, in estimating the number of settlements in this county, recourse has had to be made to a modern list of parishes.[78] An analysis of these documents provides the following estimates of the number of settlements in the counties in the thirteenth century: Bedford, 146; Kent, 405; Norfolk, 698; Oxford, 376; and Warwick, 257.

Estimating the actual number of people in these areas in the thirteenth century is even more fraught with difficulty. In the case of the two major cities of thirteenth-century England, estimates of 40,000 for London[79] and 17,000 for Bristol[80] have been adopted. For the counties of Bedford, Norfolk, Oxford, and Warwick, the estimates have been based on the 1086 Domesday Book.[81] The number of people recorded in the survey has been multiplied by five to take into account servants, family members, and those not enumerated.[82] This number in turn has been multiplied by two and one-half to allow for population growth between 1086 and the end of the thirteenth century. In estimating the population of Kent, the Domesday survey was not used. Instead, the list of names given in the 1334 Kent lay subsidy was utilized. Unlike the returns for the other counties in 1334, those for Kent list all the individual taxpayers within the county. This figure was multiplied by ten. The results of these calculations are as follows: Bedford, 43,400; Kent, 107,400;* Norfolk, 348,900; Oxford, 89,100; and Warwick, 31,900.

Since these estimates are very crude at best, a second calculation has been made, using the material collected by J. C. Russell. Russell has made estimates, using the 1377 poll tax returns, of the population of each county in England.[83] If it is assumed that the population of England in 1377 had declined by a third from what it had been at the end of the thirteenth century, the population of the five counties, ca. 1280, based on Russell's figures, should have been: Bedford, 45,762; Kent, 134,327; Norfolk, 220,089; Oxford, 61,512; and Warwick, 68,094. By way of contrast, the population of these counties in 1801 was:[84] Bedford, 63,393; Kent, 308,667; Norfolk, 273,479; Oxford, 111,977; and Warwick, 136,128.†

The unreliability of the estimated figures for the thirteenth century should be obvious. Whether one should multiply numbers derived from the Domesday Book or later surveys and tax lists by five or some other figure has produced an entire literature of its own.[85] To multiply that already suspect figure by two

---

* If the population of Kent is calculated in the same way as for the other counties, the figure arrived at is 164,225.

† This figure does not include the 70,670 people living in Birmingham.

and one-half is also an act of faith. Exactly how much England's population grew between 1086 and the end of the thirteenth century is not known. And certainly population growth was not uniform throughout the country. In old settled areas such as the plains of Oxford, much of Norfolk, and Kineton Hundred in Warwick, the population probably grew very little after 1086. At the end of the eleventh century the land already supported almost all the people that it could. Therefore, population estimates for these regions are probably high. However, in areas where colonization was possible, such as the fenland areas of Norfolk, the Weald of Kent, and the Forest of Arden, population growth was undoubtedly more pronounced.[86] The same is probably true of those regions where partible inheritance prevailed. Here noninheriting sons did not have to leave the village or resign themselves to a dependent and possibly celibate role in the village. They could set up households on their scraps of land, marry, and produce children. Therefore, the estimates for these areas are probably less than what they should be.

These, in brief, are the areas whose patterns of homicide will be scrutinized in this essay: Oxford and Bedford with their predominantly common-field social system; Kent, Norfolk, and the Chiltern Hills, where personal freedom and partible inheritance were common; the frontier areas of the Kentish Weald and the Warwickshire Forest of Arden; and the growing urban areas. Much of this essay will be concerned with trying to relate the patterns of homicidal behavior that emerge from an analysis of the eyre rolls to the social structures of these regions. Unfortunately, medieval social history is still a relatively new field of study. A very great deal about medieval social structures is unknown. Consequently, the explanations that will be advanced for the varying patterns of homicide to be found in the records can inevitably be only partial and tentative. Many factors, some of which modern historians may not even be able to imagine, undoubtedly influenced the violent conduct of medieval Englishmen. Unfortunately, these factors cannot take their rightful place in the analysis to follow. Despite these difficulties, the study of homicide in thirteenth-century England and its relation to different social structures is illuminating. For homicide is one of the few social relationships involving a large number of people which the state of the surviving documentation permits us to study in more than a single area. As such, it reveals with a clarity that few other phenomena can match many of the aspects of medieval life that are at once the most interesting and the most mysterious.

2. The Frequency of Homicide

"So violent and motley was life, that it bore the mixed smell of blood and roses. The men of that time always oscillated between the fear of hell and the most naive joy, between cruelty and tenderness, between harsh asceticism and insane attachment to the delights of the world, between hatred and goodness." [1] The glittering paradoxes of Johann Huizinga have for long summarized the tenor of life in medieval Europe. Late nineteenth- and early twentieth-century historians in particular saw the Middle Ages as a period when the iron rules of a Hobbesian state of nature held undisputed sway in Europe. For the French historian Achille Luchaire, the medieval period was the age of the war of all against all: "Imagine a social state in which security for property and person does not exist; no police, and little justice, especially outside of the larger cities; each one defends his purse and his life as best he can." [2] Across the Channel in England, T. F. Tout, the pioneering historian of the medieval English administration, wrote, "Not only were medieval criminals more numerous than their modern counter-parts, but by reason of their numbers and importance they excited much more general sympathy than they do nowadays, and were as a rule dealt with by society in a more lenient manner. . . . It is hardly going too far to say that homicide was the special misdeed [of the knightly class] and forgery the particular peccadillo of the [priestly class]. Few self-respecting gentlemen passed through the hot season of youth without having perpetrated a homicide or two." [3]

More recently, the judgment of historians has become more sober and less gracefully expressed. But most still perceive the Middle Ages as a period peculiarly prone to violence and brutality. For Marc Bloch "violence [was] the distinguishing mark of [the] epoch and [the] social system." [4] He portrayed medieval men as emotionally unstable, given to violent outbursts of rage and equally extravagant displays of repentance and contrition. And he wrote of the "despairs, the rages, the impulsive acts, the sudden revulsions of feeling" of the men of the time and of the "constant acts of violence" that these unstable characters perpetrated.[5] Georges Duby, Bloch's most distinguished successor, luridly described the "savagery of these men, accustomed to struggling against wild beasts, incapable of controlling their rage. . . . The fields which the *chansons de geste* describe are littered with severed heads and scattered brains." [6] Similarly, Marie-Thérèse Lorcin, in a study of crime in the region of Lyon in the fourteenth and fifteenth centuries, maintained that "brutality . . . marked all social behavior." [7] And Roger Vaultier, in his study of French folklore during the Hundred Years' War, characterized French peasants as *"rudes batailleurs."* [8]

English historians have agreed with their French counterparts. Looking back from a society in which interpersonal violence is remarkably rare to the time of their forefathers, they have been struck by the prevalence of violence. Gwyn Williams, having surveyed London politics in the thirteenth century, concluded that "violence was endemic." He found a seething city where trivial quarrels often ended fatally, where ill-paid and often idle private chaplains itched for a fight, where tournaments could stop all work in the city for a week, and where a wrestling match could result in the destruction of one of Clerkenwell priory's walls. For Williams, the "most immediate and vivid characteristic" of thirteenth-century Londoners was their "capacity for reckless violence." [9] The foremost modern historian of rural England, R. H. Hilton, has agreed with this view of medieval English life. For Hilton, the society that existed in the West Midlands in the thirteenth and fourteenth centuries was one "where violence, bribery and corruption were normal means of settling the issues which arose between men," [10] a society where "the expectation of life was short and . . . death in all its forms was always present." [11]

These opinions, perceptive as they may be, are almost all founded solely on impressionistic evidence. Medieval chronicles and letters are indeed filled with stories of murder and rapine. But chroniclers and other writers, like most people, were interested in recording the unusual and the dramatic. Literary sources may testify to a preoccupation with violent death, but they cannot reveal how common in reality such phenomena as violence and homicide were. For this purpose, the eyre rolls with their virtually complete lists of murder victims are indispensable. Simply to sum the number of bodies, however, is insufficient. If the relative incidence of homicide in the different regions of thirteenth-century England is to be grasped, the proportion that the victims of homicide constituted of the entire population of each area must be determined. In modern sociological and criminological literature this is usually expressed as the number of people in every 100,000 of the population who were murdered in a year. Accordingly, rates calculated on this basis have been derived for each of the twenty eyres under study here. The results of these calculations are in Table 2.

Obviously these rates are, at best, only approximations. As has been pointed out in Chapter 1, the population estimates on which they are based are vague. Despite their crudity, these estimated homicide rates are nevertheless interesting. If the population estimates made by the author are used as the basis of calculation, it is found that the homicide rate varied from a high of 64/100,000 per annum reported at the 1232 eyre of Warwick to a low of 4/100,000 per annum reported at the 1227 and 1248 eyres of Bristol. Of the rural areas, Warwick consistently had the highest homicide rates, with an overall rate of about 47/100,000

Table 2. *Estimated Homicide Rates*
(Per 100,000 population per year)

County	Eyre	Number of victims	Rate			
			Author's estimates	Russell's estimates	1801 figures	Per 20 settlements
Bedford [a]	1202	22	13	12	8.9	0.8
	1227–28	58	15	15	10.6	0.9
	1247	69	23	22	15.7	1.4
	1276	172	28	26	18.9	1.6
ALL		321	22	21	15.0	1.3
Bristol	1227	11	4	—	—	—
	1248	5	4	—	—	—
ALL		16	4	—	—	—
Kent [b]	1227	173	20	16	6.8	1.0
	1241	112	21	16	7.1	1.1
	1255	209	28	22	9.8	1.5
ALL		494	23	18	7.9	1.2
Norfolk	1250	127	7	11	9.0	0.7
	1257	193	9	13	10.9	0.9
	1268–69	399	11	17	13.5	1.1
ALL		719	9	15	11.7	0.9
Oxford	1241	59	12	17	9.2	0.5
	1247	116	20	29	15.9	0.9
	1261	134	18	26	14.5	0.9
ALL		309	17	25	13.5	0.8
Warwick	1221–22	158	38	18	9.0	1.0
	1232	114	64	30	15.0	1.6
	1247	104	48	22	11.2	1.2
ALL		376	47	22	10.9	1.2
London	1244	54	8	—	—	—
	1276	145	15	—	—	—
ALL		199	12	—	—	—

SOURCE: Figures are based on extrapolations from J. C. Russell's estimates of the population in 1377 in *British Medieval Population* (Albuquerque, N.M., 1948), pp. 132–33; and for 1801 from Great Britain, Parliament, *Parliamentary Papers (Commons), 1852–53*, vol. 85 (*Accounts and Papers*, vol. 29), Cmnd. 1631, "Population of Great Britain: Volume I," p. ccviii.

NOTE: Figures for the author's and Russell's estimates are rounded to the nearest whole number.

[a] Since the pleas held at Dunstable for the liberty of the priory of Dunstable have not survived, the rates given for the 1202 eyre are somewhat lower than they should be.

[b] Since the pleas of the Cinque Ports have not survived, the rates given for this country are somewhat lower than they should be.

per annum for the 25 years covered by the three eyres. Norfolk had the lowest rate, 9/100,000 per annum for the 23 years covered by the eyres. If the estimates based on J. C. Russell's figures are used as a basis for calculation, some differences appear. Although the highest homicide rate still remains that of the 1232 Warwick eyre, it is much reduced, being only 30/100,000 per annum. And the overall rate for Norfolk is found to have increased to 15/100,000 per annum. If we assume that the counties in question had the same population in the thirteenth century as they did in 1801, the homicide rates found are still high. The highest, however, is that for the 1276 eyre of Bedford, 18.9/100,000, and the lowest is 6.8/100,000 for the 1227 eyre of Kent.

Because the population estimates upon the basis of which these homicide rates have been figured are very imprecise, homicide rates have been calculated on yet a fourth, and considerably different, basis. Instead of using population as a basis for estimating homicide rates, I have used the number of settlements within the county. Homicide rates have been calculated in terms of the number of homicides per twenty settlements per annum. For example, in the four years covered by the 1202 Beford eyre there were 22 homicides reported. Since there were about 146 settlements in Bedfordshire, this means that for every twenty settlements in the county the figure was 0.8 for homicides committed every year. Similarly, in the eleven years covered by the 1268–69 Norfolk eyre, 399 homicides were reported. Since there were 698 settlements in Norfolk, this means that for every twenty settlements there were 1.1 killings every year. With calculations on this basis, the 1232 Warwick eyre and the 1276 Bedford eyres show the highest rate, of 1.6 homicides committed every year for every twenty settlements. The 1241 Oxford eyre now shows the lowest homicide rate, with only 0.5 in every twenty settlements each year.

Unreliable as they are, these homicide rates gain further meaning when they are contrasted with those in other societies. The most reliable figures come from the modern industrialized nations with their statistical habits of mind and their elaborate police bureaucracies. It appears that, for the most part, modern industrial societies, especially European ones, have low homicide rates. Since 1930 the homicide rate in Great Britain has remained fairly stable at the low figure of 0.4/100,000 per annum. In 1974 the rate in the United States was 9.7/100,000. Homicide rates in various American cities fluctuate rather widely. In the years between 1948 and 1952, Philadelphia had a rate of 5.7/100,000 per annum and Miami had a rate of 15.1/100,000 per annum.

Estimating homicide rates for modern agrarian societies presents many of the same problems that are encountered in estimating them for medieval England. Population size is often unknown and many homicides are unreported. The problem is further confused by the fact that some writers compute homicide rates in terms of victims, the practice followed in this essay, and some in terms of offenders. However, in broad outline it is possible to gauge the amount of homicide in many rural societies. Table 3 shows homicide rates ranging from a low of 0.7 per 100,000 for offenders among the BaLuyia of Kenya to the nearly incredible rates of more than 200 victims per 100,000 in some Mexican villages.

Cross-cultural comparisons of the frequency of murder are in some ways an exercise in comparing apples and oranges. Homicide rates are influenced heavily by the types of weapons available and the quality of health care. A study of homicide in Chicago has shown that guns are five times as likely to inflict fatal wounds as knives.[12] However, despite the lethalness of the techniques available in industrial societies for taking human life, the advanced methods of treating major traumatic injuries and handling infection have lowered homicide rates. Bearing in mind the uncertainty of the estimated rates for the thirteenth century and the difficulties of making cross-cultural comparisons, it is nevertheless clear that England in the thirteenth century was a violent country. If the streets of medieval England did not run with blood, and if thirteenth-century Englishmen did not

Table 3. *Homicide Rates in Various Societies*
(Per 100,000 population)

Society	Period	Rate	Society	Period	Rate
Great Britain	1930–39	0.4	Belgium	1951–56	0.8
	1940–49	0.4	Sri Lanka	1957	5.9
	1950–54	0.4	BaSoga of		
	1955–56	0.4	Uganda	1952–54	4.0
	1957	0.4	BaLuyia of Kenya	1949–54	0.7–7.9
	1958	0.3	Amba of Uganda	1945–54	1.1
	1959	0.4	Sebei of Uganda	1945–54	11.6
United States	1974	9.7	Middlesex, Eng.	1580–1603	6.3
Philadelphia	1948–52	5.7	Nottinghamshire,		
Milwaukee	1948–52	2.3	Eng.	1530–58	3.8–14.8
Miami	1948–52	15.1	Mexican mestizo		
Italy	1951–56	1.2	village	c. 1928–60	300–395
Japan	1951–56	2.2	Mexican Indian		
France	1951–56	0.7	village	c. 1961–65	251.2

SOURCE: Great Britain—Terence Morris and Louis Blom-Cooper, *Murder in Microcosm* (London, 1961), p. 3. United States—U.S. Federal Bureau of Investigation, *Uniform Crime Reports: Crime in the United States, 1974* (Washington, D.C., 1975), p. 15. Philadelphia, Milwaukee, and Miami—M. E. Wolfgang, *Patterns in Criminal Homicide* (New York, 1966), p. 25. Italy, Japan, France, and Belgium—A. L. Wood, "Crime and Aggression in Changing Ceylon: A Sociological Analysis of Homicide, Suicide and Economic Crime," *Transactions of the American Philosophical Society*, 51, pt. 8 (1961), p. 57. Sri Lanka—*ibid.*, p. 57. Uganda and Kenya—Paul Bohannan, ed., *African Homicide and Suicide* (Princeton, N.J., 1960), pp. 237–38. Middlesex and Nottinghamshire—P. E. H. Hair, "Homicide, Infanticide, and Child Assault in Late Tudor Middlesex," *Local Population Studies*, 9 (1972), pp. 43–44. Mexico—Lola Romanucci Schwartz, "Conflict Without Violence and Violence Without Conflict in a Mexican Mestizo Village," in *Collective Violence*, ed. by J. F. Short, Jr. and M. E. Wolfgang (Chicago, 1972), p. 155; and June Nash, "Death as a Way of Life: The Increasing Resort to Homicide in a Maya Indian Community," *American Anthropologist*, n.s. 69 (1967), p. 456.

NOTE : The rates for Uganda and Kenya are for offenders, not victims, and as such are not strictly comparable with the rates for thirteenth-century England or for the other societies in this table. Since somewhat more people in these societies tended to be involved in homicide as offenders than as victims, the homicide rates in terms of victims per 100,000 population would be slightly smaller than the rates for offenders.

murder each other with the same frequency as Mexican peasants today, nonetheless, they were more violent than their modern descendants, and more violent than many modern agrarian peoples.

One may not choose to put much trust in homicide rates based on what are no more than informed guesses about the size of thirteenth-century populations. Yet a consideration of the number of homicides committed in every twenty settlements per annum makes it clear that murder was a frequent phenomenon in medieval England. As has been pointed out above, the number of homicides in every twenty settlements oscillated between a high of almost 1.6, reported at the 1276 Bedford eyre and the 1232 Warwickshire eyre, and a low of 0.5, reported at the 1241 Oxford eyre. In other words, there was a good possibility that there would have been a homicide in every settlement in these counties once every twenty to forty years. Therefore, it is possible that every person in England in the thirteenth century, if he did not personally witness a murder, knew or knew of someone who had been killed. There was an even greater chance that an Englishman would have encountered someone who had killed a man. The eyre rolls give the names of 2,434 victims. They also list 3,492 people accused of having participated in a homicide in some fashion. But these 3,492 people represent only a fraction of the total number of people who committed murder. In many cases when the jurors reported a killing, they claimed that they did not know the identity of the slayers. Indeed, 531 of the victims, 21.8 percent of the total, were stated to have been killed by unknown assailants. It is therefore certain that experience of homicide in one form or another was widespread in thirteenth-century English society. In studying the patterns of homicide, we are concerned with one of the major social phenomena of the age.

3. Homicide and the Medieval Household

Early in the fourteenth century the scholars of the Norman nation at the University of Paris met in convocation. "There it was put to a vote, whether it pleased those who were present that the stronger members . . . should arm themselves and attack the members of another nation. And whoever found this agreeable should raise his hand and say, 'Yes.' " The students voted for the resolution, and in the following fight one clerk was killed and another mutilated.[1] The papal letter that tells us of this incident illustrates one of the most striking features of medieval homicide, its markedly collective character.[2] In thirteenth-century England, of the 3,492 people accused of homicide who were named in the eyre rolls, only 1,120 (32.1 percent) did not have a named companion (see Table 4). If we exclude the people whom the jurors described as "accomplices," and who may not have taken part in the actual killing, the number of those who acted without a companion rises only to 1,184 of 3,013, or 39.3 percent.*

* It might be thought that these percentages are deceptive, for it is possible that almost all victims were slain by lone individuals, and that only a few unfortunates were murdered by hordes of killers. However, if we consider the number of people by whom the victims were murdered, collective homicide still remains a very important phenomenon. Of the 1,903 victims whose killers were known to the jurors, 735 (38.6 percent) were killed by two or more assailants. If those people described as accomplices are excluded from consideration, the number of people killed by at least two assailants becomes 667 (35 percent).

Table 4. *Collective Homicide*

Number committing a homicide [a]	Killers (incl. accomplices)		Killers (excl. accomplices) [b]		Victims killed (incl. accomplices)		Victims killed (excl. accomplices)	
	Number	Percent	Number	Percent	Number	Percent	Number	Percent
0	1,120	32.1%	1,184	39.3%	—	—	1 [c]	0.1%
1	601	17.2	589	19.5	1,168	61.4%	1,235	64.9
2	457	13.1	426	14.1	329	17.3	323	17.0
3	268	7.7	232	7.7	174	9.1	160	8.4
4	215	6.2	139	4.6	85	4.5	78	4.1
5	192	5.5	174	5.8	45	2.4	33	1.7
6–10	295	8.4	219	7.3	81	4.3	67	3.5
11–20	166	4.8	17	0.6	15	0.8	5	0.3
21 & over	178	5.1	33	1.1	6	0.3	1	0.1
TOTAL	3,492		3,013		1,903		1,903	

[a] This is the number of companions with whom a homicide was committed or the number of killers by whom the victim was slain.

[b] This column includes only those people accused of being principal assailants. Therefore the total is less than that for the first column. There are more people in the zero row in this column than in the first column because some people committed their assault only with companions whom the jurors labeled accomplices. Although these people were counted in the first row as having more than zero companions, in this column they have been counted as having zero companions.

[c] The seemingly impossible fact that one person was killed by no one is explained by the fact that this column includes only those persons who were killed by people whom the jurors labeled principals. In one case, the jurors had no clue to the identity of the victim's principal assailant, but did suspect someone of having been an accomplice to the deed.

To the sensibilities of a citizen of a modern industrial state, such a finding is shocking. But that homicide in medieval England should have had such a markedly collective character is hardly surprising, for the bonds of mutual dependence and support that united people in medieval society were exceedingly strong. Every individual in every society, of course, participates in an intricate web of relationships that unites him to others—to kinsmen, friends, neighbors, tradesmen, members of the same cult, etc. These networks * differ in their importance. The bonds that unite a man to some of his family members, with whom he spends much of his time and with whom he shares the major experiences of life—birth, marriage, death—are far more important and continuous than those that unite him to a merchant to whom he sells grain or from whom he buys iron for his plow. In medieval Europe, these bonds of family, friendship, and neighborhood were much more important than they are today. In a society where a rudimentary technology barely allowed men to feed and clothe themselves, where disease and uncertainty were common features of life, where the government provided none of the social services it does in the modern world, men turned of necessity to their families, their friends, their neighbors, their lords and retainers for support and assistance. Loyalty and friendship were therefore two of the most prized virtues in medieval Europe.[3]

The strength of the bonds that united individuals to one another inevitably drew groups of people into violent conflict. One man's, or one woman's, quarrel easily became his kinsmen's, his friends', and his neighbors' quarrel also. Whether people cold-bloodedly joined together with their friends or relations to carry out a premeditated assault or automatically and unreflectingly

---

* Some readers may be puzzled by the use of this word to describe social groupings. I have borrowed this term from the social anthropologists. A network may be conceived of as a scattering of points connected by lines. The points are individuals and the lines indicate interactions. As can be readily grasped, a network is theoretically boundless. Each individual within a society also has his own unique network, depending on such factors as age, sex, and occupation. See Jeremy Boissevain, *Friends of Friends: Networks, Manipulators and Coalitions* (Oxford, 1974), p. 24.

came to the aid of one of their own who had become involved in
a brawl, large numbers of people often became involved in violent conflict in thirteenth-century England.

The ranks from which a killer recruited his helpers were
many and diverse, including fellow villagers, fellow workmen,
and people from neighboring villages. For the moment attention will be focused on only those relationships involving kinsmen and members of the household. See Table 5.

Kinsmen played a major role in the commission of homicide.
Of the 2,372 persons who had a companion when they murdered someone, 479 (20.2 percent) acted in the company of a
relative. Relatives, perhaps more than anyone else, were ready
to come to the aid of one of their own who had been attacked.
One day in the county of Norfolk, Nicholas at the bridge and his
son Gregory were in a shop in the village of Stow Bardolph with
ten other people.[4]

And John Leueday came up with his wife seeking aid from them, saying
that he had been threatened by the men of Shouldham. He sat with them,
so that . . . John Stalewrtheman came there crying, "Where is that traitor John Leueday; he is a dead man if I find him." John, hearing this,
hid himself with his wife. But the aforesaid John Stalewrtheman stayed
there always crying out and striking everyone near him so that he struck
the aforesaid Gregory with an axe in the head . . . so that he fell to the
ground. The aforesaid Nicholas his father, seeing this, wished to help
his son, but he was placed in a corner of the shop so that he could barely
cry out a warning. To keep himself and his son and the others who were
with them from being killed, in self-defense he struck John Stalewrtheman in the head with an axe, of which wound he died.

The readiness of kinsmen to assist one another, as in this incident, or to retaliate for an injury was undoubtedly a major factor in the regulation of conflict within the community. A man
could not expect that he would be able to injure an enemy with
impunity. Although the formal, institutionalized blood feud had
ceased to be a feature of English society by the thirteenth century, kinsmen on occasion still exacted revenge for the death of
one of their relatives. In the second quarter of the century William of Radwell was hanged in Wiltshire on the accusation of

Table 5. *Relatives with Whom One Committed Homicide*

Relative	Male killers		Female killers		Total	
	Number	Percent	Number	Percent	Number	Percent
Husband/lover			63	47.4%	63	13.2%
Wife/lover	63	18.2%			63	13.2
Father	46	13.3	10	7.5	56	11.7
Mother	23	6.6	17	12.8	40	8.4
Son	39	11.3	19	14.3	58	12.1
Daughter	8	2.3	15	11.3	23	4.8
Brother	192	55.5	13	9.8	205	42.8
Sister	14	4.0	21	15.8	35	7.3
Uncle	1	0.3	4	3.0	5	1.0
Aunt	—	—	1	0.8	1	0.2
Nephew	1	0.3	—	—	1	0.2
Niece	2	0.6	1	0.8	3	0.6
Mother-in-law	2	0.6	—	—	2	0.4
Son-in-law	—	—	2	1.5	2	0.4
Brother-in-law	4	1.2	2	1.5	6	1.3
Sister-in-law	2	0.6	2	1.5	4	0.8
TOTAL	346		133		479	

NOTE: Since some people committed a homicide with more than one relative, they have been counted twice. Therefore, the columns sum to figures greater than the totals given and the percentages to figures greater than 100.0 percent.

William of Bowden Hill. If the suspicions of the jurors are to be believed, William of Radwell's kin came one night to William of Bowden Hill's house and in retaliation killed both him and his son.[5]

Although the family, with its threat of potential vengeance, probably deterred some from violent action, it nevertheless could also encourage some forms of violence by providing support for its members once they had become involved in a quarrel. In 1297 Simon Whetebred and Nicholas le Rede, both from Helmdon in Northamptonshire, fought over a debt that Nicholas owed Simon. Simon fatally wounded Nicholas with a stick. When Nicholas' wife Isolda tried to raise the hue and cry to have Simon arrested, his sister Matilda enabled him to escape by throttling Isolda.[6]

The willingness of family members to come to one another's aid could rapidly turn trivial incidents into battles between two families and their respective groups of friends. Early in the four-teenth century William of Buckwell, his brother Geoffrey, and William Swete took part in a penitential procession in Kent. As they passed the house of Richard of Brennesham, John Ruck-ing, one of their companions, shot an arrow at Richard's dog. Richard and his brother immediately rushed out of the house. They and some of their neighbors pursued the penitents into Littlebourne and wounded them. William of Buckwell died of his wounds three days later, and Richard of Brennesham and his brother promptly fled.[7]

Within the family, not all relatives were of equal importance; siblings were the relatives to whom one turned most commonly. Of the 479 people who acted with a relative, 238 (49.7 percent) committed murder with a sibling (some with both a brother and a sister); 205 people (42.8 percent) did so with a brother, and 35 (7.3 percent) with a sister. Lifelong companions in the home and in the fields, often with a common stake in the management and protection of the family holding,[8] brothers and sisters had ample reason to aid one another in violent conflict.

The next most important group of relatives were one's parents or children. Of this group, 162 people (33.8 percent) killed someone in company with either a parent or a child, 56 (11.7 percent) with their fathers, 40 (8.4 percent) with their mothers, 58 (12.1 percent) with their sons, and 23 (4.8 percent) with their daughters. (Of the foregoing people, eleven commit-ted a murder with both their fathers and mothers and four with both their sons and daughters.) Just as parents, like Nicholas at the bridge in the incident related earlier, came to the aid of their children, so children came to the aid of their parents. For ex-ample, some time around 1272 in Devonshire, Thomas Kouke and his wife Mabel went to Rose of Buckland's tavern in the village of Sutton. Margery de Totewell, whom the members of a special inquest jury thought to be Thomas's mistress, also ap-peared at the tavern. Mabel quarreled with her husband's para-mour. Eventually Alard, the tavern keeper's son, threw Mabel out. She went to her son Nicholas to complain that it was a "great shame" that Margery had treated her thus, especially in front of her husband. Nicholas went to the tavern to give Margery a thrashing. Alard threw him out too. Nicholas then went to get his brother. Together they attacked the tavern, firing arrows at it. Ultimately, when Nicholas broke down the tavern door and tried to enter, Alard shot him with an arrow'and killed him.[9]

Although people cooperated with parents and children in the commission of homicide slightly less often than with siblings, this difference may be due more to demographic causes than to the fact that the ties uniting siblings were stronger than the bonds between parents and children. Since people tended to die at an early age,[10] many parents must have died when their offspring were still relatively young, and before they were old enough to be effective as auxiliaries in a fight. Indeed, if this is true, it would appear that the bonds between parents and children might well have been just as strong, if not stronger, than those between siblings.

Only 126 people (26.3 percent) killed someone in company with their spouse or lover. This figure is surprisingly low, since one would have expected that the strongest ties within the family would have been those between husband and wife. One could attempt to explain this pattern by arguing that marriage in thirteenth-century England did not produce very strong bonds between spouses. For confirmation of this argument, one could point to the records of the church courts, mostly from the fourteenth century and later. These seem to provide evidence of much adultery,[11] desertion, and bigamy.[12] Yet these high rates of bigamy and adultery may not be signs of weak marriage bonds but simply of peasant customs that did not fit into the patterns that canon law and the clergy sought to impose. Both may in fact be signs of marriages that in the eyes of at least one of the participants had already been dissolved. The fact that the church courts termed the new relationships adulterous or bigamous may simply indicate the inability of the church to recognize the dissolution of one marriage and the formation of a new.[13]

Probably the chief reason for the relatively low level of cooperation among spouses was the fact that women in medieval England were far less prone to engage in violent behavior than men, as will be seen presently. Women as a whole were only rarely involved in violent conflict, constituting only 8.6 percent of the accused killers and 19.5 percent of the victims. Males formed the overwhelming bulk of those who committed murder, and they turned only rarely to female relatives for aid. Whereas 192 turned to brothers, only fourteen turned to sisters. Similarly, 46 turned to fathers but only 23 to mothers; 39 went to sons for aid, but only eight to daughters. The relative lack of cooperation among spouses was thus only a reflection of the general lack of cooperation among male and female relatives. Yet one's spouse was the most important relative of the opposite sex to whom one turned for aid. Indeed, for women the husband was the single most important relative, 63 (47.4 percent) acting with their husbands. Even for men, wives were the second most important relative, after brothers. In all, 63 men (18.2 percent) acted in company with their wives. Thus the low overall figure for cooperation between spouses is not a reflection of any weakness of husband-wife bonds, but of the general reluctance of women to become involved in homicide and the strong nature of other kinship ties, especially those between siblings.

Although the bonds between spouses were not as weak as an initial consideration of the eyre rolls suggests, the links that marriage created between different sets of kin were definitely of negligible importance. Only fourteen people, scarcely 2.9 percent of the total, committed a killing with an in-law. It is possible that the records may often fail to specify kinship relationships that fell outside the bounds of the nuclear family and those immediately connected to it, but it is more likely that the silence of the records reflects the true state of affairs. A significant amount of marriage in thirteenth-century England was exogamous with respect to the village.[14] Therefore, in-laws seldom came into contact with one another. Thus they did not have the opportunity to establish the close, intimate bonds that would have made them turn to each other for assistance.

Despite the importance of family ties, they were only one of several networks of dependencies and alliances that bound people together in medieval England. Within many households there was another group on which one could rely for aid—servants. Great lords lived in the midst of a huge swarm of servants and retainers. Lord Thomas II of Berkeley (1281–1321), a major figure in West Midland society, maintained a household and "standing domestical family" of more than 200 persons—knights, esquires, servants, and pages.[15] Even at the bottom of the social scale, it was not uncommon for peasants, at least the wealthier ones, to employ help. Although it is impossible to determine how many servants any one peasant family had, their names appear so frequently in manorial court rolls as to make it clear that their employment was far from uncommon.[16] The ties that bound masters and servants to each other could be extremely strong. Servants were often taken into their master's household at a young age and treated in many ways like the children of the household.[17] Strengthened by years of shared experience, the ties between masters and servants must often have been stronger than those between some kinsmen.

The fellowship of master and man was even found fit to be a subject for popular balladry. In "Robin Hood and the Monk," the earliest known version of which exists in a manuscript of the mid-fifteenth century but which undoubtedly goes back to earlier sources, much of the tale turns on the loyalty of servant to master.[18] At a shooting match, Little John, Robin Hood's man, won 5s. from Robin.

> A ferly strife fel þem betwene,
>   As they went bi the wey;
> Litull John seid he had won fiue shillings,
>   And Robyn seid schortly nay,
>
> With þat Robyn Hode lyed Litull Jon,
>   And smote hym with his hande;

> Litul Jon waxed wroth þerwith,
>   And pulled out his bright bronde.

> 'Were þou not my maister,' seid Litull John,
>   þou shuldis by hit ful sore;
> Get þe a man where þou wilt,
>   For þou getis me no more.'

Shortly after this incident, Robin was captured in Nottingham, an event that reawakened Little John's loyalty. Together with another outlaw named Much, Little John waylaid the monk who had brought about Robin's capture and who had set off with his page to inform the king.

> 'He was my maister,' seid Litull John,
>   þat þou has browȝt in bale;
> Shalle þou neuer cum at our kyng,
>   Ffor to telle hym tale.'

> John smote of þe munkis hed,
>   No longer wolde he dwell;
> So did Moch þe litull page,
>   Ffor ferd lest he wolde tell.[19]

Just as the faithful servants and companions of balladry took revenge for a wrong done to their lord, so did the real servants of the thirteenth century. On September 25, 1205, William of Bramfield, subdean of Lincoln cathedral, was murdered by another cleric in front of St. Peter's altar. William's servants promptly cut the killer down. His body was hacked into pieces before being unceremoniously thrown out of the minster.[20] Similarly, when Beatrice Swalwechine, an Oxford whore, stole books from the lodgings of some of the university's scholars, their servants beat her to death.[21] Later in the century, on Sunday, August 16, 1254, a similar incident occurred in London. William of Wenden in Essex was playing chess with Robert son of Bernard, also of Essex, a knight, at Robert's house. The two quarreled over the game. Apparently they were on the point of coming to blows, for Robert's armiger, also named Robert, attacked William. William killed him with his knife and fled.[22]

Lords also used their servants in more deliberate ways to prosecute their quarrels. On October 26, 1271, in Bedfordshire, Osbert of Bath distrained Richard of Colesden, Adam of Basmead's man, by seizing a cow. Adam ordered his servants, Walter of Hook Wood and William the cook, to recover the beast. Together with John Chanu, the king's bailiff, they went to Wyboston. Outside Osbert's curia they met Thomas Snou of Somerset, one of Osbert's servants. Walter asked him who had the cow, striking him "lightly" on the shoulder with a staff. Osbert, who had been plowing in the fields, came to the rescue with Nicholas of Bath and Walter Smod of Somerset. A fight began, and in the melée Walter Smod fatally wounded Walter of Hook Wood with an axe.[23] An analogous incident occurred in London in 1305. John of Orpedman had fallen two years behind in his rent to the master of the Hospital of St. Giles Without Cripplegate. When the master came to demand the arrears, John assaulted him. When he returned a second time, John set his servants on him.[24]

Masters also enlisted their servants in settling grudges. Ketel of Warwick and James the merchant of Warwick had been in a fight. With Henry the clerk, Gilbert the weaver, and John the cook, Ketel broke into James's house, beat him, and carried him off to John's house, where he was kept prisoner. James died after this episode, and his widow appealed Ketel and his servants of his murder. Although the jurors acknowledged that Ketel had ordered his men to attack James, they refused to find them guilty of his death.[25]

In many instances masters sent their men out not merely to beat or intimidate an opponent, but with specific orders to kill him. Sometime around 1146 Simon de Novers, who was heavily in debt to Eleazar, a Jew of Norwich, decided to get rid of his creditor. He sent one of his squires to fetch the Jew on the pretext that Simon was prepared to pay what he owed. The unsuspecting Eleazar was led to a wood, where he was killed by a group of de Novers' servants. When King Stephen came to Norwich, the Jews accused Simon of the murder. The local bishop defended Simon, and in turn denounced the Jews, including the murder victim, for having killed the boy William of Norwich in 1144. The case was adjourned to London, where it was postponed *sine die*.[26] Similarly, in 1211 Ralf son of Thorold and Walter de Grantcurt disputed the possession of some land in Wood Norton in Norfolk. Walter came to the land with his servant Roger Test. "And . . . he ordered Roger to defend that tenement so that Ralf should not come onto it and that, if he did, he should shoot at him and make it so that he would not henceforth come onto it; and . . . he gave him two arrows and ordered him to kill Ralf with them." Two weeks later, when Ralf appeared on the land, Roger shot and killed him.[27]

The bonds that united the servants of a common master to one another were also strong. Servants were quick to take their fellows' part. In 1278 an esquire of the court of the king of Scotland rode by the house of John de Grendon, a burgess of the city of Durham, with two dogs. A dog came out of John's house and barked at the other two. The squire pursued the dog into the house, killed it, and went on toward Scotland. When the other members of the household passed by, one of John's maids complained to them. In reply, they promptly attacked John's house, beat him, tied him up and carried him off, and held him prisoner until the prior of Durham and his neighbors were able to secure his release.[28] In 1276 some of Edward I's falconers were lodged in the priory of Dunstable. One day they got into an argument with one of the priory's chaplains. That evening the falconers cornered him in the guest house and fatally wounded him. The priory's janitor tried to keep them from reentering the courtyard. They beat him up, and proceeded to run riot through the priory, attacking anyone whom they encountered, including the canons and the *conversi*. The great bells of the church were rung and the people of the town flocked to the church ready to do battle. Only with difficulty was the prior able to prevent a major fight.[29]

At times masters found themselves drawn into their servants' quarrels. One day in the fields of Great Tew in Oxfordshire there was a riot between the men of Master John de La Lade and Drogo de Pratellis. When William de Tatkel, one of Drogo's men, appealed some of his opponents for assault, John had him excommunicated, "so that he feared that he would be taken on the king's order and for fear did not press his appeal." [30]

Many lords did not stop at merely trying to protect their servants from the king's courts, but showed themselves ready to take part in the fray themselves. On October 13, 1272, two squires and four servants came to the prior of Lanthony's house in Henlow in Bedfordshire and sought entertainment for their lord, John le Burk the elder. None of the servants at the house dared grant it to them because the warden, Brother Philip, a Lanthony canon, was away. One of Burk's men struck Henry de Rolle. They also threatened to put the place to the torch, but eventually went away. The next day John himself came to Henlow. While his servants attacked the household, breaking the arm of Robert son of Walter of Henlow and fatally wounding Henry son of Adam of Henlow, John threatened the canon Philip, who had taken refuge in the church.[31] Similarly, sometime in the last half of the thirteenth century, the Cistercian abbot of the mother abbey of Fountains in Yorkshire paid a visit to the abbey's daughter house at Woburn in Bedfordshire. The servants of the two abbots fell to quarreling. The abbot of Woburn came with one of his monks, named William de la Graue, to stop the disturbance. William took a direct approach to the problem and hit one of the Yorkshire abbot's servants in the head with a hatchet. A man named John in turn shot the monk with an arrow, killing him instantly.[32]

An incident that occurred in London in 1276 illustrates how a chance quarrel initiated by a group of servants could escalate and involve an entire knightly household.

On . . . Sunday, after curfew rung, it happened that one Richard Moys, going along the King's highway, came to the door of John le Chaloner, next to the house of Agnes de Essexe, near Fancherche; in which house lodged Robert de Munceny and Arnulph, his son, with his household; and so, trying to make entrance therein, he knocked, shouted, and made a noise. On seeing which, four of the household

. . . , who were standing at the hostel of the knights before-mentioned, and of whose names [the jurors] are ignorant, being moved thereat, requested him to cease making his noise, and go away; and as he refused to do so, they cried out that he must leave forthwith; whereupon, hearing the outcry . . . , Robert and Arnulph, and all of Robert's household, came out, that is to say, John de Munceny, John son of Robert, John Fauntilun, Robert de la Rokele, Henry de Ginges, John Curteys, John de Hakone, John le Wyte, Hugh de Hoddone, Hachard de Garbodesham, and Robert de le Lo, some with swords, and some with other arms. And all of them, save only the said Robert, who stood at the door of his hostel, followed the said Richard, who fled to the house of Alice le Official; in which house many persons were seated drinking, with the door open, among whom were Richard de Parys, now dead, and one Henry Page; and Richard Moys concealed himself between two wooden vessels there. And the said Arnulph, on entering, met at the door the said Richard de Parys, who cried out,—"Who are these people?"—whereupon Arnulph struck him with his drawn sword, already stupefied as he was at the sight of the sword. Then rushing into the house, he gave him a wound in the back, between the ribs of the body, two inches in breadth, and penetrating to the intestines; and another small wound under the left breast. From which wounds he languished, and survived until the Thursday following, on which day, at the hour of Matins, he died. And immediately after perpetrating this felony, Arnulph went forth and joined his accomplices, and they went together to his hostel, John and Hachard excepted, who took to flight; and there they remained in his house.[33]

The figures that can be gleaned from the eyre rolls show that 105 (4.4 percent) of those who murdered someone with a companion did so with a master or a servant. This figure probably does not reflect the true extent of cooperation between masters and servants in prosecuting violent conflicts. In many instances the names of masters who had in fact ordered a servant to carry out an assault that resulted in a fatality may not have been entered in the rolls. In any case, of the 105 people named at the eyres as having committed a murder with a master or a servant, 40 cases (38.1 percent) were of servants who had committed a murder with a master, 37 (35.2 percent) were of masters who had committed homicide with their servants, and 40 (38.1 percent) were of servants who had committed murder with a fellow servant. (As is apparent, some of these people committed a homicide with both a master and a fellow servant.)

The ties of blood and service were strong and durable in medieval society. But the same factors that made these ties so strong—long, intimate experience of one another, shared interests and goals—also contained seeds of discord. Murder within the medieval kin group and household was not uncommon. To put the phenomenon in its proper perspective, it is necessary to glance briefly at intrafamilial conflict among some other peoples. In many modern societies homicide primarily involves people who are in close daily contact, especially members of the same family. In Denmark in the years 1934–39 and 1946–51, 98 of 172 murderers (57 percent) killed relatives.[34] In Philadelphia between 1949 and 1952 a quarter of all homicides involved members of the same family.[35] Similar patterns are found in nonindustrial societies. Among the Tiv of central Nigeria, 48 of the 122 homicide victims recorded between 1931 and 1949 were killed by relatives.[36] In 99 cases recorded among another African people, the Gisu, 38 of the victims were related to their murderers.[37] And among the Maria of India, 62 of the 100 victims studied by Verrier Elwin were slain by relatives.[38]

At first glance, the situation in thirteenth-century England seems to contrast with this pattern. Of the 2,434 victims listed in the eyre rolls, only 159 (6.5 percent) were killed by relatives. If the number of persons killed by relatives per year is estimated, the rates found are 2.0/100,000 per annum for Kent, 2.1/100,000 for Warwick, 1.6/100,000 for Oxford, 1.2/100,000 for Bedford, 0.4/100,000 for London, 0.6/100,000 for Norfolk, and 0/100,000 for Bristol.* Since most sociologists and anthropologists do not provide comparable rates for the groups they

---

* These figures, which encompass all the eyres for each region, are based on the author's population estimates. If rates are calculated using population estimates based on Russell's figures, the following rates are found: Bedford, 1.1/100,000; Kent, 1.6/100,000; Norfolk, 0.9/100,000; Oxford, 2.4/100,000; Warwick, 1.0/100,000. If the rates are calculated using the 1801 population, the following results are found: Bedford, 0.8/100,000; Kent, 0.7/100,000; Norfolk, 0.7/100,000; Oxford, 1.3/100,000; Warwick, 0.5/100,000. Finally, if the number of homicides committed every year in every twenty settlements is calculated, the following are found: Bedford, 0.07/20; Kent, 0.10/20; Norfolk, 0.06/20; Oxford, 0.08/20; Warwick, 0.05/20.

have studied, it is difficult to make valid comparisons. However, it appears that the rates for thirteenth-century England are fairly high, at least in terms of modern American experience. Between 1948 and 1952 Philadelphia had a homicide rate of 5.7/100,000.[39] Of 550 victims whose killers' identities were known to the police, 24.7 percent were murdered by relatives.[40] This works out to be a rate of approximately 1.4/100,000 per annum. The counties of Kent, Warwick, and Oxford exceeded this rate, whereas Bedford and Norfolk and the cities of London and Bristol fell below it. Medieval Englishmen thus appear to have killed their relatives with fairly great regularity. Yet because of the generally high level of homicidal activity, the people killed by their kin formed only a relatively small proportion of all homicide victims.

An analysis of the patterns of homicidal strife within the family reveals that the relationship most likely to produce a slaying was that of husband and wife. See Table 6. Of the total of 159 people killed by relatives, 96 (60.4 percent), 32 men and 64 women, were killed by their mates or lovers.[41] Contemporaries were aware that marriage could produce bloody conflicts. Thomas of Chobham, subdean of Salisbury and author of a work on penitence, explained the fact that the penance for uxoricides was heavier than that for parricides, not because uxoricide was worse than parricide, but because husbands were far more prone to kill their wives than sons to kill their fathers.[42] Our knowledge of marriage and the roles that husbands and wives were expected to play is so scanty for the Middle Ages that it is difficult to interpret the figures that emerge from the eyre rolls. Infidelity may have played a role in some of the murders, although the records are largely silent on this point. A few such cases, however, do exist. In a Herefordshire case tried in the *curia regis* in 1207, a woman named Marjorie, a notorious adulteress, was accused of having arranged for the murder of her husband, Hugh Dobin, with whom she had often quarreled about her behavior.[43] Similarly, at the 1227 eyre of Kent the jurors of Bewsborough Hundred reported that Robert Fortin

Table 6. *Victims Slain by Relatives*

Relative who killed victim	Male victims		Female victims		Total	
	Number	Percent	Number	Percent	Number	Percent
Husband	—	—	64	80.0%	64	40.3%
Wife	32	40.5%	—	—	32	20.1
Father	7	8.9	3	3.8	10	6.3
Mother	3	3.8	3	3.8	6	3.8
Son	4	5.1	4	5.0	8	5.0
Daughter	1	1.3	1	1.3	2	1.3
Brother	27	34.2	3	3.8	30	18.9
Sister	5	6.3	—	—	5	3.1
Uncle	1	1.3			1	0.6
Father-in-law	1	1.3			1	0.6
Mother-in-law	1	1.3			1	0.6
Son-in-law	1	1.3	1	1.3	2	1.3
Son-in-law's brother			1	1.3	1	0.6
Daughter-in-law			1	1.3	1	0.6
Brother-in-law	1	1.3	2	2.5	3	1.9
Sister-in-law	5	6.3	—	—	5	3.1
Stepson	1	1.3	2	2.5	3	1.9
Stepdaughter	1	1.3	1	1.3	2	1.3
TOTAL	79		80		159	

NOTE: Since some people were killed by more than one relative, they have been counted twice. Therefore, the columns sum to numbers greater than those given and the percentages to more than 100.0 percent.

had disappeared. They went on to state they suspected that his wife Agnes and her servant Wymarca had killed him because Agnes had fallen in love with another man, and Robert had often gone to stay with his parents because of the great hatred between him and his wife. The jurors, however, refused either to convict or acquit Agnes, pleading their ignorance of the true state of affairs, and at least one person told the justices that Robert had drowned in the sea.[44]

There is evidence that some killings may have grown out of the desertion of one spouse by another, especially the desertion of a husband by his wife. The disapproving attitude of society toward such conduct can be gathered from an incident in which Hugh, bishop of Lincoln, was involved. A young married woman of Oxford had become enamored of another man, abandoned her husband, and begun living with her lover. Hugh ordered her to return to her husband. Supported by her mother, she refused. Hugh tried to reconcile the husband and wife before the altar of a church. The rebellious wife, however, not only refused to give her husband the kiss of peace, she spat in his face, an act that the assembled ecclesiastics took as an affront to themselves. Hugh immediately excommunicated the woman. When she died a few days later, the saint's biographer approvingly noted that "her illicit and temporary delights were exchanged for perpetual torments as she richly deserved." [45]

The Bedfordshire coroners' rolls tell of two men, apparently separated from their wives, who took violent revenge on their spouses. On the evening of May 5, 1269, Richard son of Robert the reeve of Staploe came to Wilden to the house of his wife, Ivette the sempstress. He asked her to go with him to his father's house in Staploe. She replied that she did not want to set out so late. Eventually, however, they left, sometime after midnight. At Witewelle in William Pinceware's field in Eaton Socon, Richard killed her with an axe and threw her body down the well. [46] Two years later Walter le Bedel of Renhold disposed of his wife in a similar fashion. On March 29, 1271, he went to his wife Isabel's house in Ravensden, and asked her to go with him back to Renhold, some miles away, so that he could give her a bushel of wheat for her children. She went with him. In a meadow named Longemade he stabbed her above the left ear with a knife. Having killed her, he threw her body into "Ravenesbrok" stream and fled. [47]

The next largest group of intrafamilial homicide involved siblings. Thirty-five people (22 percent) were killed by their brothers or sisters. Although siblings were the most important relatives to whom medieval Englishmen turned for aid, they were nevertheless a group among whom strife was frequent. The opportunities for disagreement between brothers and sisters must have been legion. Noninheriting sons may often have felt resentment against the son who inherited all of their father's holdings. Sons who did not inherit land were entitled to a portion of their father's movable property when he died. If a son left home during his father's lifetime, this portion was often settled on him in advance. This practice undoubtedly caused conflict among some brothers, because the elder tried to keep down the amount of money and goods that his younger sibling received. The management of the family property also occasioned disputes. In 1270 in the manor of Halesowen in Worcestershire, Ranulf the clerk cut down some of his brother's trees. His brother Thomas Simon denounced him, and in the following scuffle Thomas wounded Ranulf in the head with an axe.[48] In at least one case a dispute about a loan between two brothers resulted in the death of one of them. At dawn on December 31, 1268, in the Bedfordshire town of Goldington, Henry and William, sons of Richard the carpenter, quarreled over a halfpenny, which one of them had lent the other. William hit Henry on the head with a crab-apple staff and killed him instantly.[49] A sibling's marriage could also result in strife. John Sali of Chalgrave in Bedfordshire married a woman from the village of Sharnbrook against his brother's will. This brother, named Walter, defamed John to his brother's new father-in-law. In this case the matter was resolved in the manorial court,[50] but in many instances such conflicts must have led to fatal blows.

Almost as many homicides involved parents and children as involved siblings. A total of sixteen people (10.1 percent) were killed by their parents—ten by their fathers and six by their mothers. Ten people (6.3 percent) were murdered by their children, eight by their sons and two by their daughters.* Although 26 people (16.4 percent) were murdered by parents or children, and 35 were killed by siblings, this number may nevertheless indicate that conflicts between parents and children were more

---

* Some people whom I have counted as having been killed by their children may have been killed by their stepchildren instead, for it is often difficult to determine from the eyre rolls whether a person is a child or stepchild. For example, the roll of the 1276 Bedfordshire eyre states that Raymond le Taylur, his son Robert and his daughter Eva were suspected of having murdered Emma, Raymond's wife. (PRO, J.I.1/10, m. 33r.). Reading through the eyre roll, one is led to the conclusion that Robert and Eva were also Emma's children. However, in the coroner's roll (*Beds. Cor. Rolls*, p. 73), although Robert is not mentioned as a suspect, it is reported that Emma was Eva's stepmother.

severe than those between brothers and sisters. Given the low expectation of life, it is probable that many parents died before their children grew to adult years and before conflicts within the family had had time to ripen. Therefore, the number of siblings killed, although greater than the number of parents and children, may actually represent less severe conflict, since one had available for a longer period of time more siblings than parents with whom to quarrel.

Slightly more children were killed by parents than parents by children, 16 as opposed to 10. The factors that led children to murder their parents may often have turned on the control of the family patrimony. Relations between sons and fathers would have been exacerbated by a father putting off his retirement and the consequent turning over of the tenement to the heir for what a son regarded as an unconscionably long time. Heirs may also have objected to the sale or leasing of parts of the holding, transactions that would have detracted from the tenement's future worth. Similarly, quarrels may have been generated by the sale of some particularly valuable resource, such as timber. In at least one instance, such a sale caused a falling out between father and son. On June 22, 1275, at Halesowen, Richard de Cakemore sold some of his wood. His son Richard came and tried to prevent the sale, claiming that he also had a right in the timber.[51]

Parents and children also on occasion came into conflict because of children's paramours. For example, Mabil, daughter of Ralph Bosse, had been living in adultery with Robert Puttoc. One day Robert went into Ralph's grange to get some corn, and Ralph tried to stop him. Together Robert and Mabil killed him. They then took his body into Derham in Norfolk and hung it in Ralph's house to make it appear that he had committed suicide.[52]

The killing of children by parents seems to have been a rare event. Although more children were reported to have been killed by parents than parents by children, at least a quarter of the sixteen child killings were accidental. Richard, the infant son of John Blechliche, was killed when his father threw a stick at his mother, which knocked a mattock off a post into his cradle.[53] Robert le Blunt of the borough of Oxford, while beating his wife, accidentally struck and killed his half-year-old daughter Isolda.[54] Ralph, son of Augustine of Taynton, died when a horse to whose tail he had been tied by his father as a punishment escaped.[55] And Stephen, son of John the miller, was fatally wounded when a knife with which his father had been eating fell out of a napkin and struck him.* Thus the number of children deliberately killed by their parents was not very large.

Despite the famous remark of John the marshal during the siege of Newbury that he did not care if King Stephen hanged his son William since he still had the anvils and hammers with which to forge better ones,[56] children seem to have been highly valued in the Middle Ages. The birth of a child was a great event, accompanied by feasts and a round of visits to the infant's mother.[57] Children were looked after as well as the rudimentary medical knowledge of the period allowed. Babies were provided with caretakers.[58] And, far from being regarded as no different in their needs than adults, they were known to require special care. The moralist Robert Mannyng of Brunne, counseling against the sin of gluttony, held that his readers should eat only two meals a day. Young children, however, he wrote, could be allowed to eat three times a day.[59]

To murder one's own child seems to have been regarded as an especially heinous act, which does not mean that it never happened. Basilia, daughter of Christina of Wroxall in Wiltshire, gave birth to an infant and immediately hid him in a ditch. A dog found the child's body, and carried it through the middle of the town.[60] Similarly, in the village of Derham in Norfolk, Amicia Haret strangled her three-day-old child.[61] But a peculiar

---

* PRO, J.I.1/569a, m. 29r. Although this story may at first seem too incredible to be true, it should not be dismissed as a fabrication. A wound that severs an artery or punctures the lung cavity in such a way as to cause the loss of the vacuum necessary for the proper functioning of the lungs can result in death in a matter of minutes. It is possible that a knife dropped from some height might cause such a wound in a very small child. Even if the wound was minor to begin with, a fatal infection may have followed.

horror does seem to have attached in contemporaries' minds to the killing of children. The monk who wrote the chronicle of Melrose, a monastery located in the lowlands of Scotland, under the year 1181 noted the killing at St. Edmund's of a boy named Robert by a Jew. In the second half of the twelfth century, accusations that Jews engaged in the deliberate killing of Christian children were beginning to spread, and the Melrose chronicler's story is in this tradition. What is interesting for the purpose of this study, however, is that, having told this story, the chronicler's mind made an associative leap to the tale of another little boy who had been murdered. But this child named Herbert, from Huntingdonshire, had been killed, not by Jews, but by his father. The chronicler even asserted that miracles had been worked through his virtue just as they had been through that of the boy killed by the Jew.[62] Thus, in at least one mind, the sense of horror engendered by the killing of a Christian child by Jews was associated with that caused by the killing of a child by his parent. So terrible an act was the murder of a child by its parent that there seems to have been a widespread belief that people who killed their children were mentally deranged, like the Lancashire man, Swayn de Hoton, who "driven by fury," seized his son Robert by the feet and smashed his head against a stone, killing him.[63]

Although in-laws constituted only a tiny fraction of those to whom one turned for aid in killing someone else, they made up a larger proportion of those killed. Twelve people (7.5 percent) were slain by in-laws (two people were killed by more than one type of in-law). Women were outsiders in the families they married into, and in a male-centered authority system had to learn to adjust their claims to the prior claims of their husbands. Conflicting loyalties were thus created.[64] In an incident in Worcestershire in 1271 a glimpse is caught of some of the conflicts that could exist between in-laws. At vespers in the manor of Halesowen, Hawisia, who had been out drinking, came home with two of her daughters. She locked the door of her house, shutting out her eldest daughter and her daughter's husband. The man broke into the house and struck his mother-in-law. The hue was raised and the neighbors turned out to answer it. In the riot that followed, at least one of the villagers was wounded.[65] Unfortunately, the terseness of the Halesowen manorial court rolls, which contain this story, makes it impossible to know more than these sketchy details. But a long history of intrafamilial conflict probably lay behind this particular brawl.

It was also not uncommon for someone who married a widow or widower to encounter hostility from his new mate's children, three people being murdered by their stepchildren (two by both a stepson and a stepdaughter). In some cases stepchildren may have been drawn into conflicts between their original parent and his or her new spouse, like Robert and Eva who helped their father Robert murder his new wife Emma in Bedfordshire.[66] In other cases fatal conflict may have been engendered by the fact that a stepparent could be a bar to a child's gaining his inheritance.[67] For example, in the fourteenth century Emma Baker of Wigston Magna in Leicestershire married John Baker. Their marriage produced a son, Richard Baker, who became a clerk. As their only son, Richard stood to inherit the capital messuage, 24 acres of land, and a yearly rent of 13½d. Emma, however, after the death of her first husband, married Robert Ley. When he died, she again remarried, this time to Adam Sutton. When Emma herself finally died, Adam enfeoffed John Weston with the tenement to the disherison of Richard Baker. As a result, Richard killed Adam on November 13, 1390.[68]

A very small proportion of victims, only 21 in all, are known to have been murdered by that other component of the medieval household, masters or servants. It was extremely rare for masters to kill their servants. Only four servants were murdered by their masters. Four people were also killed by their fellow servingmen. The most common occurrence, however, was the slaying of masters by servants, thirteen people dying in this fashion. When the sources allow a glimpse into the nature of the conflicts between masters and servants, it appears that they often turned on the questions of pay and performance of duties. For example, the following incident, recorded at the 1242–43 eyre of Somerset, illustrates a fight that grew out of a quarrel over the quality of a servant's work. John of Mells had employed Hugh de Hogeford as a plowman. One day he ordered Hugh to plow some of his land. Either through mistake or for some reason not specified, Hugh plowed in the wrong place. As a result, John threatened him. Hugh decided to quit and went to get together his clothes, which seem to have been kept in John's house. John tried to keep him from leaving, and in the following fight Hugh hit his master on the head with a club.[69] Although John survived, other masters were not so fortunate. In either Barford St. John or Barford St. Michael, both in Oxfordshire, a dispute over wages resulted in the murder of a master by a servant. Andreas of Radford killed and robbed his mistress, Basilia of Barford, "because for some time she [had] held back his pay." [70] A similar event occurred in Wiltshire. However, in this case it was the servant who died. Apparently, Robert de Cruce owed his servant Robert Hathewy back wages. At least Robert Hathewy threatened him several times in connection with them. Finally, on the evening of February 10, 1269, he attacked Robert de Cruce as he came from the house of the parson of Nettleton. Robert de Cruce fought back at first with a rock, and then with a knife. He managed to kill Robert Hathewy and fled.[71]

Servants could also become involved in the domestic quarrels of their masters and wind up taking the side of one against the other. When John de Loundoneston killed his wife Agnes on April 20, 1242, in London, suspicion fell on John Clerk, Thomas Marsh of Barking, William de la Cheniere, Ralph of Sawbridgeworth, Maud of Southwark, and Maud of Shenley, all six members of John's *familia*. Since they had been present at the killing, had remained with John until he fled, and had not raised the hue or given information to the sheriff or the chamberlains concerning the murder, the justices suspected them of complicity in the deed.[72]

The household and the kin group were but two of the networks of which thirteenth-century English society was composed. Medieval Englishmen belonged to a large number of different communities. But the household and the family, with their complex of ties between kin, masters, and servants, were perhaps the most important social organisms to which a man or woman could belong. It was to the members of these groups that a man frequently turned when confronted by a problem to which violence seemed the only answer. Almost a quarter, 578 of 2,372 (24.4 percent), of all those who killed with a partner did so with someone from these groups. The obligations of blood and service were indeed compelling in this society. But at the same time, and in large part because the duties owed to the members of the household and to kin were felt so strongly, there was much violent conflict within the medieval *familia*. It was all too easy for a man to feel that his relatives, masters, or servants had defaulted in their obligations to him, that he had been wronged by them. Therefore, the woman who slew her husband, or the man who killed his brother or his master, was, lamentably, an all too familiar figure in thirteenth-century England.

4. Social Status and Violent Conflict

The willingness of a person to resort to violence is heavily influenced by his social status. Some groups within a society have better access to means of settling their conflicts than others. Some can draw upon a wide array of institutionalized means of settling differences whereas others cannot. Different groups within a society also have different attitudes about the use of violence. Among some status groups violence may be shunned as uncouth and unmannerly, the man or woman engaging in it rendering himself a pariah. Yet for others within the same society, violence may be highly esteemed and combativeness regarded as a sign of manliness.[1] Different levels of violence among different social groups are thus indexes of the different norms by which the members of those groups order their intercourse with one another.

Unfortunately, for thirteenth-century England, the social status of murderers and their victims is very difficult to determine. Not until the middle of the fourteenth century were court clerks required to specify in the records they kept the status of those who appeared for trial. Occasionally, but extremely rarely, the eyre rolls and coroners' rolls of the thirteenth century state that a man is a freeman, lord, knight, or villein. Nor do the rolls generally provide much other information with which to gauge the social status of the people named in them. For both killer and victim the rolls may give an occupational surname. But simply because someone is labeled a smith or a plowman does not necessarily mean that that was his full-time occupation. Although occupational surnames in the thirteenth century were still in large part functional, some undoubtedly were only nicknames or family names. Even in those cases where occupational surnames actually designate their bearers' vocations, they are still not reliable indications of social status. A man called a spicer might have been anything from a petty shopkeeper to a wealthy and influential merchant.

The eyre rolls provide somewhat better information about the social status of accused killers than about that of victims. The king was entitled to the movable property of convicted felons or outlaws and to a year and a day's waste of any freehold land that they possessed. The information about freehold property, however, is not very helpful in determining someone's standing in the community. The mere possession of freehold land did not necessarily imply a high social position. Although the richest peasants tended to be freeholders, many impoverished cottars were also members of this group. Even when the jurors reported on the value of a free tenement, it is not clear that they valued all the landed wealth of the individual in question. Often it appears that they limited their assessment to the accused's freehold land within their own hundred or county. If the man held land in other counties, this would on occasion be noted. But often such information must have been left out of the records. In the cases of unfree tenants, some of whom were substantial and influential members of their communities, there is of course no indication of the extent of their land holdings in the rolls.

Therefore, the most important single index the rolls provide for determining a person's social position is the value of his movable property. But the drawbacks of using the assessed value of a felon's chattels as an indication of his social status are obvious. Chattels were often deliberately undervalued by jurors. The property of married women or adult sons living with their parents was often regarded as that of their parents or husbands. Other motives and opportunities for concealment and undervaluation must have been legion. Even if it could be assumed that chattels were accurately recorded in the eyre rolls, they would still indicate only wealth and not social status. Although some peasants of more substantial means may have been almost as wealthy as the lesser gentry, a great gulf nevertheless separated the two groups in their ways of life, legal privileges, expectations, and views of the world.

Although the assessed value of chattels is an unreliable guide, it is the only consistent one that the eyre rolls provide. In order to understand these figures, however, we must know something of the purchasing power of money in thirteenth-century England. Unfortunately, medieval wages and prices are a vexed and confusing question. Nevertheless, some guidelines are available. R. H. Hilton has found that, in the West Midlands at the end of the thirteenth century, the daily wage in cash of a skilled worker, such as a carpenter, was 3*d.* This was paid if the worker provided his own food. If his employer fed him, the wage was 1*d.* to 1½*d.* Permanent farm servants received different wages depending on their skills. Plowmen and carters usually received about 5*s.* a year in cash, with an issue of a quarter of mixed grains every ten to thirteen weeks.[2] The price of an eight-bushel quarter of wheat, the most expensive grain, used for the making of white bread, varied from a low of 2*s.* 2½*d.* in 1213 to a high of 16*s.* 8*d.* during the famine year of 1315.[3] In the Hampshire village of Crawley, the average buying price of a cart horse in the years between 1231 and 1314 was 16*s.* 1½*d.* The selling price of the same animal was 10*s.* 3*d.* Oxen cost an average 10*s.* 11¾*d.* per animal and sold for 9*s.* 4¾*d.* In the same period the buying price of cows was 7*s.* 1¼*d.* per animal and the selling price 6*s.* 3¼*d.* A ewe cost 1*s.* 3*d.* and sold for 10½*d.**

* Gras and Gras, pp. 64–65. Farmer (in "Some Livestock Price Movements," pp. 2–5) has calculated buying and selling prices of livestock for England as a whole. His data show the purchasing price of a cart horse fluctuating between 8*s.* 2*d.* (in 1210) and 28*s.* 11*d.* (in 1309), that of an ox varying between 6*s.* 1¾*d.* (1210) and 17*s.* 8*d.* (1321), and that of a ewe ranging from 8*d.* (1224) to 2*s.* ¼*d.*

Table 7. *Value of Confiscated Chattels*

Value of chattels	Number of accused	Percent of total	Cumulative percentage
0	1,044	60.6%	60.6%
1*d.*–5*s.*	299	17.3	77.9
5*s.*1*d.*–10*s.*	119	6.9	84.8
10*s.*1*d.*–15*s.*	80	4.6	89.4
15*s.*1*d.*–20*s.*	36	2.1	91.5
20*s.*1*d.*–25*s.*	28	1.6	93.2
25*s.*1*d.*–30*s.*	26	1.5	94.7
30*s.*1*d.*–35*s.*	10	0.6	95.2
35*s.*1*d.*–40*s.*	9	0.5	95.8
40*s.*1*d.*–45*s.*	13	0.8	96.5
45*s.*1*d.*–50*s.*	9	0.5	97.0
50*s.*1*d.*–55*s.*	4	0.2	97.3
55*s.*1*d.*–60*s.*	3	0.2	97.4
60*s.*1*d.*–65*s.*	1	0.1	97.5
65*s.*1*d.*–70*s.*	7	0.4	97.9
70*s.*1*d.*–75*s.*	2	0.1	98.0
75*s.*1*d.*–80*s.*	4	0.2	98.3
80*s* & over	30	1.7	100.0
TOTAL	1,724	99.9%	

The eyre rolls give the value of confiscated chattels of 1,724 people, seen in Table 7. The average value of these chattels was about 8*s.*8*d.* (exactly 104.4 pence). This might not seem an extremely low figure. Yet if the chattels are arranged in groups of 5*s.*, a very different impression emerges. The great majority of the 1,724 people, 1,044 (60.6 percent), had no movable property at all); 299 had some property, but worth less than 5*s.* In all, 77.9 percent had property worth less than 5*s.* Since an ox cost about 10*s.*11¾*d.*, these people would have been unable to afford even one of these basic plow beasts. Another 119 people had between 5 and 10*s.* worth, and those who came near the top of this group might have been able to possess an ox. But they were not wealthy enough to own a horse. Indeed, only 10.6 percent of the accused had more than 15*s.* worth and could have afforded a horse.

(1298). The selling price of these animals varied from 2*s.*9½*d.* (1294) to 14*s.*¾*d.* (1313) for cart horses, from 4*s.* 7½*d.* (1215) to 17*s.* 1½*d.* (1310) for oxen and from 5½*d.* (1213) to 1*s.* 5¾*d.* (1319) for ewes.

Thus it appears that the majority of killers, or at least of those whose chattels were confiscated, came from the lower ranks of society. In an agrarian society where the cultivation of the land by the plow was the basis of the economy, they lacked the capital to provide themselves with one, let alone two, of the indispensable plow-beasts. Therefore, their economic situation must often have been extremely marginal, and their position within the community one of low prestige and authority.

That violence should have been the tool of the relatively poor is not surprising. For the poor man or woman in thirteenth-century England, violence was one of the few available means of influencing the behavior of one's antagonist in a dispute, although it was a desperate and probably a not very efficient means. Wealthy freeholders and peasants had access to courts, whether royal or manorial, in which to settle their conflicts. They also had at their command many extra-legal methods of coercing their poorer neighbors. The wealthy villein, elected to office as reeve or juror of the manorial court, could manipulate the seigneurial power of his lord and of the manorial court to suit his needs. Also, by virtue of his superior economic resources, he could discipline his fellow villagers by granting or denying them access to wage labor or by granting or refusing the loan of the animals and implements without which the poorer villagers could not till their land. The poor peasant, even if he were free, had not the resources to take his disputes before the royal courts. Even if he could afford to bring his case to the county or hundred court, these had in the course of the twelfth and thirteenth centuries been stripped of many of their original powers.[4] In the manorial courts, the voice of a near-landless laborer who had to work for others to survive would not have counted for much against that of a wealthy tenant. Violence was therefore often the work of the poor and the impotent. Indeed, a poor peasant had relatively little to lose by resorting to violence. Should his victim die and he be forced to flee for safety, his lot might not have been materially much worse than before. He simply became a laborer in a different village. A wealthy peasant, on the other hand, would have had to give up his home, his animals, his tools, his land, and accept a catastrophic loss of social position.

Of course, examples of wealthy and powerful people who engaged in homicidal activity can be found. For example, on October 5, 1270, Hugh Bossard of Knotting took seisin of Souldrop church in Bedfordshire with its lordship and advowson after buying from its patron some land belonging to it. That night brother Hubert of Chelsham, master of Melchbourne hospital, arrived and asked Hugh and his companions what they were doing on the hospital's fee. Hugh replied that he was there as of right. Hubert then called on him and his followers to leave the church. When they refused, Hubert and his men attacked, and tried to set fire to the church. Hugh and his men fought back, killing Roger le May with an arrow.[5] A similar dispute over a church in Thame in the diocese of Lincoln produced a series of incidents in the 1290's. Bishop Oliver de Sutton of Lincoln in September 1292 collated Master Thomas of Sutton, one of his relatives, to the Thame prebend. A royal clerk, Edward St. John, disputed this collation, claiming a prior papal provision for himself. Sutton declared the provision invalid. This did not prevent Edward and his followers from seizing the church by force in early November. Either at this time or shortly thereafter, one of St. John's followers, Peter of Wyresdale, was killed. The bishop excommunicated St. John and his men. Thomas of Sutton managed to regain the church, but St. John returned to the attack. With an army of 200 men he assaulted the church, piled timber in the porch, lighted it, and pulled stones from the church walls so that arrows could be fired at the men within. His forces eventually managed to enter the church and wounded two clerics. Sutton renewed his sentence of excommunication. To prevent its publication, St. John's followers broke into the neighboring church at Long Crendon during matins and beat the officiating clergy. They also attacked the monastery of Notley. Eventually, this dispute found its way into the royal courts. In October 1294 the king ordered the lands and prebends restored to Thomas of

Sutton and issued a general pardon to all those involved in the killing of Peter of Wyresdale.[6]

The most notorious incident of violent conflict among the nobility involved John de Warenne, earl of Surrey, and Alan de la Zouche. The two had been disputing the possession of a certain manor for some time. On June 19, 1270, the case was tried in the hall at Westminster before the king's justices. Warrenne, Alan, and Alan's eldest son began quarreling. Eventually, the earl's men set upon the Zouches, seriously wounding Alan. Henry III and the Lord Edward, who were in the neighboring palace, were incensed by this violence. The earl fled to Reigate Castle. Edward pursued him there and threatened to besiege him, a threat that persuaded the earl to surrender. On July 6 he submitted himself to the king's mercy. He was required to pay a fine of 10,000 marks. On August 3 he purged himself with 25 oath helpers, and on August 4 he was pardoned. Alan de la Zouche died six days later. Although the earl suffered no further trouble as a result of this, it was widely regarded as a scandal that he had been treated so leniently.[7]

It will be noted that almost all these incidents are drawn from sources other than the eyre rolls. It can be suspected that the rolls may not give a complete picture of violent activity among the aristocracy. If any group was able to avoid being named as accused of homicide by the jurors, it would have been this one.* Only investigation into sources other than the eyre rolls can reveal the full extent of conflict among the nobles and how this conflict was structured. Although such research may reveal a greater propensity for bellicose display on the part of the nobles than do the eyre rolls, it is unlikely that it will show them to have been noticeably homicidal. Among the 3,492 killers, of those

---

* The eyre rolls, of course, do not record homicides committed in the course of wars with the Welsh, French, or Scots. But the killing of members of a rival out-group is very different from the killing of members of one's own community, the type of homicide that is the object of this study. There is not a necessary correlation between high levels of domestic homicide and high levels of intergroup or international conflict. Twentieth-century Europeans seldom murder their fellow citizens, but in the course of the two major wars of this century they have systematically slaughtered several million people.

people who there is reason to believe from their titles may have
been of some social importance, there were only one sheriff, two
sheriff's serjeants, one constable, nine monks, two abbots, four
canons, and one royal clerk. Similarly, among the 2,434 victims
there were one sheriff's serjeant, six monks, one canon, and five
masters, two of whom taught at Oxford. No one described as a
knight or a lord is to be found among the victims. Undoubtedly,
some of the people who appeared in the records were members
of the ruling classes who cannot now be identified as such. But
the impression derived from the eyre rolls is that members of
the ruling elites did not personally participate in violent conflict
to any significant degree.*

This reluctance to engage in direct violent conflict with their
fellow nobles contrasts startlingly with the behavior of other European nobles. On the continent as well as elsewhere in the British Isles, conflict within the ranks of the various nobilities seems
to have been much more frequent and to have persisted into a
much later period. Although by the thirteenth century the formal blood feud had ceased to exist in England among the aristocracy, it persisted in other countries. For example, it appears
that even after Berry had been brought under the control of the
French monarchy by Philip Augustus, feuds among the local nobility persisted in the thirteenth century.[8] In the Romagna in fif-
teenth-century Italy the blood feud was still practiced.[9] In Ger-
many as late as 1453 a feud could divide an imperial counselor,
Georg von Pucheim, against his master, the Emperor Frederick
III.[10] In Britain itself, outside of the confines of England, the
noble feud continued to be practiced with zest. In the fourteenth
and fifteenth centuries feuding was endemic among the Scottish
nobility. For example, in the year 1478 there were serious feuds
going on between the earl of Buchan and the earl of Atholl, between the master of Crawford and the lord of Glamis, and between the lord of Caerlaverock and the lord of Drumlanrick.
There was also a lesser feud going on that involved the lords of

* For references to some violent conflicts in which English nobles became involved, see below, p. 77.

Caithness, Ross, and Sutherland.[11] In the Welsh marches, the unsettled border area between England and Wales, private war was a jealously guarded custom, and it required drastic action on the part of Edward I in 1291 to halt the fighting between the earls of Gloucester and Hereford.[12] But within England itself such outbreaks of violent conflict among the nobility appear to have been virtually nonexistent. Even when two nobles fell out, they appear to have been very reluctant to push matters to a violent conclusion. For example, in 1269 John de Warenne, earl of Surrey, and Henry de Lacy, earl of Lincoln, quarreled over their respective rights to a pasture. Both earls assembled their armed retainers and prepared for battle, but, as the chronicler who recorded these events noted, "they feared to come together." Ultimately the issue was settled by royal justices in a royal court.[13]

It thus appears that the behavior of the English nobility in the thirteenth century was very different from that of their counterparts in the rest of Europe. That this should be so is hardly surprising. Although the great English lords were exceedingly rich, unlike their European counterparts they did not rule over compact, coherent territorial blocks like the castellans of France. Their estates were scattered about England. This made it difficult to mobilize support for a violent quarrel. More important, the English nobles lived in a country with the most developed administrative machine and legal system in Europe. With access to a nearly ubiquitous, flexible, and, for the age, sophisticated, system of courts, there was less need for members of the gentry and aristocracy to turn out with arms to defend their interests. And with powerful monarchs on the throne, there was often a very great incentive to refrain from violence. This system did not work perfectly, and when it did break down, as it did in the reigns of John, Henry III, and Edward II, the nobility could be divided against itself. But these outbursts, which were of fairly short duration, more resemble civil wars, which pit two large factions against one another in a struggle to control the state, than they resemble the chronic, drawn-out feuds conducted by two or three lords against one another elsewhere in Europe.* Apart from these major political crises, the English nobles appear to have preferred to settle their disputes in some fashion other than by personally assaulting their enemies.[14]

In addition to these major factors which made for a generally nonviolent ruling class in thirteenth-century England, some other forces were at work as well. In part, it may well have been the fear of one another that helped keep the ruling groups peaceful. That suspicion and apprehension for one's physical safety acted to restrain conflict, at least among the ranks of the great churchmen, is made abundantly clear in the records they have left. The clerics who move through thirteenth-century chronicles seem to have been eager to spy out threats to their lives. When Samson was abbot of the great house of Bury St. Edmund's, he became embroiled with his monks in what he thought to be a potentially deadly dispute. During one of his absences, the monks deprived Ralf the gatekeeper, who had been the subject of complaints by some of the obedientiaries, of his pay, although they allowed him to keep the corrody which belonged to his office. Ralf, however, complained to Samson that

* Joel Rosenthal (in "Mediaeval Longevity and the Secular Peerage," *Population Studies,* 27 (1973): 288) has found that of 434 peers, i.e. men individually summoned to parliament between 1350 and 1500, 83 (or 19.1 percent) died violently. This finding might seem to disprove the thesis that I have argued here. However, Rosenthal lumps together all violent deaths, including those of persons who died in hunting accidents, who were killed in battle by the Scots or the French, or who were slain by their fellow Englishmen. It is thus impossible to gauge the amount of domestic noble conflict from his figures. The question is further confused by the fact that the number of people who received individual summonses to parliament decreased drastically in the late Middle Ages as the notion of a peerage crystallized. By the end of the Middle Ages, Rosenthal is dealing with a very small group. Of the 35 peers born after 1451, 9 (25.7 percent) died violently. As the richest and most powerful individuals in England, these people were obviously in a dangerous position if they should be on the losing side in a faction struggle. The same, however, is probably not true for the average noble or member of the gentry, whose head did not stick up far enough to be cut off. I think it is significant that in the largest of the birth cohorts into which Rosenthal divided his peers, and therefore the most representative of the fate of the average member of the English ruling elite, only 3.5 percent of 86 peers born before 1325 died violently.

he had been deprived of his corrody, an act that he claimed was especially to the abbot's dishonor since it had been done without consulting him. When Samson confronted the monks and ordered Jocellus the cellarer to return all that had been taken from Ralf, Jocellus refused. Samson immediately went into exile. From his retreat, he sent a letter to his monks in which, according to Jocelin of Brakelond, he wrote that "he would not come among us because of the conspiracies and oaths, which he said we had made against him, to slay him with our knives." [15] In 1237, when the papal legate Otto held a council at St. Paul's in London at which he planned to act against pluralists, he so feared for his life that he had to be provided with an armed guard by the king, which included Gilbert, the earl marshal, John, earl of Lincoln, and Simon de Montfort.[16]

The section of the chronicle of Evesham abbey written by Thomas of Marlborough is eloquent on the fear that could pervade ecclesiastical circles. Thomas's story is largely concerned with the struggle that he and the other monks of Evesham waged against their abbot, Roger Norreys, who had been prior of Christ Church, Canterbury, before he came to Evesham. When Thomas protested the gift of an assart by the abbot to his nephew, his superior had him arrested. "And then my abbot seized me to put me in prison at Amberesley, to kill me as I thought. For he had done the same thing to the monks at Canterbury and to our man Augustine de Salford whom he had killed with much torture, and therefore I feared greatly, knowing his tyranny." Eventually, however, Thomas did get out of prison alive. At the same time that Roger and his monks were fighting one another, they were contesting the bishop of Worcester's claim of jurisdiction over them. In 1205 Roger and Thomas left England for Rome to conduct the monastery's case in the papal courts. Thomas, who did not trust his abbot's intentions, traveled separately. After a period of wandering about Italy, he finally went to Roger's lodgings in Rome for an interview. He also took the precaution of bringing with him several people to keep watch to see that he came out of the house again.

At the interview Thomas, who was rapidly running out of money, asked his abbot for permission to stay with him. Roger, who apparently had his own suspicions of Thomas, exploded, and denounced him as an enemy and a traitor, saying, "Should I allow you into my house so that you can kill me?" Nevertheless, he eventually agreed to let Thomas stay with him for fifteen days. One night a chaplain who shared Thomas' room told him that the abbot was plotting his murder. The next day, Thomas and the abbot encountered each other, and Roger denounced the monk for blocking his efforts toward the papal curia, and exclaimed, "By the queen of the angels I will be revenged on you." Thomas, who had prudently secreted a knife on his person, succeeded in calming his enraged abbot, and the two managed to get through the rest of their stay together in Rome without coming to blows.[17]

Since the lay nobility were not as inclined to literary pursuits as the upper levels of the clergy, it is difficult to discern with what mistrust they viewed one another. But what evidence is available leaves the impression that they also feared one another. To an extent, this fear was warranted, for the members of this class, which liked to conceive of itself as devoted to the exercise of arms, were fond of engaging in physical threats. The royal courts even allowed a man who had been threatened a remedy by which he could have the culprit bound to obey the peace, an action that appears to have been fairly common. For example, in late thirteenth-century Bedfordshire, Lord John Enslye and Master Walter Covlye waged peace to Hugh of St. Edward, Geoffrey of Carlton did the same to Master Matthew of Dunstable, and Ralph Pirrot waged peace to Miles Thekin, John of Pattishall's parker.[18]

Whenever trouble seemed imminent, the nobles conducted themselves warily. For example, when Henry III held his Christmas court at Winchester in 1239, his doormen denied entrance to Gilbert the earl marshal and his men, threatening them with blows. The earl immediately "perceived that doubtlessly some whisperer had sewn discord between himself and the king." He quietly returned to his lodgings and the next day sent messengers to Henry to inquire why he had been treated in this way. The memory of the revolt of Gilbert's brother Richard was still fresh in the king's mind, and he responded with intemperate words. When these had been reported to the earl, he immediately left Winchester.* The suspicion of one another's intent by great churchmen and important lords, and the circumspect activity it inspired, served the function of enabling them to avoid situations in which they might have come into physical conflict with one another. Convinced that they might indeed be in danger, they took evasive action, action that not only removed them from potential harm but also allowed tempers to cool and paved the way for subsequent agreements. Abbot Samson's eight-day absence from his abbey was the prelude to a tearful reconciliation and a tacit agreement on the part of everyone involved to forget the causes of the dispute.

The structure of knightly households also reduced direct physical conflict among the nobility. Lords, especially rich and powerful ones, lived surrounded by a great retinue of friends, retainers, servants, and hangers-on. This swarm of attendants in effect insulated lords from physical conflict with one another. For one thing, if it appeared that a dispute was about to come to a physical resolution, there was almost always someone present to step between the two combatants. On two different occasions, when William de Valence, King Henry III's half-brother, denounced Simon de Montfort as a traitor, an insult that prompted Simon to attack him, Henry prevented violence by stepping between the two.[19]

The swarm of retainers that surrounded a lord was also a de-

---

* Paris, 3: 523–24. The stories in Paris, whose love of the dramatic and the scurrilous makes his chronicle so entertaining, must often be approached with caution. (For differing views about Paris's reliability, see Richard Vaughan, *Matthew Paris* [Cambridge, Eng., 1958], p. 134, and M. T. Clanchy, "Did Henry III Have a Policy?" *History*, 53 [1968]: 205–8.) Yet even if the evidence that Paris provides, especially the speeches he puts into people's mouths, has been embroidered by his fertile imagination, it nevertheless can be used to explore what may have been widely held attitudes about various people, events, and types of behavior.

terrent to violent conflict, since an attack on a master would have provoked instant retaliation from his followers, a fact of which contemporaries were aware. At a stormy parliament held in London in February 1251, Henry III denounced one of his justices, Henry of Bath, for perverting justice. In an excess of rage, Henry declared, "If anyone kills Henry of Bath, let him be quit of his death." Having spoken these words, the king stormed out of the meeting. According to Matthew Paris, there were many people present who were willing to attack Henry. However, the justice had taken the precaution of coming to the meeting with a large group of his friends and supporters. Before anyone could act, John Mansel, one of the king's most trusted clerks, spoke up. He observed that the king might regret his words once his temper had cooled. And, he went on to point out, if anyone assaulted Henry, the knights who were with him would take immediate "revenge" on his attackers. These words calmed the parliament, and Henry of Bath was allowed to depart unharmed after promising to pay the king a large sum of money.[20]

A lord's retainers also gave him a means of injuring his opponents indirectly without his own physical involvement. Quarrels between members of the upper classes were often fought out by their retainers. For example, in Norfolk John Lovel claimed the liberty of hanging handhaving thieves on either his own gallows or those of the church of Holy Trinity, Norwich. One day at Docking John's men caught a thief, who was judged to death. As John and his men were preparing for the execution, word reached them that the prior's men intended to prevent them from exercising John's liberty. Therefore, John sent John de Elecumb and others out on a reconaissance. They encountered the prior's men, and in the ensuing fight, John de Elecumb wounded Reyner Shad of Sedgeford with an arrow.[21] A similar event occurred in Kent late in the reign of Henry III. Matilda de Acsted held a tenement in gavilkind from Alice de Helles in Petham. Because her rent was in arrears, Alice came and seized the goods in Matilda's mill. As a counter-blow, Matilda sent Ralph de Acsted, John Beneyt, and Nicholas de Eywelested to

Reginald de Cobham's house in Petham, where they beat Alexander, one of Alice's servants, and destroyed her bread, beer, and meat which were stored there.[22]

On the rare occasions when the gentry personally engaged in violence, they often directed their aggression not against their real enemies, but against their enemies' servants. Geoffrey de Childewike was at loggerheads with abbot John of St. Albans (1235–60) over his right to free warren. One day Geoffrey encountered one of the abbey's *famuli*, a man named John, as he was traveling from Bedford to St. Alban's with a gift of venison from the archdeacon of Bedford. Geoffrey denounced him as a thief and a traitor, and accused him of having taken the venison in the king's forest. As a member of the king's *privata familia* and as one of his marshals, he announced that he could not tolerate this. He knocked John from his horse, and made off with it and the venison. John appealed him for robbery and assault, but at the intervention of the king and members of his court, the appeal was dropped.[23]

Some members of the gentry were willing to pay for the assassination of their opponents. In Kent seven thieves attacked a house belonging to the Cistercian monks at Boxley. They wounded three men and killed Brother Gregory. At the 1227 eyre Adam de Berewurth was accused of having given 40*s.* to Robert de Hillinglegh, one of the thieves, to kill the monk. He was convicted and hanged.[24] Some years later Robert le Norreys was accused in the same county of having similarly given Eustace of Suffolk 10*s.* to kill one Richard, a task that Eustace carried out successfully. In this case, however, Robert was acquitted.[25]

The nobility were also able to avail themselves of a ritualized form of aggression, the tournament, which undoubtedly served to vent much ill will. The tournament of the twelfth and thirteenth centuries, which had been legalized in England by Richard I, was little different from war. It was usually fought with unblunted weapons and a minimum of rules. Individual combat was the exception and massed bodies of knights, often aided by foot soldiers, fought one another for hours at a time.[26] Although

Henry III attempted to forbid tournaments during much of his reign, they were often held in spite of his prohibitions.[27] That thirteenth-century tournaments were not mild exercises, but deadly serious games, is shown by a brief glance at some of the men, among them members of the most powerful families in England, who died in them. In 1216 Geoffrey de Mandeville, earl of Essex and one of the leaders of the opposition to King John, was killed in a tournament at London.[28] In 1241 Gilbert Marshal, son of the great tournier William Marshal, was fatally injured during a tournament at Hertford.[29] In 1252 Arnald de Munteinny was killed by Roger de Leyburne, later a fast friend of Edward I.[30] In 1286 William de Warenne, the heir of John de Warenne, earl of Surrey, was killed at Croydon.[31] And in 1304 outside Leicester, Thomas Basset of Welham killed a man during a joust.[32]

Tournaments were often fought between individuals or groups who had reason to dislike one another. In 1249 at Brackley the "aliens" led by the king's half-brother William de Valence fought against the native English lords, led by Richard, earl of Gloucester. The English lost.[33] Two years later, however, they had their revenge outside Rochester when they routed the aliens and pursued them into the city.[34] Other tournaments pitted northern English against southerners.[35] The thinly disguised hostilities that must often have been the real reasons for holding some tournaments were revealed by the suspicions that immediately arose following fatal accidents. Earl Gilbert's death had been caused in 1241 when the reins on his destrier broke and he fell from the animal. Matthew Paris, always a scandalmonger, reports that there were people present at the tournament who believed that the reins had been deliberately cut by someone hoping to injure the earl.[36] When Arnald de Munteinny was killed in 1252, the combat was supposed to have been fought under the new rules, first introduced in 1216, which required blunted weapons. However, when the lance that had killed Arnald was removed from his throat, it was found not to have been blunted as it should have been. As a result, suspicion arose that

Roger de Leyburne had killed him deliberately, especially since in an earlier joust Arnald had broken Roger's leg.[37] Similarly, when William de Warenne was killed in 1286, there was widespread belief that his enemies had brought about his death.[38] Although tournaments ended fatally for some, on the whole they probably served to reduce violent conflict among the lay nobility. Even if the sources of conflict between certain nobles could not be resolved in tournaments, at least the animosities they engendered could be dissipated by a socially approved and satisfying, although probably not fatal, display of brutality.

Beyond the fact that members of the nobility do not seem to have frequently involved themselves directly in murderous assaults, it is difficult to tell if there were any occupational or status groups that were peculiarly prone to homicidal behavior. With the exception of clerics, whose status was invariably specified in the records since they were subject to special treatment in the courts, it is only by chance that the eyre rolls give any indication of the occupation or status of an individual. Probably the great majority of people whose names do not contain an occupational element, 2,039 victims and 2,699 accused, were peasants. See Table 8. A large proportion of those whose names give some indication of occupation were probably peasants also, who happened to pursue a craft as a means of picking up some extra cash. And in the case of some, their occupational surnames may only have been nicknames or family names. Even when these difficulties are taken into account, it is readily apparent that clerics of one sort or another, including their wives, were the single largest occupational or status group involved in homicidal conflict. Of the victims, 67 (2.8 percent) were ecclesiastics, and of the accused, 265 (7.6 percent) were also clerics.* Churchmen

---

* This figure may be artificially inflated. A man accused of homicide could have had a very real interest in claiming to be a cleric, even if he were not in orders. Clerics were supposed to be released to their bishops to stand trial in a church court. Since a church court could not impose a death penalty, there were decided advantages to being able to claim benefit of clergy. Since this privilege extended to all clerics in all orders and not just to those in holy orders, it was not unknown for some laymen to have their heads tonsured while in prison and then try to persuade the court that they were clerics. (For an example, see Leona C.

Table 8. *Accused Killers and Victims with Surnames Indicating Possible Occupation*

	Accused killers		Victims	
Occupational group	Number	Percent	Number	Percent
None	2,699	77.3%	2,039	83.8%
Officials	17	0.5	2	0.1
Manorial officials	20	0.6	14	0.6
Dealers and traders	15	0.4	21	0.9
Manufacturers or sellers of provisions	77	2.2	48	2.0
Cloth workers	56	1.6	35	1.4
Leather workers	28	0.8	20	0.8
Metal workers	64	1.8	31	1.3
Wood workers	23	0.7	20	0.8
Masonry and roofing workers	11	0.3	3	0.1
Stone, crockery, and glass workers	1	0.0	4	0.2
Physicians and barbers	2	0.1	2	0.1
Agricultural workers	25	0.7	24	1.0
Transport workers	20	0.6	14	0.6
Ecclesiastics	265	7.6	67	2.8
Miscellaneous	169	4.8	90	3.7
TOTAL	3,492	100.0%	2,434	100.2%

probably formed about 2 percent of the entire population of thirteenth-century England.[39] Therefore, the fact that almost 3 percent of all victims were clerics is what one would expect if all occupational and social groups were represented equally among the victims. But the fact that they formed 7.6 percent of all accused killers requires explanation.

It is clear that the bulk of those clerics who committed homicide were from the lesser clergy. Of the 265 ecclesiastics and their wives accused, only 26 were from the middling to higher ranks: nine monks, two abbots, two *conversi,* four parsons, four vicars, four canons, and one royal clerk. It is noted that 207 were merely clerics, 21 were chaplains, six deacons, two subdeacons, two "presbyters," and one the wife of a cleric. England in the thirteenth century had an overabundance of churchmen for the

Gabel, *Benefit of Clergy in England in the Later Middle Ages* (Smith College Studies in History, Northampton, 1928, 14: 64.) Thus it is possible that the figure for accused clerics given here may include a few impostors.

jobs available. For example, in the late thirteenth and early four-teenth centuries, the diocese of Worcester contained 445 parishes and some 30 chantries. To serve these churches, there were approximately 2,000 men who had been ordained sub-deacon, deacon, or priest.[40] Although those who had secured a church of their own and some of those who served one as a sub-stitute for an absentee were often substantial peasants,[41] the bulk of the clergy had to eke out a meager and precarious living as assistants to incumbents or as ill-paid chantry priests. In addi-tion to the fact that the livelihood of many priests was relatively insecure, priests of all degrees of wealth and social standing were probably less amenable to the normal means of social con-trol. The very poorest, like the poorest elements of any society, were beyond the normal suasions of family, friends, and associ-ates because of their very rootlessness. Similarly, some parish priests, who were fortunate enough to have secured prosperous livings, may have been able to defy the social pressures of their neighbors because of their wealth, their free status, and their clerical privileges, jealously guarded by the hierarchy. For ex-ample, on the manor of Lewes, when the bailiffs of the lord of the manor, the earl of Surrey, tried to enter the house of William the vicar of Rottingdean to discover if he was harboring men against the king's peace, the priest, together with his nephew William, refused them entry and fired on them with crossbows. From February of 1266 through July of the same year the ma-norial court of Lewes repeatedly and fruitlessly ordered the cleric's distraint to force him to appear in court to answer to the earl. William successfully defied the villagers and the earl and ul-timately got away with everything.[42]

The unruly nature of medieval clerics is illustrated most strik-ingly by the extremely high incidence of homicide in the borough of Oxford. In the city of Norwich, which probably had a population of about 13,000 at the beginning of the fourteenth century,[43] there were 47 homicides committed in the 22½-year period covered by the eyres. This means that the homicide rate was roughly 16.1/100,000 per annum, a high rate in itself. In the

20½-year period covered by the three Oxfordshire eyres of 1241, 1247, and 1261, 58 homicides were committed in the borough of Oxford. If it is assumed that Oxford had a population of about 8,000, this means that the homicide rate in this small town was a staggering 35.4/100,000 per annum.* To a large extent, this was the work of the student population. Whereas outside Oxford 7.4 percent of all accused killers were clerics (252 of 3,399), in Oxford they made up 14 percent (13 of 93) of all accused murderers.† Elsewhere clerics made up 2.6 percent (61 of 2,376) of of all victims. In Oxford, however, they constituted 10.3 percent (six of 58) of the total.‡ Although the clerks who came to Oxford to study were certainly more prosperous than the men who served rural parishes as chaplains, the fact that they were in most cases isolated from the restraining influences of their native communities and were members of a privileged organization accentuated their quarrelsomeness. The students frequently fought among themselves, with fatal results. For example, David de Trempedhwy was assassinated by a group of unknown clerics on December 10, 1296, while he was picking up a prostitute.[44] Quarrels between groups of scholars often resulted in small battles. In 1298 John Barel, a clerk from Ireland, was drinking late at night in a tavern with some of his fellows. Nicholas de Uilers, another Irish clerk, and John of Suffolk were drinking with a different group in the same tavern.

* The estimate of about 8,000 people in Oxford in the mid-thirteenth century is H. E. Salter's in "The City of Oxford in the Middle Ages," *History*, n.s. 14 (1929–30): 98. If Russell's estimate in *British Medieval Population*, p. 285, of from 4,000 to 4,500 in 1279 is accepted, the homicide rate works out at between 62.9/1000,000 and 70.7/1000,000 per annum.

† For this distribution, Yates's chi-square = 4.67 with 1 degree of freedom; $p = .031$; phi = 0.04. Contingency coefficient = 0.04. Lambda (asymmetric) = 0.0 with the area as the dependent variable, 0.0 with occupation as the dependent variable. Uncertainty coefficient (asymmetric) = 0.01 with the area as the dependent variable, 0.0 with occupation as the dependent variable. For a brief explanation of these statistics, see the Appendix.

‡ For this distribution, Yates's chi-square = 10.05 with 1 degree of freedom; $p = 0.002$; phi = 0.07. Contingency coefficient = 0.07. Lambda (asymmetic) = 0.0 with the area as the dependent variable, 0.0 with occupation as the dependent variable. Uncertainty coefficient (asymmetic) = 0.01 with the area as the dependent variable, 0.01 with occupation as the dependent variable.

The two parties began to argue. They all went out of the tavern and in the street Barel attacked Nicholas with a sword. Nicholas and John of Suffolk fled, raising the hue as Barel chased them through the streets. The two finally turned, and Nicholas, who also had a sword, wounded Barel in the forehead while John gave him a fatal wound with an axe.[45] These battles between clerics could reach such proportions that the university officials had to intervene to maintain peace, as they did in 1252 after disturbances between scholars from the north of England and Ireland.[46]

When the scholars were not battling each other, they were often fighting the townsmen. On the Feast of the Purification in 1297, Michael, manciple of the clerks living at the Bolehall in the parish of St. Aldath, John de Skurt, a clerk, and Madoc, a Welsh clerk, went through the streets armed with swords and bows attacking everyone they met. The hue was raised and when John Metesharp came to answer it, he was shot and killed by Michael.[47] Similarly, in 1298 a group of clerks and their manciples came into the High Street between the churches of All Saints and St. Mary armed with bows and arrows, swords and bucklers, slings and stones, and assaulted all the laymen they could find. They also looted homes and shops. When a group of them tried to force entry into Edward de Erkalewe's house, Edward fired an arrow from an upper room and hit Fulc Neyrnyt (or Neyrmithe), rector of the church of Picklesthorne,[48] in the left eye as he peeped over the top of his shield and killed him.[49]

After the ecclesiastics, the next largest occupational group involved in homicide was that composed of servants: 136 servants (3.9 percent) were accused of having committed homicide, and 60 people (2.5 percent) described as servants were killed. In light of the large number of servants in medieval society, their often precarious economic and social position, and their propensity to become involved in the quarrels of their masters and their fellows, this high proportion is not surprising.

Another occupational group that bulked large in the eyre rolls was that of people engaged in the preparation and sale of food or food-related products. Of these, 77 people (38 millers and their wives, a butcher and a butcher's wife, 18 cooks and their wives, three brewers and their wives, eleven bakers and their wives, two vintners, one candlemaker, one soap-maker, and one spicer) were accused of having committed murder. And 48 were the victims of homicide (28 millers and their wives, one spicer's wife, one taverner, one puleter's wife, eight cooks, one brewer, five bakers and their wives, two vintners, and one soap-maker's wife). In a society where most people lived on the margin of subsistence, it was inevitable that specialists in the processing of food should be drawn into violent conflict. The preponderance of millers is especially striking. Grain was the staple of life for medieval Englishmen. Therefore, almost inevitably suspicion and hostility attached itself to millers. A German proverb neatly expressed this distrust: "Why do storks never nest on a mill? Because they are afraid that the miller will steal their eggs." [50] Not only did peasants regard millers as by nature dishonest; they also saw in them a very real and especially vexatious manifestation of seigneurial power. On most manors the mill was the lord's monopoly, and the peasants were required to grind their grain there, a service for which they had to pay. Medieval social life was marked by a relentless struggle between lords who were determined to collect everything that they felt was coming to them and peasants who were equally determined to grind their grain in their own mills. [51] The men who burnt the prior of Coventry's mill at Lillington in Warwickshire, killed three men, and wounded Thomas the miller must have met with at least some tacit approval from some of the local peasants. [52]

To a very large degree, much homicide involved truly rootless people. Of the 2,434 victims, 234 (9.6 percent) could not be identified by the jurors. Two more were called "vagabonds" and 39 "outsiders." Of the accused killers, 67 were labeled vagabonds, 157 outsiders, and 12 "unknown," a term that appears to have been used as a synonym for "outsider." Thus, 6.8 percent of all killers were strangers in one way or another to the communities in which they committed their crime.

It would be interesting to know how much homicide was committed across status lines, whether people tended to choose victims of the same social standing as themselves, or from a higher or lower group. However, given the state of the documentation, this is almost impossible to discover. Yet here and there the records allow glimpses of some of the conflicts between lords and peasants which historians such as R. H. Hilton have claimed embittered the life of thirteenth-century England as lords tried to reduce the peasantry to an ever greater state of dependence and submission.[53] Lords and their officials did not scruple to use violence and the threat of violence in efforts to coerce the peasants. In east Sussex the prior of Hastings brought a suit of villeinage against his tenants at Burwash. His effort to deprive his men of their legal freedom failed in the courts. He therefore decided to take direct action. With some 30 men, including Ralph Harengod—who had also brought a suit of villeinage against his tenants in the nearby village of Iklesham—and some other members of the local gentry, Simon de Sumery and John de Pepplesham, he attacked Burwash, destroyed the villagers' houses, and carried off their goods.[54] Such conflicts could also involve townsmen with lords who claimed authority over them. Early in the fourteenth century the Berkeley family claimed that the men of Redcliffstreet in Bristol owed suit of court to them. To enforce their claim, Thomas and Maurice of Berkeley came to Bristol in 1305, attacked and wounded some of the men of the city, "dragged some out of their houses and threw them into a pit, beat their wives when they came to their aid and trampled them so that some of them died, wounded and maimed the king's bailiff of that town in the high road at Frampton on Severn because he defended the king's estate against them, and treated him so shamefully that he died shortly after." The same two also besieged the town of Tetbury during the fair held there and beat the burgesses of Redcliffstreet who were in attendance.[55]

It appears that all too often the exalted social status of these gentlemanly ruffians protected them from the law. On December 3, 1274, John of Rushall, a knight, and his squire Henry of Hastings were entertained at the parson of Melchbourne's house in Bedfordshire. Henry took provisions for his lord from several men in the vill. When they came to demand payment, John and Henry answered that they had no cash with them and asked the townspeople to send a man with them to Cambridge to be paid there. The villagers elected to send Ellis of Astwood. Outside Melchbourne, the knight and his household cut Ellis's throat. It appears that John and his retinue never suffered any inconvenience for this act.[56]

The peasants responded in kind. In addition to rent strikes and refusals to appear in the manorial courts, they resorted to violence, much of it directed against manorial officials and other agents of seigneurial exploitation. Among the victims of homicide were two serjeants, four reeves, seven haywards, and one beadle. In 1303 when the archbishop of Canterbury sent Richard Christian, the dean of Ospringe, to Selling in Kent to make citations, the villagers attacked him, "threw him into filthy mud, and with his face turned to his horse's tail, holding the tail in his hand instead of the bridle, led him with songs and dances through the middle of the town of Selling, and afterwards cut off the tail, ears, and lips of his horse, and threw him into filthy mud, and prevented him from exercising the office committed to him by the archbishop."[57] Similarly, Hugh le Bercar of Wydehay, a shepherd, and his brother William, together with other men, killed William le Surreys and burnt the buildings of their lady, Lucy of St. Amand, in two different villages in Berkshire.[58] Peasants on occasion even attacked lords directly. On November 12, 1303, Henry Bobbe of Lower Caldecote in Bedfordshire hanged Robert le Bole on his gallows near Biddenham. As he went toward Bedford, Thomas son of Gervase the cobbler came and struck him three times with his hand. Simon son of Roger le Bercher of Wilshamsted hit him in the back with a staff. When Henry took refuge in William Bascat's croft, Richard of Old Warden stabbed him in the chest with a fork and killed him.[59] And sometime in the first quarter of the thirteenth century the people of the village of Sandford in Somer-set combined to kill their lord, Nicholas de Arundel. According to the report of the jurors of Taunton and Milverton hundreds, the entire population of the vill, with the exception of four men, chased Nicholas through the town to the church, where he tried to take refuge. The chaplain slammed the door shut in his face. His pursuers killed him, carried him to his house, and set fire to the building to make it appear that he had died in the blaze. For this deed, fifteen men and women were drawn and hanged. Six others fled and were outlawed by order of the king's courts.[60]

This last tale is emblematic of all homicide in thirteenth-century England. Violence was a tool resorted to by the poor and the weak. It was largely a peasant means of settling conflict. For the most part, the rich and the powerful, although bred to an ethic that glorified military prowess, refrained from direct physical assaults on one another. In the proliferating law courts they had an effective means of settling their disputes. Should they wish to step outside the limits of the law, their bands of servants and retainers allowed them to engage in bloodletting by proxy. It was the poorer members of society, cut off from the royal courts and increasingly from the old, local, community courts which had been stripped of many of their original powers, who had to resort to violence and killing to solve their quarrels. Like the peasants of Sandford, when they ran foul of their lords, their fellows, or men from neighboring villages, they often had no recourse but the knife, the stick, and the arrow. That so many found it necessary to kill reveals that in England in the thirteenth century justice and order were all too often the monopolies of the privileged few.

5. The Accused Slayer in Court

Murder was an event that radically altered the social network. The death of a person left a gap that had to be dealt with in some fashion. Together with a man's body, his social personality survived his decease. The living were faced with the task of adjusting the social relationships in which he had participated to take account of the fact of his death.[1] This task was complicated by the fact that his death had been sudden, "unnatural," and had come before his associates had had time to prepare themselves for it. One of the sets of relationships that the survivors had to adjust were those involving the victim's slayer. In thirteenth-century England, all homicide, except that which was in self-defense or clearly accidental, was in theory punishable only by death. Therefore, a killer's standing in his community was automatically called into question and in a very real sense radically endangered.

Medieval English society dealt with the problem of homicide in a variety of ways. Some of these will be considered later in a section on social control. In this chapter attention will be focused on the narrower question of legal adjudication, which illuminates some of the prevalent attitudes of medieval Englishmen toward violence.

Few of the people who were accused of having taken a human

life in thirteenth-century England ever suffered the penalty for their deed that the law required, as can be seen from Table 9. In fact, to kill someone appears to have been a safe thing to do. Twenty murderers were themselves slain without benefit of trial, ten being fatally wounded by their victims, five killed as they tried to escape, and another five captured and summarily beheaded. Only 285 people of 3,492 accused (8.2 percent) were punished for their deed by a court of law. Of these, 38 were clerics who were found guilty, but who, in accordance with the privileges of their order, were released to their ordinary to undergo trial in an ecclesiastical court, where a death penalty could not be imposed. Thus, only 247 people, 7.1 percent of all accused, were executed in accordance with the judgment of a court. When it is realized that a large proportion of all victims of homicide, 531 (21.8 percent), were slain by people all or some of whom the presenting jurors could not identify, it is clear that only a tiny minority of those who killed ever paid the penalty prescribed by the law.

Since comparable information on the frequency with which murderers are punished does not exist for modern agrarian societies, comparisons can only be made with industrialized societies. In Philadelphia between 1948 and 1952, 621 suspected killers were known to the police. Only fourteen of these had still eluded capture when Marvin Wolfgang studied them in the mid-1950's. Of the 607 who had been apprehended, 404 (66.6 percent) had been convicted of murder or manslaughter, and 122 (20.1 percent) had been acquitted.[2] This high proportion of suspects who were apprehended and punished contrasts startlingly with the situation in medieval England.

As for the execution of those thirteenth-century killers who were judged to death, very little hanging was done at the eyres themselves. Only 84 of the 247 (34 percent) executed for homicide were hanged before the justices in eyre. As with most of their activity dealing with criminal affairs, the justices contented themselves with recording action that had been taken elsewhere. Most of those people who were executed were tried and con-

Table 9. *Disposition of Accused*

Disposition	Number of accused	Percent of total
Acquitted	944	27.0%
Executed	247	7.1
Killed by victim or by pursuers	20	0.6
Transferred to church court:		
Guilty	38	1.1
Innocent	26	0.7
Unspecified	14	0.4
Pardoned	56	1.6
Outlawed	1,444	41.4
Abjured	258	7.4
Fled	49	1.4
Escaped from jail	7	0.2
Died before trial	93	2.7
Other	137	3.9
None given	159	4.6
TOTAL	3,492	

victed at the periodic local gaol deliveries which emptied the prisons of medieval England. Eighty people (32.4 percent) were executed at these sessions. A further 51 (20.6 percent) were executed elsewhere than at the eyres, and although the records are not specific, it is likely that they too were condemned at gaol deliveries. Nine (3.6 percent) were tried either before the curia regis sitting at Westminster or at a delivery of one of the London gaols to which on occasion accused criminals from the countryside were sent for trial. The old local communal courts, which in the course of the twelfth century had been deprived of their right to try capital crimes, seem to have only rarely attempted to reassert their old prerogatives. One person was hanged in a county court and two in hundred courts.

On much of the European continent when the old communal courts, to which the English hundred and county courts were analogous, decayed, much of the criminal jurisdiction they had exercised passed, in altered form, to the new *seigneuries banales*. In England this process never came to fruition, as is revealed by the fact that only 20 people (8.1 percent) were executed in courts held by local lords. Although executing a murderer in a local court, whether of shire, hundred, or local lord, may have satisfied the community's desire for a speedy rendering of justice or have given some lord a sense of power, any such attempts to infringe on the jurisdiction of the royal courts invariably brought retribution. For example, sometime in the 1240's or 1250's Thomas de Hauekenese and John le Noreys slew Hugh de Shope in Faversham Hundred in Kent. John was captured and imprisoned in the abbot of Faversham's prison. With the exception of only four men, the entire population of Faversham broke open the abbot's prison and carried John into the town, where they in turn imprisoned him. The archbishop of Canterbury's bailiff came to the town and tried to claim John as belonging to the homage and liberty of the archbishop. The men of Faversham refused to surrender him. Instead, they set up their own court, in which every man in the village individually (*nominibus*) passed judgment on him. Having convicted him, they erected gallows, which the hundred jurors claimed had never before been set up in Faversham, and hanged him. They were promptly excommunicated by the archbishop's official and forced to pay £100 to buy their way back into the church's fold. This, however, was not the end of their troubles, for when the justices learned of Faversham's trespass against the royal prerogative, they amerced the town.[3]

Altogether, 1,251 people appeared in one court or another to stand trial. In the thirteenth century, criminal trials were not conducted by the interrogation of witnesses or the examination of evidence. In the case of an appeal, the issue could be decided by a judicial duel, provided that the appellor was male and in a condition to fight and that no technical grounds were found for quashing the appeal. In practice, however, virtually no judicial duels were fought. The question of guilt or innocence was settled almost exclusively by trial by jury. A thirteenth-century jury trial, however, was very different from one in a modern American or British court. For one thing, several juries were often involved in rendering judgment. When an individual was tried at one of the eyres, the hundred jury that had named him as a suspect in its veredictum was sworn a second time (the first time had been at the beginning of the eyre, when they had taken an oath to answer truthfully all questions put to them) and was required to decide on the accused's guilt or innocence.* If the jury found him guilty, the reeve and four men from each of the four townships neighboring the place where the crime had been committed were also asked for their verdict. If they agreed with the hundred jury, sentence was passed on the guilty party. Since there were several juries present at an eyre, the justices would often also turn to another such jury for its opinion about the guilt of an accused. In F. W. Maitland's opinion, by the end of Henry III's reign, the question of the guilt or innocence of an accused was regularly being submitted to the presenting jury, another hundred jury, and the men from the four townships.[4]

This plethora of jurors who sat in judgment, unlike their modern descendants, were not supposed to be ignorant of the facts of the case before the trial and were not bound to consider only the evidence presented in court. Indeed, in most cases there was probably no critical dissection of testimony in court.[5] Instead, the jurors were expected to be familiar with a case even before they came to court.[6] But, in addition to the "facts" of the case, the jurors, drawn from the communities where the killings had taken place, would have been informed about many other things—the relations that had existed between the victim and his alleged slayer, their relations with other members of the community, and the general opinion of the community about them. In short, they would have known something, and often a very great deal, of the total social personalities of those involved in the homicidal event. Therefore, it was probably very easy for the jurors to manipulate what information they had about a killing in light of their feelings about the characters of the people involved and about what behavior they believed to be appropriate and normative in the context of the social relationships with

---

* However, it is not the case that the jurors were judging an accused twice. In their veredictum they were not required to pass on the guilt or innocence of the accused felons, but only to indicate who was *suspected* of having committed a crime. The question of guilt or innocence was determined later and separately.

which they were familiar.[7] This process would have been facilitated by the fact that their deliberations were not limited by any formal rules about the admissibility or reliability of evidence. Therefore the verdicts that they rendered on those accused of homicide can be used to explore attitudes about violence held by medieval Englishmen.

Medieval juries were reluctant to send someone to the gallows for murder. Whether large numbers of innocent people were accused of homicide in the thirteenth century, or jurors were unwilling to judge to death people who had killed in what were regarded as mitigating circumstances, or because violence was regarded as a normal mode of behavior, the fact remains that it was only the unlucky few who were punished for having killed. According to Table 10, only 247 of the 1,251 people (19.7 percent) who appeared in court were found guilty and executed. Thirty-eight clerics (3 percent) were also found guilty and released to a bishop's official to stand trial in an ecclesiastical court. The majority of defendants, 794 (63.5 percent), were acquitted.[8] Although in most cases an accused cleric whom the jurors felt to be blameless was simply released, 26 (2.1 percent) were found innocent but were nevertheless turned over to the bishop's official. Fourteen others (1.1 percent) were sent to the church courts to stand trial without the jurors' venturing any opinion on their guilt or innocence.

Forty (3.2 percent) of the people who appeared in court produced royal pardons.[9] In 49 (3.9 percent) instances the court took some action other than that of acquitting, convicting, remanding to an ecclesiastical court, or enrolling a charter of pardon. Four accused murderers confessed their crimes, turned approver, and were therefore returned to prison to await the time when they could fight judicial duels with their former accomplices, whom they had now denounced. One person, accused of being an accomplice, was required to find pledges to guarantee his appearance before the justices at a later date. In two cases the jurors professed their complete ignorance of the circumstances surrounding a killing and no action was taken.

Table 10. *Verdicts on Those Who Appeared in Court by Appeal and Indictment*

	Appealed		Indicted	
Verdict	Number	Percent	Number	Percent
Acquitted	398	75.2%	396	54.8%
Executed	31	5.9	216	29.9
Transferred to church court:				
Guilty	7	1.3	31	4.3
Innocent	19	3.6	7	1.0
Unspecified	6	1.1	8	1.1
Pardoned	14	2.6	26	3.6
Other	21	4.0	28	3.9
None given	33	6.2	10	1.4
TOTAL	529		722	

NOTE: Chi square = 150.25 with 7 degrees of freedom; $0.001 > p$. Cramer's $V = 0.35$. Contingency coefficient = 0.33. Lambda (asymmetric) = 0.0 with verdict as the dependent variable; 0.07 with appeal/indictment as the dependent variable. Uncertainty coefficient (asymmetric) = 0.06 with the verdict as the dependent variable; 0.10 with appeal/indictment as the dependent variable.

Seventeen people were transferred to another court for trial. One man, a Londoner, was ordered to wage his law, i.e. prove his innocence with the assistance of oath-helpers, and by the time the roll was drawn up he had apparently not yet done so. One person who refused to put himself on a jury was returned to prison. Another man, who also refused to submit to a jury trial, was allowed to abjure the realm.[10] In one case the court ruled that the killing had occurred during time of war and that therefore no action could be taken. In four cases the court ruled that the killings had been accidental and either took no action or reserved judgment until the king could be consulted. Two other cases were also reserved for discussion with the king. Nine people, appealed of murder, had come to an agreement with their appellors to have the appeal dropped. They were arrested and required to pay a fine before being released. And six people were simply returned to prison without standing trial. In the case of 43 persons (3.4 percent), there is no indication in the eyre rolls of what disposition, if any, was made of their cases. It will be recalled that there were two ways in which a homicide case could come into the king's courts, by appeal or by indictment. In the first and most ancient way, a relative or lord or retainer of the victim could make a formal appeal of the people whom he believed to have committed the murder. Of the 3,492 killers, 1,200 (34.4 percent) were appealed. Of the victims, the deaths of 438 (18 percent) were brought into court on appeal. In 410 cases the appellor's relation to the victim can be determined. Wives made the most appeals, 191 (46.6 percent). The next largest group was composed of parents, 81 in all (19.8 percent). Siblings made 80 appeals (19.5 percent), husbands nine, sons eleven, uncles and daughters six each, and aunts and nephews five each. One guardian, one niece, one grandfather, one sister-in-law, and one father-in-law also made appeals. Ten other appeals were made by approvers who accused their accomplices. And one was brought, shortly before her death, by the victim herself, a girl who had been raped and beaten.

Most appeals were not prosecuted to their end. The appeals of less than half of those accused in this manner were prosecuted to the end, 579 (48.3 percent). In some cases the appellor may have feared to prosecute because of threats received from the accused's friends or relatives. In Blackheath Hundred in Kent a woman named Emma appealed Richard de Heltham and Ralph le Page for the death of her son Alexander. However, she did not dare to press her appeal in the county court as the law required. For when she appeared, the sheriff, Roger de Grunnestan, for reasons that are unfortunately not specified, imprisoned her and two of her brothers.[11] In some cases appeals were not prosecuted because the killers and the appellor had come to a settlement out of court. When Adam of Muleton was killed in the county of Norfolk, his wife Estrild prosecuted only one of his alleged killers. The others who were implicated in his slaying—Roger de Snape, Henry Perer, and Robert Wrythe, all of Stretton—came to an agreement with her that she should not sue them.[12]

As can be seen in Table 10, the vast majority of those who

were appealed and who appeared in court to stand trial were acquitted, 398 (75.2 percent). Another 19 clerics (3.6 percent) were remanded to an ecclesiastical court for further trial, but were nevertheless declared innocent by the jurors. Only slightly more than one in twenty of the appellees who came into court were executed, 31 (5.9 percent). Another seven clerics (1.3 percent) were declared guilty and released to the bishop's official.

The other way in which someone was accused of homicide was by indictment. If the suspicion of the community held that someone had committed a particular killing, the jurors reported this suspicion. Two-thirds of all persons named in the rolls, 2,292 people, were accused in this fashion; and 722 of them appeared in court. The majority of these were also acquitted, 396 (54.8 percent). However, a person who had been indicted was almost five times as likely to die on the gallows as someone who had been appealed. Almost three-tenths, 216 (29.9 percent), of all those indicted were executed.*

There were perhaps two reasons for the fact that jurors apparently looked askance on appeals. Many appeals seem to have been lodged maliciously, with the design of using the threat of a possible trial in the king's courts as a means of extortion. In Canterbury a man named Hubert Mulling died some time in the 1240's or 1250's of consumption. The city bailiffs, John Digge and Richard Samuel, however, accused Arnald the goldsmith of having fatally beaten him. To be left in peace, Arnald was forced to give them a mark.[13] Private citizens also tried their hand at manipulating the system for their own ends. Early in the thirteenth century, again in Kent, Tristram son of Theobald got drunk at a local tavern. Ralph son of Viward and Hamo of Elne put Tristram on his horse and tried to take him home. In his inebriated state Tristram fell from his mount and was killed. Tristram's father Theobald appealed Ralph and Hamo of hav-

---

* If only those who were executed or acquitted are considered, Yates's chi-square for this two-by-two distribution equals 108.25 with 1 degree of freedom; $0.001 > p;$ phi $= 0.32$. Contingency coefficient $= 0.31$. Lambda (asymmetric) $= 0.0$ with the verdict as the dependent variable; 0.0 with appeal/indictment as the dependent variable. Uncertainty coefficient $= 0.11$ with the verdict as the dependent variable; 0.09 with appeal/indictment as the dependent variable.

ing killed him. The jurors, however, acquitted the two, and informed the justices that Theobald had appealed them *"pro denariis habendis."* The justices promptly ordered his arrest.*

It is of course impossible to determine how widespread such malicious appeals were. That they were not infrequent, however, appears certain, as revealed by even a cursory glance at the Hundred Roll inquests from the early part of the reign of Edward I with their long list of complaints about false arrests and malicious appeals.[14] Beyond the fact that the jurors may have doubted the good faith of some appellors, it is possible that they may also have been reluctant to involve themselves in what they perceived as the private quarrels of different groups of family members and friends. The homicides that resulted in appeals may have been of the kind that the community felt were either justified or at least not extremely culpable, and they may have preferred to let the aggrieved kin of the slain man or woman come to a private arrangement with the killer and his kin rather than proceed to the final and irrevocable step of executing the slayer.

People accused of being accomplices—of having held a victim while he was killed, of having counseled a killing, or of receiving a felon after the commission of his deed—fared much better in court than people accused of being principals. As Table 11 shows, 564 of 960 accused principals (58.8 percent) were acquitted; fifteen clerics were also declared innocent before being released to the bishop's official. The acquittal rate for accomplices was substantially higher, 230 of the 291 accomplices (79 percent) being found innocent. Eleven clerics were also acquitted before being consigned to church courts to purge themselves. What is even more striking is the fact that accused principals were almost eighteen times as likely to be executed as accused accomplices:

---

* PRO, J.I.1/358, m. 23r. It is possible that this incident may reveal not extortion but a late attempt to get a blood composition, a common practice in England at an earlier date. Theobald may have felt that Ralph and Hamo had not killed his son deliberately but had nevertheless been in some way responsible for his son's death, if only through their negligence. He may therefore have used the threat of an appeal in an effort to obtain a composition from the two. For a similar incident, see above, p. 84.

Table 11. *Verdicts on Accused Principals and Accomplices Who Appeared in Court*

Verdict	Principals		Accomplices	
	Number	Percent	Number	Percent
Acquitted	564	58.8%	230	79.0%
Executed	243	25.3	4	1.4
Transferred to church court:				
Guilty	34	3.5	4	1.4
Innocent	15	1.6	11	3.8
Unspecified	14	1.5	0	
Pardoned	37	3.9	3	1.0
Other	39	4.1	10	3.4
None given	14	1.5	29	10.0
TOTAL	960		291	

NOTE: Chi square = 145.08 with 7 degrees of freedom; $0.001 > p$. Cramer's $V = 0.34$. Contingency coefficient = 0.32. Lambda (asymmetric) = 0.0 with the verdict as the dependent variable; 0.05 with principal/accomplice as the dependent variable. Uncertainty coefficient (asymmetric) = 0.06 with the verdict as the dependent variable; 0.13 with principal/accomplice as the dependent variable.

243 principals (25.3 percent) were hanged, whereas only four (1.4 percent) of the accomplices were executed.* Thirty-four clerics accused as principals were also found guilty, whereas four accused as accomplices were convicted. In a surprisingly large number of cases the court simply failed to take action when dealing with accomplices. For 10 percent no disposition of the case was recorded. In the case of principals, this percentage was only 1.5 percent.

The reasons for this high acquittal rate are readily understandable. In thirteenth-century English society, where the bonds that united one man to another were especially numerous and strong and where one seldom embarked on any important action without first consulting friends, relatives, and neighbors,

---

* For a two-by-two table composed only of executed and acquitted principals and accomplices Yates's chi-square = 79.30 with 1 degree of freedom; $0.001 > p$; phi = 0.28. Contingency coefficient = 0.27. Lambda (asymmetric) = 0.00 with the verdict as the dependent variable; 0.00 with principal/accomplice as the dependent variable. Uncertainty coefficient (asymmetric) = 0.10 with the verdict as the dependent variable; 0.10 with principal/accomplice as the dependent variable.

suspicion must easily have fallen on a wide network of people after a killing had occurred. Many of these people—friends, servants, relatives—whom the community initially suspected, must indeed have been innocent of any wrongdoing, a fact that was tardily recognized in court.

In the case of friends or relatives who received a killer after he had committed a murder, the jurors may also have been unwilling to convict someone who they realized was only fulfilling the obligations imposed upon him by blood and friendship, although in law an accessory after the fact was just as culpable as the principal. Obviously, no jury would convict a father who received his son, as did John the miller of Barlichway Hundred in Warwickshire, who sheltered his son William after he had killed Richard Jacob.[15] Again, sometime in the late thirteenth century Brother Richard of Sharnbrook, a conversus of the priory of Newnham in Bedfordshire, came into the priory's fields in Fenlake and found a boy named Philip, the son of Nicholas le Warner, gathering straw. Richard, angered by this, threw a stone at him. It hit Philip in the head and he died later the same day. Brother Richard went back to his priory. There the "prior and his men removed his habit and dressed him in secular clothes and put him outside the priory's gates and thus permitted him to escape." Despite the fact that this action was clearly a violation of the law, the prior and his men escaped without even an amercement from the justices.[16]

Those who had killed their relatives were treated harshly in the courts. See Table 12. Forty-six people, 28 men and eighteen women, accused of having slain a relative, appeared in court to stand trial. Less than half of these were acquitted, 19 (41.3 percent), and 21 (45.7 percent) were executed (twelve of the men and nine of the women). Yet of those who had not been accused of having killed a relative, 775 (64.3 percent) were acquitted. And, whereas almost half of those accused of having killed a relative were executed, only 226 (18.8 percent) of this group were hanged.* Although thirteenth-century juries treated those who

---

* For a two-by-two table including only executed or acquitted people according to whether or not they had killed a relative, Yates's chi square = 17.41 with 1

Table 12. *Verdicts on Those Who Appeared in Court Accused of Having Killed a Relative*

Verdict	Killed relatives		Killed nonrelatives	
	Number	Percent	Number	Percent
Acquitted	19	41.3%	775	64.3%
Executed	21	45.7	226	18.8
Transferred to church court:				
Guilty	1	2.2	37	3.1
Innocent	0		26	2.2
Unspecified	0		14	1.2
Pardoned	1	2.2	39	3.2
Other	4	8.7	45	3.7
None given	0		43	3.6
TOTAL	46		1,205	

NOTE: Chi square = 26.16 with 7 degrees of freedom; $p = 0.005$. Cramer's $V = 0.14$. Contingency coefficient = 0.14. Lambda (asymmetric) = 0.00 with the verdict as the dependent variable; 0.00 with relative/nonrelative as the dependent variable. Uncertainty coefficient (asymmetric) = 0.01 with the verdict as the dependent variable; 0.06 with relative/nonrelative as the dependent variable.

slew their relatives harshly, they appear to have been far more tolerant of those who killed someone from the same village. See Table 13. Of the 40 people who indisputably killed someone from their home village, twenty (50 percent) were acquitted and eight (20 percent) were hanged. These figures do not differ appreciably from those for the group as a whole, whose appearance in court saw 63.5 percent acquitted and 19.7 percent executed. Indeed, the jurors treated those who had killed someone from another village in exactly the same way in which they treated those who had killed someone from their own community. Of these 213 people, 115 (54 percent) were acquitted and 46 (21.6 percent) were hanged.*

It will be recalled that a very large proportion of all homicide

degree of freedom; $0.001 > p$; phi = 0.14. Contingency coefficient = 0.13. Lambda (asymmetric) = 0.01 with the verdict as the dependent variable; 0.0 with relative/nonrelative as the dependent variable. Uncertainty coefficient (asymmetric) = 0.01 with the verdict as the dependent variable; 0.05 with relative/nonrelative as the dependent variable.

* For a two-by-two table composed of those executed and acquitted according to whether or not they had killed a fellow villager, Yates's chi-square = 0.05 with 1 degree of freedom: $p = 0.82$. This is not a statistically significant distribution.

Table 13. *Verdicts on Those Who Appeared in Court According to Whether They Had Killed Someone of the Same Village*

Verdict	Killed someone of same village		Killed someone of different village	
	Number	Percent	Number	Percent
Acquitted	20	50.0%	115	54.0%
Executed	8	20.0	46	21.6
Transferred to church court:				
Guilty	2	5.0	6	2.8
Innocent	0		13	6.1
Unspecified	3	7.5	3	1.4
Pardoned	2	5.0	15	7.0
Other	3	7.5	8	3.8
None given	2	5.0	7	3.3
TOTAL	40		213	

NOTE: Chi-square = 9.93 with 7 degrees of freedom; p = 0.19. This is not a statistically significant distribution.

was collective in nature. The jurors were far more lenient with people who had killed in company with someone else than they were with those accused of acting alone. As will be seen from Table 14, of the 225 people accused of having slain someone single-handedly, 95 (42.2 percent) were acquitted, and 75 (33.3 percent) were executed. But of the 1,026 accused of having combined with someone else to carry out their deed, the majority, 699 (68.1 percent) were acquitted. Only 172 (16.8 percent) were executed.* Undoubtedly, many of the slayings carried out by groups of people were regarded as justified. In a society where the formal institutionalized means of settling conflicts were not numerous, a man who had made himself odious to his neighbors may not have aroused much concern when he was slain by a group of those same neighbors.

* For a two-by-two table of those executed and acquitted according to whether or not they had killed with a partner, Yates's chi-square = 43.34 with 1 degree of freedom; $0.001 > p$; phi = 0.21. Contingency coefficient = 0.21. Lambda (asymmetric) = 0.0 with the verdict as the dependent variable; 0.0 with the number of companions as the dependent variable. Uncertainty coefficient (asymmetric) = 0.04 with the verdict as the dependent variable; 0.05 with the number of companions as the dependent variable.

Table 14. *Verdicts on Those Who Appeared in Court According to the Number of Accomplices*

Verdict	Killed alone		Killed with one or more accomplices	
	Number	Percent	Number	Percent
Acquitted	95	42.2%	699	68.1%
Executed	75	33.3	172	16.8
Transferred to church court:				
Guilty	11	4.9	27	2.6
Innocent	2	0.9	24	2.3
Unspecified	5	2.2	9	0.9
Pardoned	25	11.1	15	1.5
Other	9	4.0	40	3.9
None given	3	1.3	40	3.9
TOTAL	225		1,026	

NOTE: Chi-square = 110.39 with 7 degrees of freedom; $0.001 > p$. Cramer's $V = 0.30$. Contingency coefficient = 0.28. Lambda (assymmetric) = 0.0 with the verdict as the dependent variable; 0.04 with the number of accomplices as the dependent variable. Uncertainty coefficient (asymmetric) = 0.03 with the verdict as the dependent variable; 0.08 with the number of accomplices as the dependent variable.

Certainly the terror of the royal courts must have dissuaded few of those who were intent on murder in thirteenth-century England. The justice that was dispensed in them was more than tempered with mercy; it was extremely lenient. Although jurors showed themselves harsh toward those who had killed their relatives, they were in general extremely reluctant to send people accused of murder to the gallows. Perhaps the harshness of medieval English law, which did not distinguish between different degrees of murder and manslaughter but punished all indiscriminately with death, may have been responsible for this. Had the jurors been able to impose lesser penalties on some killers, they might have done so with greater frequency. But to a large extent the leniency shown to those accused of homicide reflected a general attitude toward violence, one that saw it as a normal means of settling certain conflicts, and one with which society was reluctant to interfere.

6. The Entrepreneurs of Violence

For many people in thirteenth-century England, homicide was a part of their trade. A significant proportion of all homicides was perpetrated by thieves in the course of robbery; 229 people (9.4 percent) were explicitly stated to have been killed by thieves or bandits. This number may mask a certain number of deaths that really occurred in other ways. Since a suicide was, according to the law, a *felo de se*, and his chattels accordingly forfeit to the king, jurors may have protected the families of some suicides by attributing their deaths to unknown thieves. Fear, favoritism, or approbation of a particular killing may also have disguised other murders as the work of brigands. Yet, even with allowance made for the possible doctoring of the records, it is probable that most people who the jurors said were killed by thieves were actually killed by them. Indeed, the number of people killed by bandits was probably larger than the figure of 229. Of the 2,205 people who were not explicitly stated to have been killed by bandits, 424 (19.2 percent) were slain by people whom the hundred jurors could not identify. Undoubtedly, some of these were killed by bandits or thieves.

Homicide committed in the course of robbery was thus a major social phenomenon.[1] In Table 15 homicide rates have been calculated for the number of people per 100,000 popula-

Table 15. *Homicide Victims Killed by Bandits*
(Per 100,000 population per year)

County	Eyre	Number of victims	Author's estimates	Russell's estimates	1801 figures	Per 20 settlements
Bedford	1202	0	0	0	0	0
	1227	0	0	0	0	0
	1247	13	4.3	4.1	3.0	0.26
	1276	23	3.7	3.5	2.5	0.22
Bristol	1221	0	0	—	—	—
	1248	0	0	—	—	—
Kent	1227	7	0.8	0.6	0.3	0.04
	1241	0	0	0	0	0
	1255	51	6.9	5.5	2.4	0.36
Norfolk	1250	5	0.3	0.4	0.4	0.03
	1257	22	1.0	1.5	1.2	0.10
	1268–69	41	1.1	1.7	1.4	0.11
Oxford	1241	1	0.2	0.3	0.2	0.01
	1247	20	3.5	5.0	2.7	0.16
	1261	21	2.9	4.1	2.3	0.14
Warwick	1221–22	5	1.2	0.6	0.3	0.03
	1232	7	3.9	1.8	0.9	0.10
	1247	7	3.2	1.5	0.8	0.08
London	1244	1	0.1	—	—	—
	1276	5	0.5	—	—	—

SOURCE: Figures are based on extrapolations from J. C. Russell's estimates of the population in 1377 in *British Medieval Population* (Albuquerque, N.M., 1948), pp. 132–33; and for 1801 from Great Britain, Parliament, *Parliamentary Papers (Commons), 1852–53*, vol. 85 (*Accounts and Papers*, vol. 29), Cmnd. 1631, "Population of Great Britain: Volume I," p. ccviii.

tion killed by bandits each year. The fluctuation of the incidence of this sort of homicide among the different eyres for a single county is at first sight puzzling, with a county like Kent showing rates that varied from 0/100,000 for the 1241 eyre to 6.9/100,000 for the 1255 eyre. This and the similar fluctuations for Bedford are probably not the result of crime waves that beset these counties at certain times, but of the fact that for certain eyres the clerks who drew up the rolls did not bother to note whether or not a killing had been committed during a robbery. If we restrict our attention to the fifteen eyres that show rates greater than 0/100,000, we find rates, using the author's population estimates, varying from a low of 0.1/100,000 per annum for the 1244 London eyre to a high of 6.9/100,000 per annum for the 1255 eyre of Kent. Of these fifteen eyres, the rate was at least 2/100,000 for seven. When these rates are compared with those for all homicides, not just those committed in the course of a robbery, for twentieth-century Philadelphia (5.7/100,000) or late sixteenth-century Middlesex (6.3/100,000), the magnitude of the medieval phenomenon appears to have been very great indeed. Since, as has been pointed out earlier, the estimates of population size upon which these medieval homicide rates have been constructed are only approximations, the number of homicides committed in the course of robbery in every twenty settlements per year has also been estimated. The 1255 eyre of Kent, according to this calculation, still shows the highest rate, with 0.36 homicide a year for every twenty settlements. The low occurs in the 1241 Oxfordshire eyre, with only 0.01 homicide.

With a move to more certain ground, it is apparent that the overwhelming bulk of murders committed during a robbery occurred in rural areas. Only eighteen people were killed by thieves in towns.* In London only six people of a total of 199 (3 percent) were murdered in the course of the commission of a robbery. In Norwich, only one of the 47 victims (2.1 percent) was killed in the course of a robbery. In the other large cities, Bristol and Great Yarmouth, the records mention no victims of thieves. This certainly does not mean that no one stole in the towns. But the urban environment was more conducive to sneak thievery, to individual burglary, than the countryside. A thief could support himself by stealing food and goods from open stalls and shops. In the larger towns, full of recent immigrants, merchants, and itinerant laborers, a thief, even if seen, might well not be recognized. In the countryside, however, where communities were small and close-knit, thieves were probably more

---

* These eighteen made up 3.8 percent of the 479 urban victims. In the countryside, 211 of the 1955 victims (10.8 percent) were killed by bandits. For this distribution, Yates's chi-square = 21.52 with 1 degree of freedom; $0.001 > p$; phi = 0.10. Contingency coefficient = 0.10. Lambda (asymmetric) = 0.0 with robbery as the dependent variable; 0.0 with location as the dependent variable. Uncertainty coefficient (asymmetric) = 0.0 with robbery as the dependent variable; 0.01 with location as the dependent variable.

likely to be recognized. Since English law at this period punished the theft of all but a very small amount of goods with death, thieves operating in the countryside may have had a greater incentive to kill their victims and any possible witnesses than did their urban counterparts.

Similarly, in the forest regions, a man could support himself by some discreet cattle lifting. This form of thievery was suitable for a small-scale entrepreneur, like the man who was apprehended driving two stolen sheep through the town of Eaton Socon in Bedfordshire.[2] Exceptionally, such small-scale activity produced a killing, as when David Haringod of Wymelingwand discovered a thief driving off some sheep in the woods of Wingham Hundred in Kent. When he tried to arrest the malefactor, he was fatally wounded.[3] The forests of England, indeed, probably saw very few people killed by bandits. In the Warwickshire hundred of Hemlingford, the heart of the Forest of Arden, only two people were killed by thieves. Similarly, in the Weald of Kent, a much less wild woodland region, only four of a total of 58 for the entire county were killed by robbers.

The thefts that produced murder were often the work of bands of robbers making concerted attacks. To be sure, some thieves, probably a majority, operated alone, like John le Ley, who was killed on March 17, 1317, when he fell from a ladder after burgling a ham from Maud Bolle's house at Dean in Bedfordshire.[4] Another free-lance thief tried to ply his trade in Bedfordshire at a slightly earlier date. When Brother Ralph the carpenter, a wood-seller, and Henry the hayward, a servant boy, were going to their lodging in Putnoe in Bedfordshire at twilight one night, they were waylaid by a felon who had been hiding among the blackthorns next to the road. He relieved them of their coats and 4*d.*, and foolishly, as it proved, let them go. They went into Putnoe and raised the hue. After a chase through the woods, the thief was killed by his pursuers.[5] Only in unusual circumstances would one of these solitary thieves murder his victim. For example, early in the thirteenth century a man stole some cloth belonging to Juliana of Withybrook in Warwickshire.

He was captured and given by the hundred serjeant to Juliana to guard. After two weeks he killed her and escaped.[6]

But the sort of robbery that resulted in a killing seems to have been the work of large groups of people and to have been of an entrepreneurial character. For 1,903 victims the number of people who killed them is known. Of the 1,781 people who were not killed by thieves, 1,133 (63.6 percent) were murdered by a single person. Of the 122 killed in the course of a robbery, only 35 (28.7 percent) were killed by a single person.* Similarly, of the 3,263 people accused of having committed a murder but not a robbery, 1,090 (33.4 percent) did not have a named companion. But only 30 (13.1 percent) of the 229 accused of both robbery and murder did not have a named companion.†

Whether these groups of bandits were organized "gangs" with formal leadership like bandit groups in modern Sicily, Brazil, and the United States, which, despite constantly changing membership, managed to maintain a sense of identity for extended periods of time, is impossible to determine from the eyre rolls. It is possible that organized, coherent bands, such as the Folvilles and the Coterels, who operated early in the fourteenth century, were exceptional, the product of the disturbed political state of the kingdom.[7] The groups of thieves the eyre rolls reveal may not have had any such continuity, being composed of men re-

---

* Of the people not killed by thieves, 648 (36.4 percent) were killed by more than one person. Of the people killed by thieves, 87 (71.3 percent) were killed by more than one person. Yates's chi-square for this distribution equals 57.29 with 1 degree of freedom; $0.001 > p$; phi = 0.18. Contingency coefficient = 0.17. Lambda (asymmetric) = 0.07 with the number of killers as the dependent variable; 0.0 with robbery as the dependent variable. Uncertainty coefficient (asymmetric) = 0.02 with the number of killers as the dependent variable; 0.06 with robbery as the dependent variable.

† Of the people accused of having committed only a homicide, 2,173 (66.6 percent) had a companion. Of the people accused of having committed a murder in the course of a robbery, 199 (86.9 percent) had a companion. For this distribution, Yates's chi-square = 39.56 with 1 degree of freedom; $0.001 > p$; phi = 0.11. Contingency coefficient = 0.11. Lambda (asymmertric) = 0.0 with the number of accomplices as the dependent variable; 0.0 with robbery as the dependent variable. Uncertainty coefficient (asymmetric) = 0.01 with the number of accomplices as the dependent variable; 0.03 with robbery as the dependent variable.

cruited in taverns and along the roads, who cooperated on an ad hoc basis for only one or two expeditions. Yet the large size of many of the groups—with 144 people (62.9 percent) of all those accused of robbery and murder operating in groups of at least four people, and 120 (52.4 percent) in groups of at least five— indicates that thieves were able to mobilize relatively large numbers of people for a raid. If organized gangs like Robin Hood's were largely a figment of myth and legend, it is still clear that someone intent on larceny in thirteenth-century England had no difficulty finding accomplices.

Homicide committed by groups of thieves was closely linked to the growth of trade and the development of a network of markets and towns. If the geographical location of homicides committed in the course of robbery is considered, it is found that they show a strong tendency to cluster near large towns and along trade routes. In Kent almost all the incidents occurred in the northern half of the county, near the Thames and on the roads leading from London to the Channel ports. Sixteen of 58 occurred in the Lathe of Sutton-at-Hone, adjacent to the city of London. Twenty were committed either in the city of Canterbury or in its hinterland. Eleven of these were in the hundreds of Faversham, Boughton-under-Blean, and Westgate, along the roads most frequently used by pilgrims coming to Becket's shrine from the north and west. In Norfolk 30 of the 68 homicides were committed in Norwich and the hundreds immediately adjacent to it: Taverham, Eynford, South Erpingham, Blofield, Forhoe, Henstead, and Loddon. Sixteen of these took place in Blofield, Henstead, and Loddon hundreds, on the River Yare between Norwich and Great Yarmouth. Another ten took place either in King's Lynn, a major grain-trading center,[8] or in its immediate hinterland in Freebridge and Clacklose hundreds. In Oxfordshire 23 of the 42 occurred in the hundreds of Thame, Lewknor, Ewelme, Pirton, Langtree, and Binfield, where the roads from the southeast crossed the Chiltern Hills. In Warwickshire fourteen of the nineteen took place in Knightlow Hundred, in proximity to Warwick, the county seat, and

Coventry,* a major crossroads and center of iron and textile manufacture.[9] In Bedfordshire the picture is less well defined, but it appears that the homicides were clustered in the valley of the Ivel, a tributary of the Ouse, not far from the main road between London and Huntingdon, and near Dunstable where the roads through the passes over the Chilterns debouched onto the plain.

The picture that this distribution conjures up is one of highwaymen preying upon the merchants and other travelers passing along the roads connecting the new urban centers. Banditry and thievery, at least the kind that resulted in murder, would then appear to have been the work of the people of the countryside preying upon the representatives of the nascent urban and mercantile culture. Certainly the pens of clerical writers, especially monastic ones, dwelt most readily on the fate of merchants and other travelers at the hands of bandits—especially since these writers were often great landlords physically immobilized by their profession and thus very dependent on a far-flung mercantile network for the efficient exploitation of their estates and the provisioning of their convents. Dan Michel in his *Ayenbite of Inwyt* spoke of thieves only in connection with this group, writing of the "robberes and kueade herberȝeres þet berobbeþ þe pilgrimes and þe marchons and oþre wayuerindemen."[10] The spectacular burning of the Boston fair in 1288 attracted the attention of many clerical chroniclers.[11] During the fair, a *buhurdicum* or *hastiludium,* a form of small-scale tournament, was held by some men-at-arms. Some of them, tempted by the goods on display, decided to appropriate them. One day at sunset they set fire to the merchants' tents. As the traders ran about trying to save their goods, the thieves proceeded to murder and steal at will. A large part of the town burnt to the ground, and, according to one chronicler, "it was said that all the

---

* In addition to Coventry, Knightlow Hundred contained three other boroughs—Bretford, Brinklow, and Kenilworth—and the market towns of Rugby, Willoughby, Southam, Napton-on-the-Hill, Bishop's Itchington, Wolvey, and Monk's Kirby. (Hilton, *A Medieval Society,* pp. 172–73.)

money in England could scarcely make good the damages. For rivers of gold and silver . . . flowed into the sea." [12]

That bandits did indeed prey upon merchants is beyond doubt. For example, the pass of Alton in Hampshire, through which the main road between London and Winchester wended, appears to have been a favorite haunt of bandits in the thirteenth century. In 1249 some Brabantine merchants were robbed there, and the entire *patria* of Hampshire banded together to protect the culprits from the law. To do justice, King Henry III himself had to come to Winchester castle. And even he had to threaten to hang two juries before he could overawe the country enough to get a presentment. Some 50 gang members and their accomplices were eventually named. Among those hanged was one of the electors of the jury for Selbourne Hundred.[13] The records afford other glimpses of bandits who had come together to rob merchants, like Nicholas de Sutton and Thomas de Hulme, who robbed a London merchant of 16s. and a gold cup, killed him with a mace, and dumped his body into the Thames, or the band that assembled in the woods at Plumstead in Kent to rob a merchant.[14]

But to conceive of banditry as an activity primarily directed by rural people against merchants and travelers is incorrect. Few of the victims recorded in the eyre rolls were merchants. Of the 229 victims of robbers, only five (2.2 percent) were described as merchants. Another victim was called a "packman" (*sumetarius*), and another was a packman's wife. Moreover, an analysis of the location of the homicides committed by bandits shows that few occurred on the open road. The overwhelming majority of bandits' victims were not travelers, but peasants killed in their houses. For the 229 people killed by bandits, the eyre rolls give the place in which 196 were murdered: 166 (84.7 percent) were killed in a house (128 in their own or in that of a relative), and only 30 (15.3 percent) were killed elsewhere. Twelve of these were killed in either towns or villages; one was killed in a cemetery; another was killed in a barn, a building usually closely attached to the dwelling house;[15] and another victim was killed in a monastery. Only fifteen were definitely killed in open country: five in fields, one in a fold, four in a forest, three on heath land, and two who were stated to have been murdered between two villages.

That the majority of homicides should have taken place inside houses is no surprise. Animals could be rustled from open country or stolen from granges,[16] but the most easily portable and salable wealth was concentrated in homes. Not only did country people usually keep their animals under the same roof with themselves; [17] they also stored in their homes what coin they had, food,[18] cloth,[19] and other goods. Although in the thirteenth century many peasants were rebuilding their houses at least partially in stone,[20] their buildings were far from impregnable. A determined band of men could easily force an entry, like the thieves who used a plowshare to break down the wall of William Bevetoun's house in Farndish in Bedfordshire on January 22, 1276.[21]

Thus the interrelationship of the development of towns and trade and banditry appears to be more complex and subtle than one would have at first suspected. Banditry, at least the large-scale type that resulted in homicide, was not directed primarily against the representatives of the nascent urban society. Most of the victims were peasants. But the growth of towns linked together by trade and manufacturing, by providing a market for stolen property and a place of refuge for thieves, enabled thievery to take on an entrepreneurial character, and allowed it to become, perhaps for some individuals, a craft. Without the development of towns and trade in thirteenth-century England, banditry would have been an insignificant phenomenon, and would have consisted almost exclusively of the stealing of foodstuffs and other necessities for direct consumption, a form of theft endemic in medieval English society,[22] as perhaps in any agrarian society.

In some instances the eyre rolls and coroners' rolls carefully detail the close connection of towns and bandits, providing glimpses of gangs that had been recruited in urban areas or that operated out of them. For example, on November 17, 1269, thieves descended on Roxton in Bedfordshire, robbed two houses, and killed six people. One of their victims, called either Azeline or Alma, before she died of her wounds, said that she had recognized some of her attackers. She named, among others, some glovers from the borough of Bedford.[23] Similarly, in Kent, Robert son of Gerard of Dover and Stephen de Bere, both from the Cinque Ports, traveled inland from the coast to the hundred of Kinghamford, where they robbed the house of Henry de Wyk. They were discovered and pursued. In their flight they killed Stephen Barun, who had answered the hue and cry. They were later caught at Dover, where Robert turned approver, appealed Stephen, and defeated him in a judicial duel.[24]

Whether or not thieves operated out of the towns, it was to them that they often fled after having committed their crimes, as did the two Kentish thieves. Of the people whom the unfortunate Azeline denounced, four—Reynold of Polebrook, Adam, Alan, and Simon Corbin—were later arrested in the liberty of Bedford. The thieves who robbed the church at Corley in Warwickshire in the early part of the thirteenth century were tracked by their pursuers as far as Coventry.[25] Similarly, when Bernard of Greenfield, Ralph of Oxford, and others committed a robbery at Cheshunt on January 15, 1236, they fled into London for safety. Bernard, Ralph, and some of the others took refuge in the church of St. Bartholomew, where they abjured the realm. One of their companions, however, was captured on London Bridge by a pursuer. As he was being taken to the sheriff of London, he killed his captor. But this did not save him; he was recaptured and hanged before the justices of the Bench.[26]

Town officials on occasion made efforts to weed out the criminals who had taken refuge within the walls or who had come to town to dispose of their goods. When John of Hathern, John of Crowley the parson of Heyford in Oxfordshire, William Bruning, Robert Christopher of Thurmaston, and John the parson of Crowley came to Leicester in 1306 with a large amount of stolen goods, the town bailiffs tried to arrest them. In the ensuing fight, they managed to escape, killing Bate Geryn's groom as they fled. The booty they were forced to abandon was valued at £5 10s. 4½d.[27]

Yet often within town walls thieves could expect aid and succor rather than harassment. On this point the roll of the 1285 eyre of Oxfordshire is eloquent. Hugh de Bolre and William de London were taken outside the north gate of Oxford for suspicion of theft and imprisoned in Headington. A great multitude of clerics, probably students at the university, came to the prison and rescued Hugh. And the bailiff of Bullingdon Hundred, Elias of Kettleburgh, later allowed William to escape.[28] The clerics were not content to stop there; they were even willing to rescue people from the very gallows. Reginald de Stretle, Thomas de Fres, Simon de Wanetyng, Henry Somer de Stoke de Insula, Henry Helle, and John son of Walter de Hayle were all condemned to death by the king's justices. But as they were being taken to the gallows, they were rescued by unknown clerks, who took them to the church of St. Giles, where they abjured the realm.[29]

The records also reveal many thieves who had committed their crimes elsewhere but who had then fled to a church in a town and there abjured the realm. London saw large numbers of these bandits from the hinterland flee to its churches. In 1238 William de Ewelme from Buckinghamshire abjured in London.[30] In 1240 or 1241 Richard Bernere, Roger son of Seman Queneman, and Richard son of Reginald of Haspesbrigges, described as "unknown thieves," abjured.[31] The 1276 eyre produced an entire catalog of abjurors: John son of Geoffrey Bosse of Warwick, Agnes Dayches of Oxfordshire, Thomas of Gloucester who had committed his theft in Essex, an unnamed man from Lincolnshire, a thief who had stolen some books from a church in Hertfordshire, a thief from Hereford, and six other people, all called "strangers."[32]

To turn for a moment from the bandits themselves to their victims, it is clear that certain groups were more prone than others to be slain by thieves. Women and children formed a disproportionate number of those killed by bandits. In general, women, compared to men, were only infrequently the victims of homicidal attacks. Of the 2,205 people who were not said to have been killed by thieves, 391 (17.7 percent) were women. However, of the 229 victims of bandits, 84 (36.7 percent), over twice as high a percentage, were women.* Children constituted only 1.6 percent of those not killed by bandits (36 of 2,205). But they accounted for 3.5 percent of those killed by bandits (eight of 229).† Indeed, almost a fifth of all children who were murdered were slain by thieves (eight of 44 or 18.2 percent). This greater tendency for women and children to be murdered in the course of a robbery was the result of a number of factors. The disproportionate number of children is undoubtedly accounted for largely by the fact that most homicides committed during a robbery took place in the victims' homes. This same fact may also account for the high number of women. Although next to nothing is known of the way in which a woman's work day was structured, it is likely that a large part of it was spent in the home, cleaning, cooking, tending the garden, minding children, making ale and cheese, and manufacturing clothing. With their activities more localized in the home than those of men, it would be natural that they were more strongly represented among the victims of homicide. It is also possible that robbers deliberately sought out women as targets. Thirteenth-century women may not have been noticeably weaker than their male counterparts, but they lacked the training in the use of weapons that their husbands and brothers, all sworn to the assize of arms, were required to possess.

* Males constituted 1,814 (82.3 percent) of the victims not killed by bandits and 145 (63.3 percent) of those killed during a robbery. Yates's chi-square for this distribution equals 46.23 with 1 degree of freedom; $0.001 > p$, phi = 0.14. Contingency coefficient = 0.14. Lambda (asymmetric) = 0.0 with robbery as the dependent variable; 0.02 with sex as the dependent variable. Uncertainty coefficient (asymmetric) = 0.03 with robbery as the dependent variable; 0.02 with sex as the dependent variable.

† Adults accounted for 221 (96.5 percent) of the victims killed during a robbery and 2,169 (98.4 percent) of the victims not killed during a robbery. For this distribution, Yates's chi-square = 3.07 with 1 degree of freedom; $p = 0.08$. This is not a statistically significant distribution.

Although the unusual age and sex distributions of thieves' victims are readily apparent, it is more difficult to appraise their socioeconomic status. For only 32 of the 229 is there any indication of their possible occupations. One would expect that bandits would by preference have chosen to rob the wealthier members of the community, or at least those who could have been expected to have on hand a supply of money or of easily transported goods for which there would be a resale market. Although to generalize from only 32 individuals is hazardous, this theory appears to be borne out by an examination of the victims' occupational surnames. The six servants may reflect more the fact that bandits preferred to attack the houses where they served rather than any wealth they themselves may have possessed. The bandits were after the goods of their masters, the very wealth that enabled them to maintain servants. Eight of the victims were engaged in mercantile exchanges or the transport of goods: five of these were merchants; one was a spicer's wife, one a packman, and one a packman's wife. All these people would have been more likely than the average villager to possess coins and easily salable goods. Two, possibly four, of the victims came from the peasant aristocracy of the village: both a reeve and a hayward—among the most important of manorial officials, usually chosen from among a village's wealthier villeins—fell victim to bandits. In addition, a cleric and his wife were also murdered.

Although the life of many thirteenth-century clerics was undoubtedly eked out on the verge of poverty, resident parish priests were often leading members of their communities, profiting from at least part of the tithes, the glebe lands, and various payments and gifts.[33] On the other hand, the one chaplain murdered by bandits was probably not very well off. Four millers, a baker's wife, and two shepherds were also murdered by thieves. All these occupational groups would have been obvious targets: shepherds whose sheep were a tempting target and whose job often took them away from the village into the woods and wastes, and millers and bakers because they undoubtedly accumulated a great deal of money from the peasants whose grain they ground and baked into bread. Five craftsmen—one fuller, two tanners, one carpenter, and one cooper—were killed by bandits. By the very nature of their trades, which consisted in producing finished goods for sale, these individuals must have had on hand a larger supply of coin than the average peasant who did not also practice a special craft. And in the case of fullers and tanners, they would have possessed a supply of raw materials and finished goods that would have been tempting. One monk, a representative of one of the wealthiest groups in medieval society, was also murdered by bandits. Thieves thus appear to have been discriminating in their choice of victim. They sought out the relatively defenseless, like women and children and those who were more likely to possess money or valuable goods.

Thieves also tended to kill more than one victim at a time during their raids: [34] 118 of the 226 people killed by bandits (52.2 percent), the number of whose fellow victims can be determined, were slain in company with someone else.* Many of these multiple killings were perpetrated in the course of raids carried out by fairly large and apparently well-organized bands of outlaws. In many cases it appears that the object of attack was not an individual person or house but an entire village. The killing of seventeen people returning home from a tavern in the fields of Great Milton in Oxfordshire may have been exceptional,[35] but there are numerous other instances in which thieves left a trail of blood and destruction extending throughout a village, and reaching even into neighboring vills. At twilight on September 1, 1267, some bandits came into the fields of the Bedfordshire hamlet of Honeydon. They caught a boy named

* Only 307 of the 2,204 people not stated to have been slain by bandits (13.9 percent) were killed in company with someone else. For this distribution, Yates's chi-square = 205.54 with 1 degree of freedom; $0.001 > p;$ phi = 0.29. Contingency coefficient = 0.28. Lambda (asymmetric) = 0.02 with the number of fellow victims as the dependent variable; 0.0 with robbery as the dependent variable. Uncertainty coefficient (asymmetric) = 0.07 with the number of fellow victims as the dependent variable; 0.11 with robbery as the dependent variable.

Philip, who was returning home from his father's fold. They took him to the house of Ralph son of Geoffrey and forced him to ask Ralph to let them in. Once inside, they wounded Ralph, killed his mother Denise and his servant William, and carried off all the household goods. They then went to the home of William Courtepie, whom they wounded and robbed. After that they broke into the widow Margery Levot's house and killed her. Then they attacked William le Messer in his home and wounded both him and his wife. Their next stop was the house of their captive's father. He, however, had heard the uproar in the village and hidden himself with his wife and other children and thus escaped with his life. The thieves then robbed Joan le Fillere's house, killed her, and pillaged William de Lodday's home. William, however, got away unharmed. Having finished with Honeydon, the bandits proceeded to the neighboring Goodwick, where they fatally wounded William Motte and set fire to his house. At this point Philip managed to escape and raise the hue. The bandits disappeared, leaving behind five dead or dying victims.[36]

In a period of three days in 1269, two other villages in Bedfordshire suffered similar raids. On November 15 thieves descended on Clifton in the southeastern part of the county. They first broke into the house of Edmund le Mastref, bound him, his wife, and his maidservant, and stole everything in the house. They then forced their way into Agnes Colbrun's house, and killed Beatrice le Sarreman and Agnes's servant John le Toutere of Daintry. Agnes they dragged along with them. When she refused to obey their order to ask permission to enter Geoffrey of Hoo's house, they wounded her in the head and arm with an axe. Geoffrey realized that they were thieves and that they were about to set fire to his house and raised the hue.[37] Two days later, on the 17th, it was the turn of Roxton, a vill in Barford Hundred near Bedford. Here the thieves robbed the house of Ralph of Bovetoun. They then forced an entry into the neighboring house and there killed Maud del Forde and Alice Pressade. They next broke into John the Cobbler's house, wounded him there, dragged him out into the street, and killed him. They also fatally wounded his wife Azeline (or Alma) and his daughter Agnes. His servant Walter of St. Neot's was also severely injured. One of John's daughters managed to get away and raised the hue.[38] Since Clifton and Roxton are only about eight miles apart, it is possible that these two raids and seven murders may all have been the work of the same band.

The socioeconomic condition of the thieves who were named in the eyre rolls is even more difficult to ascertain than that of the people whom they killed. Some writers who have considered the problem have concentrated on the relatively well-documented gangs of the early fourteenth century and have emphasized the gentry element in their composition. Noticing that the leaders of the gangs he had examined were drawn for the most part from the ranks of the gentry, the knights and esquires, John Bellamy observed that "the activities of the bands, we may suspect, represented the will to power among the gentry, the determination to achieve a position of privilege or re-achieve an old one in county society by fair means or foul." [39] Rodney Hilton in his study of the West Midlands noted that "members of the gentry appear [in the court records] with such considerable frequency, in proportion to their total numbers, that disorder appears almost to be a by-occupation of the class." [40] The eyre rolls contradict this impression. The condemned or outlawed thieves whom they reveal were clearly poorer than the average killer. The mean value of the chattels of 1,642 people accused of homicide alone was 8s. 10d. (106.9 pence exactly). That of 82 people accused of having committed a murder in the course of robbery was only slightly more than half of this—4s. 6d. (54.2 pence exactly).

This impression of the low social and economic status of bandits may nevertheless be deceptive. A person's social status may ultimately depend on the control of wealth or the means of production, but a status group is more than an economic group. It is equally a group that shares common values and a common way of life. It is possible that the records obscure the extent of gentry participation in banditry. For one thing, they record only the wealth of those bandits who had the misfortune to be caught or outlawed. The success of a bandit depends on the extent of the protection he receives. Peasants, being the least powerful members of society, can offer the least protection.[41] Therefore, it is possible that peasant bandits were caught and brought to trial more frequently than bandits of more gentle background. They lacked the support and protection of the powerful groups within society that could have kept them safe from the clutches of the law. And whatever support they might have received from their fellow peasants was quickly lost, since it was upon this group that they, like other bandits, preyed. Gentry bandits, on the other hand, may have been protected from the law by their social connections.

It is also possible that some of the people who appear in the records, although poor, were not peasants or artisans but impoverished gentry. The line that differentiated the poorer gentry and the richer peasants economically was often very fine and difficult to discern.[42] And in the twelfth and thirteenth centuries the economic position of the poorer knights was being steadily eroded. Possessing small manors with a limited number of villeins, they were far more dependent on wage labor to work their land and hence were often at a disadvantage in the marketplace. To a large extent, they also lacked access to the other profits of lordship. Owning few villeins, they were deprived of the money to be obtained from heriots, licenses to marry outside the village, licenses for the alienation of land, and tallage. Many did not possess courts and thus lacked one of the most effective means of disciplining the peasants and extorting money from them. At the same time the lesser knights were caught in the vise of rising prices and the rising level of consumption required by the lifestyle thought to be appropriate for members of the ruling classes. Faced with the prospect of being depressed into a lower social class, some apparently turned to banditry in an effort to preserve their position. In the thirteenth century, for example, the Basoc family in Sussex was losing control of its land. Early in the century Robert Basoc, lord of Sedlescombe, both leased and sold land to Battle Abbey. When he died, his widow Milisent sold the abbey her rights in his land for half a mark and a life corrody. By the end of the century this family of petty lords had disappeared from the records. The last mention of any of its members is of two brothers who had turned to crime and been hanged.[43]

Occasionally other glimpses of gentry bandits appear in the sources. Under the year 1236 Matthew Paris referred to a group of young men, all "*nobiles*," who had formed a conspiracy to devastate England "after the fashion of brigands and nightwalkers." Their "captain," Peter de Buffera, the king's doorkeeper, was betrayed and executed.[44] In 1251 Matthew also mentioned a Robert de Chandos, a knight of the *familia* of John of Monmouth, who, apparently because of a falling out with his lord, had turned to rapine until he had been captured by the earl of Gloucester's men.[45] According to the Dunstable chronicle, when the archdeacon of Richmond's manor near Exeter was robbed in 1293, several *nobiles* were hanged for the deed. The same chronicle noted that when the justices in eyre sat at York that year, they had another *nobilis*, Simon le Constable, arrested for his many robberies.[46] And, in 1272 or 1273 Guydo le Taylur, a master at Oxford, together with Robert de Boyton and Adam de Weston, stole 24 cows and five horses from Oseney Abbey.[47]

The presentment of the jurors of Barlichway Hundred in Warwickshire at the 1262 eyre reveals the activities of a gang that counted among its members some of the local gentry.[48] Robert de Castello, Thomas de Raggel, and Maurice son of the lady of Coughton had committed many robberies in the area near the Worcesterhire border, apparently with the connivance of the sheriff, William de Maunsel. Although the sheriff had held an inquest on the Alcester bridge, at which the culprits had been denounced, he had failed to capture them, perhaps because they had paid him a 100s. bribe. Remigius de Arundel, the under-sheriff, had also been bought off by the gang. Among their other crimes, Robert, his brother Henry, Thomas,

Maurice, Dobbe de Coughton, Walter de Lennak, William Strech, Roger of Alcester, and Robert de Shelfhull had stolen a casket belonging to Chadde of Alcester from the Alcester abbey church. They had taken this casket to Robert de Chandos's house in Alcester,[49] broken it open, and shared out its contents. Robert de Chandos and Robert de Udicote, a monk of Alcester, were suspected of having been accomplices in this theft. In another robbery this group combined with Richard Scot of Ipsley, Ranulf de Castello, Robert the parson, John de Teshal, and Cok of Kinwarton to carry out a theft at Norton in Worcestershire. On their way back from this deed, they killed the abbot of Bordesley's forester. For this exploit Robert de Castello, his brother Henry, Thomas de Raggel, Maurice, Dobbe de Coughton, William Strech, and Robert de Shelfhull were all hanged. Some of the members of this band were fairly substantial members of the local gentry, Robert de Castello in particular. His chattels were valued at £8 19s. 2d. His freehold land in Coughton and Kinwarton was worth £3 11s. 4d. a year. In addition, he owned a mill and apparently had the right to hold a court for his tenants.[50] Maurice was probably the son of Agnes the widow of Simon de Bruly who had held half a knight's fee in Coughton.[51] Thomas de Raggel had chattels worth £4 6s. 8d. and freehold land worth 10s. a year. Their suspected accomplice, Robert de Chandos, in 1251–52 had held half the town of Alcester[52] and possibly part of a knight's fee at Finmere in Oxfordshire.[53]

Although some bandits, perhaps especially the leaders of some outlaw bands, may have been of gentry background, the occupational surnames given for 48 accused in the eyre rolls indicate that most thieves were recruited from a lower social stratum. The two largest groups involved were clerics with nineteen representatives and servants with eight. A substantial number appear to have been artisans, which supports the idea that banditry was in large part a consequence of urban growth. Two were tailors, two were carpenters, and there was one each of soap-makers, criwelers, shoemakers, cutlers, weavers, turners, and comb-makers. Only four had indisputably rural occupations. One was a hayward, one a gardener, and two foresters. There were two charcoal-burners, who certainly pursued their craft in the forests but who prepared a product destined for a largely urban and artisanal market. The one marshal recorded may have been a specialist in the care of horses. However, the same term was also applied to a kind of metal-worker. And among this group of accused bandits there were also one ventusser, a man who assisted a surgeon in letting blood, and two millers.*

Some of these lower-class people may have operated in bands that were protected by the nobility or gentry. A noble could often have had a use for a band of rough necks, and may have been willing to condone some unsavory activities by his retainers. Contemporaries certainly felt that some lords maintained bands of criminals. In 1272 Archbishop Walter Giffard of York (1266–79), one of the men to whom the Lord Edward had entrusted the care of his kingdom while he was on crusade, wrote to his proctor in Rome that one of his chief tasks was to combat thieves and brigands, whose numbers had grown exceedingly great, and who he feared had powerful supporters.[54] A later archbishop of York, William Melton (1317–40), felt that he had been wronged by a group of powerfully backed bandits. Melton and Bishop Beaumont of Durham were embroiled in a dispute over the spiritualities of Allertonshire.[55] When Melton tried to carry out a visitation in Allertonshire, the bishop of Durham turned out with a "not small army" which threatened to kill the archbishop's men. Among this army of excommunicates, Melton complained to the pope that there had been many "brigands and robbers."[56] In 1276 the jurors of the borough of

---

* In her deposition to the coroner, the moribund Azeline (or Alma) of Roxton said that among the people who had robbed her and killed her husband and daughter were men who that autumn had collected tithes for the prior of Caldwell in Roxton field. (*Beds. Cor. Rolls*, p. 12.) This remark indicates that some bandits may have been recruited from among the ranks of the middlemen who served to link the traditional structures of the village with the new structures of the kingdom and the international church. It is from an analogous group that Anton Blok claims the Sicilian *mafiosi* of the nineteenth and twentieth centuries were recruited. (Blok, *The Mafia of a Sicilian Village*, pp. 6–8.)

Luton in Bedfordshire reported an incident in which the servants of a rich man had committed a robbery with his connivance. Hugh de Kaldewell, John de Kaldewell, Gilbert de Ossyngton, and Richard de Ossyngton, all of the mainpast, or household, of David de Ossyngton, stole two horses belonging to John le Cowe and killed John's servant Henry. The jurors claimed that the culprits had gone out to commit the deed from David's house and had returned there, that David had had a share of the proceeds of the theft, and that he had ultimately taken the four with him to Ireland.[57]

In addition to the ties of lord and retainer, master and man, thieves were also united by family bonds. Of the 199 people accused of having committed a robbery and homicide with a partner, 39 (19.6 percent) did so with a relative.[58] The relatives involved in this form of homicide were all members of the nuclear family. As was true of the entire population, sibling ties were far and away the most important. Twenty people cooperated with their brothers and sisters in committing their crimes. Fifteen people committed their crime with either a parent or a child: six with their sons, one with his daughter, and four each with their mother and father. Some of these familial bands of robbers can be seen at work in the Bedfordshire coroners' rolls. At twilight on August 1, 1265, John son of Richard Herebert of Gamlingay and his concubine Helewise, together with William son of Nicolas Prechur of Huntingdon, a clerk, and his sister Edith tried to rob Margery the wife of Thomas of Beachampstead, her sister Margaret and her son John as they went from the fair of St. Neot's toward the leper hospital at Sudbury. The hue was raised and the thieves pursued to Hail Bridge below Sudbury. There, before they were captured, John killed William the shepherd, who had joined the hue.[59] On April 28, 1272, Adam of Deddington in Oxfordshire, Isabel of Moreton in Buckinghamshire, Walter Scot of Berwick-upon-Tweed, and his wife Joan of Stratford outside London arrived in the town of Dunton. Walter tried to sell a pelt, but no one would buy it. The group then sought hospitality in the town, but were turned away everywhere. They went to a place outside the vill known as "Godeshull," where Walter and Adam quarreled. Adam killed Walter with a knife and Joan raised the hue. Isabel, who was still in Dunton, heard the hue, took her child and fled to the church. There she confessed that she and the others were thieves and abjured the realm. Adam was subsequently hanged at Great Barford. Joan was also arrested, but she was acquitted of any wrongdoing at a Bedford gaol delivery.[60]

Just as thieves cooperated with their relatives in committing homicide, so they combined with their fellow villagers. The home villages of 70 of the accused thieves can be determined from the eyre rolls. Thirty-four (48.6 percent) committed their crime with someone from the same village, which is a slightly smaller figure than for those who committed homicide only (54.7 percent, or 423 of 773). As is evident from the fact that 51.4 percent of the accused thieves acted with someone not from their home village, thieves also established networks that could stretch into several counties. In 1221 the jurors of Tamworth in Warwickshire denounced Richard the reeve of Sutton Coldfield for robbery and receiving. According to them, William de Hauekesford of Leicestershire regularly brought him stolen cattle, horses, and other goods. In return, Richard took stolen goods to William in Leicestershire.[61]

The ramifying networks of allegiance that united thieves to one another and on occasion to powerful men made it difficult for the government to deal with the problem of banditry. Some bands were apparently successful in terrorizing the countryside into a kind of submission. The tactics that could be used by bandits to cow the countryside are revealed by an incident that occurred on March 30, 1270. After some thieves robbed the house of Muriel le Braceresse in Astwick, Bedfordshire, Richard the clerk said that he had been threatened by one of the bandits, Richard le Husser, whom he had recognized by his voice.[62] A group of bandits operating around Taunton in Somerset early in the thirteenth century appears to have enjoyed a large measure of success in defying the countryside, at least for a period of time. In 1225 Gorwy Budde, Walter de la Sterte, Gilbert son of Jordan de Cumb, Osbert son of Roger Chelemund, Herbert son of Roger, William Counte, and Alice Black were accused of harboring these thieves. The jurors said of them that the bandits they were supposed to have received had often been attached by the bailiffs of Taunton and had "often promised to go away so that the aforesaid accused did not know whether they should be on their guard or not." They specifically said of Alice Black that she had taken food to the thieves in the forest, but only out of fear. One of the thieves had eventually been arrested. However, he had escaped from Taunton castle and the others had never been apprehended.[63]

Even after thieves had been captured, their friends, relatives, and neighbors often attempted to save them from the gallows. When Henry Dolfin was taken for theft and receiving in Blackheath Hundred in Kent, his wife Salerna and his sons John and William threatened to kill the hundred jurors and burn their houses if they convicted him.[64] In another case the kinsmen and associates of some accused robbers endeavored to aid them by killing their accusers. John de Colham and John of Bridgnorth, both from Shropshire, stole some animals belonging to a woman of Levedale in Staffordshire. They were caught and imprisoned at Shrewsbury. The woman and some of her neighbors went to Shrewsbury to recover her beasts. On their return, eight men, "partners and kinsmen" of the accused thieves, attacked them and killed William, Richard, an unnamed chaplain from Pencrick, and Henry son of Robert le Hus of Wolgarton. The killers tried to disguise the real nature of their deed by claiming, ironically enough, that their victims had themselves been bandits.[65] In some cases the thieves' companions resorted to a direct attack on the prison where the thieves were lodged. When Robert Stede was captured and imprisoned in the borough of Thame in Oxfordshire, Robert de Slochtre came with a multitude of armed men, broke open the prison, and rescued him.[66] It is not surprising, then, that in 1283, when William, a renegade monk of Wenlock who had become a bandit leader, was taken to stand his trial in the liberty of Oswaldslaw, he was conducted thither "with horse and arms, lest he be stolen away by other brigands." [67]

The wide extent of banditry and the difficulty of dealing with it were apparent to contemporaries. The awareness of the existence of bandits and the fear of them were widespread. Although they preyed largely on peasants, this fear extended even to the upper levels of society. For although the nobles were probably not sought out as targets as readily as peasants, they knew that they too were potentially vulnerable. For example, in 1244 thieves attacked the house of Simon of Edlesborough, a member of the Buckinghamshire gentry. Although a number of the bandits were killed, they murdered Simon's son and made off with much of his property.[68] Similarly, on August 1, 1267, at Renhold in Bedfordshire, a band of at least fourteen attacked the house of Simon the Red, one of the county coroners. According to the confession of one member, they intended to kill Simon and his entire family. Simon and some of his family were indeed wounded, but in what became a small battle involving men from several neighboring townships, the bandits were beaten off.[69]

The clearest expression of this fear of bandits was naturally given form by the literate elites. In the late twelfth century Richard FitzNeale explained the king's support of confessed felons who had turned approver as a means of eradicating the thieves who abounded in the land, a superfluity that he attributed to England's great wealth and the "inveterate drunkenness of the inhabitants." [70] Early in the reign of Henry III, Pandulph, the papal legate, wrote to the bishop of Winchester and the other members of the regency council to complain that no one could travel in the area around Winchester without running the risk of being either robbed or murdered.[71] In 1246 when the clergy protested Innocent IV's request for half of their ecclesiastical revenues for three years to help him in his Italian wars, one of the reasons they advanced against his demand was that the English church had to support an "infinite number" of paupers. If the church's funds were drained off to aid the pope, many of the poor would starve to death. Others, "who could not dig and were ashamed to beg," would turn to theft "from which would follow many homicides, tumult among the people . . . and uproar in the entire kingdom." [72] And in 1285 the canons of Lincoln cathedral complained to Edward I that they scarcely dared to go to midnight services for fear of being robbed and murdered by malefactors who haunted the cathedral precincts. [73]

The peasants, unlike the educated minority, could not record their fears. However, there is evidence that they too feared for their lives. The coroners' rolls reveal that people went about heavily armed after dark, like John Dreu, who, when he went out one night in 1271 to check on a cartload of his corn, took with him haqueton, helmet, and lance. [74] At Wigston Magna in Leicestershire the fear of bandits left its mark on the very names of the fields. By the fourteenth century one part of the fields was known as Shakresdale, which in the local dialect meant "the robbers' valley," and another was called the Saturilese, "the robbers' pasture." [75]

Since there was no effective police force to protect them, the peasants were forced to take collective action on their own to ensure their safety. In May 1271 the court of the manor of Halesowen in Worcestershire ordered everyone, on pain of the very heavy fine of 20s., to keep watch because of the passage of robbers through the country. [76] A village by-law of 1319 from Great Horwood in Buckinghamshire required each villager to keep the fences around his portion of the fields in good repair, not with an eye to keeping out rooting pigs and wandering cows, but so that "wrongdoers" could not enter the village except by the king's highway [77] and thus be seen.

People were so frightened of bandits they consciously organized their lives to minimize the chances of being robbed and murdered. Bracton wrote that no one should have to travel so far from his home to a market that he could not transact his business and return before dark, because once the sun sank, a traveler ran the risk of being ambushed by thieves.[78] In 1295, indeed, as a pious act, Matthew of Dunstable founded a chantry dedicated to St. Mary and St. Katherine on the Biddenham Bridge in Bedfordshire "for the safety of travellers who were in danger from thieves." [79]

In such a climate of fear, suspicion fell easily on strangers. Thieves were thought to travel in disguise, like the two who came to Bridgwater in 1225 dressed as clerics.[80] To grant a traveler hospitality, an act of charity that was regarded as a moral duty,[81] might easily prove fatal. At least eight of the 229 people (3.5 percent) killed by thieves were slain by their guests. For example, an unknown man and his wife lodged one night with Richard Paternoster in Dunton. In the middle of the night they smashed in his head, and those of his wife and daughter, the last fatally, with a hammer and stole all their goods.[82]

Those who had no visible means of support, those who "watch by night and sleep by day and frequent taverns and it is not known whence they live," as a list of articles for a view of frankpledge put it,[83] were regarded with considerable suspicion. For someone, especially an outsider, to behave in the least exceptionally was often to invite retaliation from a frightened community. In the reign of King John a serjeant of the sheriff of Oxford and the bailiff of the borough of Oxford arrested two men suspected of "evil-doing," largely , it seems, because they ate and drank by night and conducted themselves "stupidly." [84] The Lord Edward himself, when he discovered the bodies of some murdered men near Canterbury in 1268, arrested several of the city's citizens, being informed that they were "willful and quarrelsome youths." A special inquest jury acquitted them, and declared that suspicion had fallen on them "because, on account of the disturbance of the kingdom [during the Barons' War], they banded themselves together, and because they went frequently with their fellows to the taverns, night and day, and played and drank there, and quarrelled on the way home both among themselves and with those who met them." [85] In 1225 the Dunstable chronicler summed up the feelings and fears of generations of thirteenth-century Englishmen when he wrote that "in all the regions of England, bandits abounded. Not only did they rob travellers of their goods, they also murdered innocent people, so that in the villages no one slept securely, nor did anyone travel in safety from one borough to another." [86]

The government was almost totally incapable of dealing with the problem of banditry. It did, however, make sporadic attempts to police the countryside. In 1223 John of Thornton was sent to Yorkshire with eight serjeants to pursue and capture the "brigands and malefactors who were wandering" about the county.[87] A year later a similar commission was given to Walter son of Robert who was charged with keeping safe the roads of Bedfordshire, Cambridgeshire, and Huntingdonshire.[88]

Such measures were much too little. The king's government lacked the techniques and the manpower with which to police the countryside effectively. The burden of providing what defense was possible fell on the local community. In contrast to the attitude toward simple killers, who appear to have been allowed to slip away unmolested for the most part, thieves were often pursued for some distance. When a band of malefactors was reported to be lurking in the Cornish woods, the men of the neighborhood assembled under the leadership of one of the hundred serjeants and scoured the forest. They discovered a band of six; two of them they killed. Three managed to escape, but one was captured.[89] On December 20, 1279, Richard le Blake of Clipstone in the Bedfordshire parish of Leighton Buzzard, a chaplain, took part in a robbery and killing at Sudbury. He was wounded in the thigh. Shortly before midnight on December 21, he was tracked to his mother's house in Clipstone by six men, including the serjeants of Hatch and Clipstone. When they called on him to surrender, he fled from the house and was killed.[90]

Similarly, when Roger le Fendour of Charwelton, Richard le Bole of Charwelton, Hugh le Messer, and Thomas Bron robbed two houses in Buckinghamshire, they were pursued across Oxford to Northamptonshire where they took refuge in a chapel in

Charwelton. When John Purcel of Newenton called on them to surrender, they pulled him into the church and killed him. They defended themselves for some time "as in a castle." Eventually they were killed and their heads cut off and sent to Northampton castle.[91]

Such local self-help was of only limited effectiveness. But when men accused of banditry were apprehended, they were dealt with severely, as is shown by a comparison of the sentences they received and those imposed on people accused of having committed murder alone. Of the 1,136 people accused of homicide alone who appeared in court, 736 (64.8 percent) were acquitted and only 198 (17.4 percent) executed. Of the 115 accused of both robbery and homicide who appeared in court, almost as large a proportion were acquitted, 58 or 50.4 percent. However, two and a half times as many people were executed, 49 or 42.6 percent.*

Homicide committed in the course of robbery was a major phenomenon in thirteenth-century England. It accounted for at least 9.4 percent of all killings. For the most part it was perpetrated by men who operated in groups and made a living stealing goods from country people, which they then disposed of in urban markets. Indeed, banditry on this organized a scale was a phenomenon that was closely connected with the development of towns and the growth of trade. Without the revival of urban markets and commercial enterprise, medieval banditry would not have taken on the entrepreneurial character that it had acquired by the thirteenth century in England.

* For a two-by-two table composed of only those executed or acquitted according to whether or not they had committed their killing during a robbery, Yates's chi-square = 30.75 with 1 degree of freedom; $0.001 > p$; phi = 0.18. Contingency coefficient = 0.17. Lambda (asymmetric) = 0.0 with the verdict as the dependent variable; 0.0 with robbery as the dependent variable. Uncertainty coefficient (asymmetric) = 0.02 with the verdict as the dependent variable; 0.04 with robbery as the dependent variable.

7. Violence and Sexual Identity

The first, and perhaps the most significant, division within society is that made according to sex. Virtually every human culture attributes different economic, political, religious, and intellectual roles to men and women. Unfortunately, scholarly interest in the role of women in medieval societies is relatively recent.[1] And, if the records that have survived from the Middle Ages seldom let us see most men as anything other than taxable and justiciable ciphers, the picture of women that they present is even more dark and obscure. The eyre rolls, with their information on thousands of different interactions, allow us to penetrate a little into this obscurity. Although the rolls certainly do not cast a flood of illumination on the question of women and their roles in medieval Europe, they do allow us to see some things more clearly.

Homicide in thirteenth-century England was an overwhelmingly male phenomenon, as can be seen from Tables 16 and 17. Of the 2,434 victims recorded in the eyre rolls, 1,959 (80.5 percent) were men; only 475 (19.5 percent) were women. Among the accused killers this disparity was even more pronounced. Of the 3,492 accused killers, 91.4 percent (3,193) were men, whereas only 8.6 percent (299) were women.[2]

To an extent, the low level of female participation in homi-

Table 16. *Sex of Killers and Victims by Region*

Region	Male killers		Female killers		Total no. of killers	Male victims		Female victims		Total no. of victims
	Number	Percent	Number	Percent		Number	Percent	Number	Percent	
Rural Bedford	334	93.3%	24	6.7%	358	240	87.9%	33	12.1%	273
Rural Kent	473	88.9	59	11.1	532	325	72.5	123	27.5	448
Weald of Kent	40	88.9	5	11.1	45	20	76.9	6	23.1	26
Rural Norfolk	998	90.2	108	9.8	1,106	508	80.1	126	19.9	634
Oxford plains	203	94.9	11	5.1	214	130	84.4	24	15.6	154
Chiltern Hills	73	88.0	10	12.0	83	57	70.4	24	29.6	81
Forest of Arden	257	97.7	6	2.3	263	203	79.3	53	20.7	256
Felden Warwickshire	89	95.7	4	4.3	93	72	86.7	11	13.3	83
Large cities	494	91.1	48	8.9	542	233	84.1	44	15.9	277
Small cities	232	90.6	24	9.4	256	171	84.7	31	15.3	202
TOTAL	3,193	91.4%	299	8.6%	3,492	1,959	80.5%	475	19.5%	2,434

cide, both as killers and victims, may be explained by the different social roles that contemporaries expected the sexes to play. The use of violence was regarded as inappropriate for women. Unlike men, women were not trained in the use of weapons from childhood. They were not sworn to the assize of arms, nor do they seem to have engaged in the forms of hunting that required the use of quasi-military weapons such as the bow or the lance. When women did resort to violence, their actions seem to have been severely frowned upon. Although the beating of wives by husbands was socially acceptable, the opposite was not true. A man who allowed himself to be struck by his wife was subjected to the derision of the community. In France in the fourteenth and fifteenth centuries, a husband who had been struck by his wife was paraded through the village on an ass.[3] Although similar charivaris have left few, if any, traces in the legal records of thirteenth-century England, in the sixteenth century and later, Englishmen who were beaten by their wives were subjected to similar humiliations by their neighbors.[4]

Table 17. *Male and Female Homicide Rates, All Eyres*
(Per 100,000 population per year)

Area	Sex	Author's estimates	Russell's estimates	1801 figures	Per 20 settlements
Bedford	Male	19.0	18.0	13.0	1.13
	Female	2.9	2.7	2.0	0.17
Bristol	Male	3.1	—	—	—
	Female	0.7	—	—	—
Kent	Male	16.6	13.2	5.8	0.88
	Female	6.2	4.9	2.1	0.33
Norfolk	Male	7.4	11.7	9.4	0.74
	Female	1.8	2.8	2.3	0.18
Oxford	Male	13.9	20.1	11.0	0.66
	Female	3.1	4.4	2.4	0.15
Warwick	Male	38.2	17.9	9.0	0.95
	Female	8.3	3.9	1.9	0.21
London	Male	9.9	—	—	—
	Female	1.9	—	—	—

SOURCE: Figures are based on extrapolations from J. C. Russell's estimates of the population in 1377 in *British Medieval Population* (Albuquerque, N.M., 1948), pp. 132–33; and for 1801 from Great Britain, Parliament, *Parliamentary Papers (Commons), 1852–53*, vol. 85 (*Accounts and Papers*, vol. 29), Cmnd. 1631, "Population of Great Britain: Volume I," p. ccviii.

Table 18. *Verdicts on Those Who Appeared in Court*
According to Sex of Defendants

Verdict	Male defendants		Female defendants	
	Number	Percent	Number	Percent
Acquitted	717	63.6%	77	62.6%
Executed	206	18.3	41	33.3
Transferred to church court:				
Guilty	38	3.4	—	
Innocent	26	2.3	—	
Unspecified	14	1.2	—	
Pardoned	40	3.5	0	
Other	44	3.9	5	4.1
None given	43	3.8	0	
TOTAL	1,128		123	

NOTE: Chi-square = 30.34 with 7 degrees of freedom; $p = 0.0001$. Cramer's $V = 0.16$. Contingency coefficient = 0.15. Lambda (asymmetric) = 0.0 with the verdict as the dependent variable; 0.0 with sex as the dependent variable. Uncertainty coefficient (asymmetric) = 0.01 with the verdict as the dependent variable; 0.05 with sex as the dependent variable.

The strong social and cultural inhibitions against the use of force by women as a means of settling disputes is reflected in the verdicts handed down on women accused of homicide. See Table 18. Men and women who appeared in court were acquitted in about equal proportions: 717 of 1,128 males (63.6 percent) who appeared in court were found innocent. Another 26 clerics (2.3 percent) were also acquitted. Seventy-seven of the 123 women (62.6 percent) who appeared in court were also set free. Women, however, stood a greater chance of being executed. Of the males, 18.3 percent (206) were hanged, whereas fully 33.3 percent of the women, 41 in all, were executed.*

* For a two-by-two table composed only of those acquitted or executed according to their sex, Yates's chi-square = 8.25 with 1 degree of freedom; $p = 0.0041$; phi = 0.09. Contingency coefficient = 0.09. Lambda (asymmetric) = 0.0 with the verdict as the dependent variable; 0.0 with sex as the dependent variable. Uncertainty coefficient (asymmetric) = 0.01 with the verdict as the dependent variable; 0.01 with sex as the dependent variable. Barbara Hanawalt in her study of fourteenth-century gaol delivery rolls ("A Study of Crime," p. 133) has found that, if one compares the conviction and acquittal rates for males

The fact that women were also much less involved than men in homicide as victims may in part be explained by the fact that women were perceived as being more enveloped in the mysterious forces of the world than men. The nurturers of life, they may well have seemed more intimately connected with forces that were difficult for medieval men to understand. It is certainly not an accident that the most powerful, and the most capricious, saint of medieval Europe was the Virgin Mary.[5] Just as women were of the same sex as the Virgin, the agent by which the savior of the world had been introduced onto earth, so they were of the same sex as Eve, the agent by which corruption and death, according to the medieval myth, had entered paradise. Thus, women were seen to be more tightly linked to the mysterious forces of the world.

Among the nonhuman creatures that peopled rural Europe in the Middle Ages—the fairies, elves, dwarfs, trolls, and kobolds—there were beneficent female spirits who patronized those households that treated them well. William of Auvergne, a bishop of Paris who died in 1249, described these creatures in his *De universo creaturarum*. According to William, these spirits, whom as a conscientious bishop he believed to be demons, took on the likeness of girls and women in shining robes and frequented woods and groves. They entered stables, bearing wax candles, and plaited the horses' manes. These spirits also visited people in their homes. If they found food and drink set out for them, they partook of it but without diminishing it, and bestowed prosperity on their hosts. If, however, they found that no food had been set out for them, they left the niggardly household in contempt. According to William, foolish old women, and some men, left their pantries open and uncovered their barrels on the nights when they expected a visit from these beings.[6]

---

and females accused of all felonies, the courts were more lenient with women. This finding makes the harshness with which the thirteenth-century courts treated women accused of homicide all the more striking. Although medieval judges and juries may have been willing to excuse many forms of deviant behavior engaged in by women, they most certainly did not extend their tolerance to violence perpetrated by women.

But not all of the female beings who inhabited the world were felt to be as beneficent as these "ladies of the night." There were also witches and sorceresses about. When the belief in and fear of witches reached their apogee in seventeenth-century England, women made up the bulk of the people accused of being witches.[7] Although witches and sorcerers did not obsess the people of thirteenth-century England as much as they did their descendants, some have left traces in the records. It is perhaps significant that virtually the only people accused of supernatural evil-doing in the records that I have examined were women. In a case tried in the curia regis in 1199, a woman named Giliena was accused of sorcery by another woman named Agnes, the wife of Odo the merchant. Giliena was sent to the judgment of the red-hot iron, passed, and was therefore acquitted.[8] A more dramatic and darker tale was reported at the 1279 Northumberland eyre. According to the jurors, an unknown woman, a sorceress, entered the house of John de Kerneslawe at vespers and attacked him. John, signing himself with the cross, fought back, defending himself "as if from the devil." He succeeded in killing his attacker with a piece of firewood. On the advice of the local clergy, the suspected witch's body was burnt. John himself went mad for a period of time. When he recovered his senses, he fled to Durham. The jurors, however, did not feel that his deed had been a felony. The justices agreed and ruled that John could return to his home if he wished.[9] All this evidence suggests that females' perceived involvement in the supernatural and the uncanny may have served to isolate them from violent conflict. But until historians better understand the role of women in medieval myth and speculation, such arguments must remain conjectural.

Regardless of the unease medieval jurors may have felt about the relationship of women to the realms of nature and supernature, they viewed harshly anyone who had slain a woman. As Table 19 shows, a person who had killed a man had a much better chance of being acquitted than did someone who had been accused of having murdered a woman. Of those who appeared in court to stand trial, 1,057 were accused of having killed a male

Table 19. *Verdicts on Those Who Appeared in Court According to Sex of Victims Killed by Defendants*

	Defendants who killed males		Defendants who killed females	
Verdict	Number	Percent	Number	Percent
Acquitted	711	67.3%	53	41.7%
Executed	160	15.1	56	44.1
Transferred to church court:				
Guilty	37	3.5	0	
Innocent	25	2.4	1	0.8
Unspecified	13	1.2	1	0.8
Pardoned	37	3.5	3	2.4
Other	35	3.3	13	10.2
None given	39	3.7	0	
TOTAL	1,057		127	

NOTE: Chi-square = 88.02 with 7 degrees of freedom; $0.001 > p$ Cramer's $V = 0.27$. Contingency coefficient = 0.26. Lambda (asymmetric) = 0.01 with the verdict as the dependent variable; 0.0 with the sex of the victim as the dependent variable. Uncertainty coefficient (asymmetric) = 0.03 with the verdict as the dependent variable; 0.10 with the sex of the victim as the dependent variable.

Only those people who were accused of killing a male only or a female only have been included; those who killed both a male and a female—67 in all—have been excluded.

only. Of these, over two-thirds, 711, were acquitted, and 160 (15.1 percent) were executed. Those who had slain women fared much worse. Of those accused of having slain a woman only and who appeared in court, less than half were acquitted, only 53 of 127. Almost half, 56, were executed.*

If men may have felt uncomfortable about the use of violence against women, this was not a feeling that women seemed to share to the same degree. The bulk of thirteenth-century English homicide consisted of the killing of males. Of the accused male slayers, 89.9 percent (2,870) killed men. Similarly, of the accused women, 77.6 percent (232) killed men. Only a small

---

* For a two-by-two table composed only of those executed or acquitted according to the sex of their victim, Yates's chi-square = 59.52 with 1 degree of freedom; $0.001 > p$; phi = 0.25. Contingency coefficient = 0.24. Lambda (asymmetric) = 0.01 with the verdict as the dependent variable; 0.0 with the sex of the victim as the dependent variable. Uncertainty coefficient (asymmetric) = 0.05 with the verdict as the dependent variable; 0.08 with the sex of the victim as the dependent variable.

proportion of male murderers killed women, 13.1 percent in all (419). However, of the accused women, over twice as many, 28.8 percent (86) killed other females.* Similarly, whereas only 10.2 percent of the male victims (160 of 1,569 whose killers' identities were known to the jurors) were killed by women, 21.8 percent of the female victims (73 of 335) were killed by members of their own sex. This greater tendency for women to attack women can in part be explained by the fact that any cultural taboos on assaulting women probably did not exert the same restraining force on women as they did on men. On a more practical and perhaps more important level, women may have felt considerably safer in resorting to the use of violence against members of their own sex than in assaulting men, who were possibly more powerful and certainly more likely to be accustomed to the use of violence. And finally, in the course of their day, women may have interacted primarily with other women—with the exception, of course, of male members of their households—and thus have been more likely to come into conflict with other females than with men.

Undoubtedly the chief reason why women were involved so much less frequently in homicide was the fact that they played a less active role in social life. The social networks in which a woman participated were far more restricted, both in number and extent, than those to which a man belonged. The bonds that women established with people outside the home were neither as numerous nor as continuous as those of their male counterparts. Men participated much more fully in the life of the village community. The by-laws that regulated the agrarian practices of many villages were drawn up by men. Together with other males, men participated in the manorial courts, where these existed, as jurors, disciplining those who had been rebellious against their fellows. It was the men who belonged to religious confraternities. And it was the men who ventured more often

---

* Some people killed both males and females. Therefore they have been counted twice and the figures given here sum to a figure greater than the 3,492 of Table 16.

out of the village, to participate in the expanding commercial networks or to look for work. Women, on the other hand, had no formal role in the management of the village or the parish. They also often moved from their home villages when they married, but in that case they were simply moving from one male-dominated family in which their existence had been encapsulated to another similar group. Unlike the physical displacement of men, that of women did not serve to generate wider allegiances for them.

The ties that bound women to the outer world were accordingly much fewer than those of men. This reduced the possibility that women would become involved in homicidal conflicts for two reasons. First, it meant that they had fewer sets of obligations to honor. Once a woman had met her obligations to her family, she had few other important duties to fulfill. This fact was apparent to contemporaries. In his *Des quatre tenz d'aage d'ome,* Philippe de Novarre (d. 1270) wrote: [10]

Women have a great advantage in one thing; they can easily preserve their honour if they wish to be held virtuous by one thing only. But for a man many things are needful, if he wish to be esteemed virtuous, for it behoves him to be courteous and generous, brave and wise. And for a woman, if she be a worthy woman of her body, all her other faults are covered and she can go with a high head wheresoever she will; and therefore it is in no way needful to teach as many things to girls as to boys.

With fewer sets of obligations to fulfill, there was less chance that a woman would fail to match the demands made upon her and thus dangerously frustrate or disappoint someone. Men, on the other hand, had a wider network of ties—with friends, neighbors, trading partners, etc. They thus had more opportunities to fail, and more chances of calling down on themselves the wrath of a frustrated partner. Second, since women did not participate in as many, or as extended, networks as did men, there was less chance that they would be attacked if two or more networks came into conflict. Men, belonging to more allegiance groups, correspondingly had more opportunities to be drawn into a conflict between different sets of friends and retainers.

Even within the context of these networks, women acted more passively. Although combining with others to perpetrate a murderous assault was a generalized cultural trait, true of both men and women, it was even more pronounced among women. About a third of all men accused of homicide (33.5 percent, 1,070 of 3,193) acted alone. But less than a fifth of the accused women (16.7 percent, 50 of 299) did not have a partner in committing murder.* Similarly, women were much more likely to be killed with someone than were men. Of the 1,955 male victims the number of whose fellow victims can be determined, 1,686 (86.2 percent) were killed alone. But of the 475 female victims, only 319 (67.2 percent) were killed alone.†

The most important network to which a woman belonged was her family. Women were far more likely to be killed with relatives than were men: 112 women (23.6 percent) were killed with a relative as opposed to 108 men (5.5 percent).‡ Indeed, many women were probably not assaulted as principal targets, but as adjuncts to their husbands or some other male relative. For example, one day John the smith, Peter the smith, Walter Storfray, and William Burgeys, all from the county of Suffolk, came to Riolf of Cambwell's house in Barnfield Hundred in the Kentish

* Of the men, 2,123 had partners (66.5 percent), as did 249 of the women (83.3 percent). For this distribution, Yates's chi-square = 34.60 with 1 degree of freedom; $0.001 > p$; phi = 0.10. Contingency coefficient = 0.10. Lambda (asymmetric) = 0.0 with the number of accomplices as the dependent variable; 0.0 with sex as the dependent variable. Uncertainty coefficient (asymmetric) = 0.01 with the number of accomplices as the dependent variable; 0.02 with sex as the dependent variable.

† Of the men, 269 (13.8 percent) were killed in company with someone else, as were 156 of the women (32.8 percent). For this distribution, Yates's chi-square = 95.11 with 1 degree of freedom; $0.001 > p$; Phi = 0.20. Contingency coefficient = 0.20. Lambda (asymmetric) = 0.0 with the number of companions as the dependent variable; 0.0 with sex as the dependent variable. Uncertainty coefficient (asymmetric) = 0.04 with the number of companions as the dependent variable; 0.04 with sex as the dependent variable.

‡ Of the men, 1,851 (94.5 percent) were not killed in company with a relative; similarly 363 of the women (76.4 percent). For this distribution, Yates's chi-square = 149.57 with 1 degree of freedom; $0.001 > p$; phi = 0.25. Contingency coefficient = 0.24. Lambda (asymmetric) = 0.0 with relative/nonrelative as the dependent variable; 0.01 with sex as the dependent variable. Uncertainty coefficient (asymmetric) = 0.08 with relative/nonrelative as the dependent variable; 0.05 with sex as the dependent variable.

Weald. They asked Riolf for some beer. When he refused, they broke a window in his house, climbed in, and helped themselves. When Riolf protested, they beat him. At this point Riolf's wife Edilda came up "shrieking." They attacked her also. In the course of beating her, William Burgeys struck her with a mace, wounding her so severely that she gave premature birth to two infants, who lived for eight days, were baptized, and died. Although John, Peter, and Walter were acquitted of any wrongdoing, William Burgeys was hanged for the death of the infants before the justices in eyre.[11]

When women committed homicide, they were three times as likely to kill someone in company with a relative than were men. Of 2,123 men who had a companion, 16.3 percent killed in company with a relative. Of the women however, fully 53.4 percent (133 of 249) acted with a relative.* Women were also killed far more frequently by their relatives than were men. Eighty of the 475 female victims (16.8 percent) were killed by relatives. Only 79 of the 1,959 men (4 percent), however, were killed by relatives.† Although women constituted only 17.4 percent of those who were killed by people other than their relatives (395 of 2,275), they made up 50.3 percent of all those killed by relatives (80 of 159). Similarly, of the 3,193 males accused of homicide, only 3.9 percent (124) were accused of having killed a relative, whereas 18.7 percent of the 299 accused females (56) were al-

* Of the men, 1,777 (83.7 percent) acted with a partner who was not their relative; similarly 116 of the women (46.6 percent). For this distribution, Yates's chi-square = 188.21 with 1 degree of freedom; $0.001 > p$; phi = 0.28. Contingency coefficient = 0.27. Lambda (asymmetric) = 0.04 with relative/nonrelative as the dependent variable; 0.0 with sex as the dependent variable. Uncertainty coefficient (asymmetric) = 0.07 with relative/nonrelative as the dependent variable; 0.03 with sex as the dependent variable.

† Of the men, 1,880 (96 percent) were not killed by relatives; similarly 395 of the women (83.2 percent). For this distribution, Yates's chi-square = 100.65; $0.001 > p$; phi = 0.21. Contingency coefficient = 0.20. Lambda (asymmetric) = 0.0 with relative/nonrelative as the dependent variable; 0.0 with sex as the dependent variable. Uncertainty coefficient (asymmetric) = 0.07 with relative/nonrelative as the dependent variable; 0.03 with sex as the dependent variable.

leged to have murdered a relative.* Although women composed only 7.3 percent of the people who were suspected of having killed someone other than a relative (243 of 3,312), they made up 31.1 percent of those accused of having killed a member of their family (56 of 180).

Within the family group, men and women interacted in different ways with different relatives. Both sexes seemed to turn to parents and children for help in committing murder in about the same proportions. Of the 346 men who killed in company with a relative, 18.2 percent (63) did so with their parents, and 14.5 percent with their children; and of the 133 women, 16.5 percent (22) acted with their parents. (Of the foregoing, six males and five females acted with both a father and a mother.) A somewhat larger proportion of women killed someone in company with their children, 32 or 24.1 percent, as opposed to men, 45 or 13 percent. (Two of these men and two of these women committed a homicide with both their sons and daughters.) There was a striking difference in the frequency with which men and women acted in partnership with spouses and siblings. Most men committed homicide with a sibling, 204, or 59 percent (two men committed homicide with both a brother and a sister). In contrast to this, the relatives with whom women most often committed murder were their husbands or lovers, 63 or 47.4 percent of the women falling into this category. Only 34 or 25.6 percent of the women killed in company with their siblings. These differences may be explained by the fact that many women left their home villages when they married, moving to the village where their husband's family lived. Thus their ties with siblings were weakened.

* Of the men, 3,069 (96.1 percent) did not kill a relative; similarly for 243 women (81.3 percent). For this distribution, Yates's chi-square = 120.23 with 1 degree of freedom; $0.001 > p$; phi = 0.19. Contingency coefficient = 0.18. Lambda (asymmetric) = 0.0 with relative/nonrelative as the dependent variable; 0.0 with sex as the dependent variable. Uncertainty coefficient (asymmetric) = 0.06 with relative/nonrelative as the dependent variable; 0.04 with sex as the dependent variable.

If the relatives whom men and women killed are analyzed, similar patterns emerge, as can be seen in Table 20. The majority of both men and women, if they killed a relative, killed their spouse or lover. Sixty-five men (52.4 percent) killed their wives, whereas 33 women (58.9 percent) killed their husbands. Both sexes killed children and parents in roughly the same proportions: 8.1 percent of the men and 3.6 percent of the women killing their parents; 8.9 percent of the men and 10.7 percent of the women killing their children. In the case of siblings, however, there was a marked disparity. Fully 29 men (23.4 percent) killed their siblings (one man murdered both his brother and his sister), whereas only 10.7 percent of the women did so. This phenomenon can also be explained by the fact that married women tended to leave their home villages. They had fewer contacts with their siblings and thus were less often drawn into violent conflict with them.

Women showed a greater tendency to kill in-laws than did men. Seven men (5.6 percent) killed in-laws. Eight women also killed their in-laws, but these eight constituted 14.3 percent of all the women who killed a relative. Women also tended to concentrate their homicidal attacks on their brothers-in-law, six of the eight women killing this relative. Four of the six killed a sister's husband, and two killed a husband's brother. Since relations between spouses were the familial relation most likely to produce homicidal conflict, it is not surprising that women were involved in their sisters' quarrels with their spouses. Similarly, since, as we have seen above, relations between brothers were often strained, it is also not surprising that some wives were drawn into conflicts with a husband's brother. Men, on the other hand, displayed a much more diffuse pattern. Of those men who killed in-laws, only one killed a brother-in-law. Two killed a sister-in-law. One killed his father-in-law, one his mother-in-law, one his son-in-law, and one his brother's mother-in-law.

The more restricted nature of the social networks in which women participated was also reflected in the fact that they tended to kill people from the same village more frequently than

Table 20. *Killers and the Relatives They Killed According to Sex of Killer*

Relative killer	Male killers		Female killers	
	Number	Percent	Number	Percent
Husband/lover			33	58.9%
Wife/lover	65	52.4%		
Father	6	4.8	1	1.8
Mother	4	3.2	1	1.8
Son	8	6.5	3	5.4
Daughter	3	2.4	3	5.4
Brother	26	21.0	6	10.7
Sister	4	3.2	0	
Nephew	1	0.8	0	
Father-in-law	1	0.8	0	
Mother-in-law	1	0.8	1	1.8
Son-in-law	1	0.8	1	1.8
Brother-in-law	1	0.8	6	10.7
Sister-in-law	2	1.6	0	
Brother's mother-in-law	1	0.8	0	
Stepfather	1	0.8	1	1.8
Stepmother	2	1.6	1	1.8
TOTAL	124		56	

NOTE: Since some people were accused of having killed more than one relative, they have been counted twice. Therefore, the columns sum to numbers greater than 124 and 56 and the percentages to more than 100.0 percent.

men did. Only 23.4 percent of the men (167 of 714) killed someone from the same village as themselves, whereas 35.5 percent of the women (22 of 62) did so.* Thus, altogether 78 women, 26.1 percent of the total 299, killed someone from either their family or the same village. But only 291 males, 9.1 percent of the 3,193, killed either a relative or someone from their home village.

The less active social role of women was also reflected in the places where they were killed or committed a murder. The eyre rolls provide information about the places where 1,053 men and

* Of the men, 547 (76.6 percent) did not kill someone from the same home village; similarly for 40 women (64.5 percent). For this distribution, Yates's chi-square = 8.87 with 1 degree of freedom; p = 0.0029, phi = 0.10. Contingency coefficient = 0.11. Lambda (asymmetric) = 0.0 with fellow villager/nonfellow villager as the dependent variable; 0.0 with sex as the dependent variable. Uncertainty coefficient (asymmetric) = 0.01 with fellow villager/nonfellow villager as the dependent variable; 0.02 with sex as the dependent variable.

315 women were killed. In contrast to men, women were killed far more often in houses: 184 women (58.4 percent) were killed in a house, but only 254 men (24.1 percent). Similarly, whereas only 29.1 percent of the accused male killers, the location of whose crime is given in the eyre rolls (407 of 1,399), killed someone in a house, 42.1 percent of the women (64 of 152) did so. And, although only 4.6 percent of the men who killed someone in a house did so in their own home, 17.2 percent of the women did so. Men displayed a much greater propensity to become involved in homicide in places where more social and economic interaction occurred. Of the male victims, 3.2 percent were killed in taverns as opposed to only 1.3 percent of the women. Although varying numbers of men were killed in folds, on ships, in stables, in meadows, on bridges, or at markets, parties, and fairs, no women were reported killed at any of these places.

The impression that these figures give is that women were far more likely to be the occasions for conflict rather than active participants. For example on May 24, 1270, Emma the daughter of Richard Toky of Southill in Bedfordshire went to a place called "Houleden" to gather wood. There Walter Garglof of Stanford tried to rape her. In answer to her cries, her father came to her help. Walter shot him with arrows in the head and stomach. Seman of Southill also arrived and demanded to know why Walter was trying to kill Richard. In reply, Walter shot him in the back. Richard died of his wounds a few hours later. Seman, although seriously wounded, apparently survived.[12] Similarly, in Somerset Nicholas le Gardiner killed Gunnilda of Norton when she tried to keep him from raping her daughter.[13]

Quarrels over a woman's sexual favors also produced killings. In 1264 or 1265 William the hayward of Newnham came to William Curtepye's house in Bedfordshire. After drinking there for a long time he left. In the middle of the night he returned to sleep with Curteype's servant, Alice, something he was apparently accustomed to do. Henry son of William the cleric, seemingly also one of William Curtepye's servants, discovered them together and fatally wounded William.[14]

Although only a small proportion of thirteenth-century England's male population, and an even smaller proportion of its female population, were ever involved in homicide, the figures derived from the eyre rolls do provide insights into the different roles the sexes were expected to play and the different ways in which they interacted with other members of their society. To a large extent, thirteenth-century Englishmen saw violence as a male preserve. Women who were accused of taking human life were far more likely to be executed than men, just as those who, of whatever sex, had been accused of killing a woman were more likely to be executed than those who had been accused of killing a man. Women did indeed participate much less frequently in homicide than men, as both victims and killers. When they were involved, they also displayed different patterns of behavior than men. Women played a much more passive role, fewer of them being willing to engage in a violent assault unaided. To a degree more marked than for men, homicide for women was centered on the family. They were less likely to cooperate with people other than members of their own family in carrying out a killing. And they were more likely to kill a relative or be killed by one than were men. Medieval England was a culture in which violence was a tool reserved largely for men. It was a means of manipulating the environment, which, even if not a particularly successful one, men were willing to resort to in a wide range of situations. Women, on the other hand, were much less willing to resort to violence as a weapon. When they did utilize it, they tended to act only as adjuncts to someone else, especially a relative. And, in many cases, they must have resorted to it only in desperation, as in familial disputes where violence was unlikely to produce positive results; where, indeed, it must often have been self-defeating.

8. Homicide and the Rural Community

Thus far we have examined the patterns of homicide in the entire population of 2,434 victims and 3,492 accused killers. No effort has been made to distinguish regional variations or to analyze the differences in homicidal behavior in urban and rural areas. In this chapter an attempt will be made to sketch the different ways in which violence manifested itself in the various agrarian societies contained within the borders of the five counties whose eyre rolls have been analyzed for this study. These counties have been divided into eight regions: rural Bedfordshire, the plains of northern Oxfordshire,* and Felden Warwickshire,† all three common-field regions containing large nucleated villages practicing communal agriculture and characterized by the prevalence of impartible inheritance and large numbers of unfree peasants; the Chiltern Hills,‡ where settlements were more scattered and individual freedom more common; rural Kent, where virtually all the peasants were free, settlement scattered, partible inheritance practiced, and agrarian activities unregulated by the village community; rural Norfolk,

* The hundreds of Bampton, Banbury, Bloxham, Bullingdon, Chadlington, Ploughley, and Wootton have been included in the Oxford plains.
† The hundred of Kineton has been included in Felden Warwickshire.
‡ The hundreds of Binfield, Dorchester, Ewelme, Langtree, Lewknor, Pirton, and Thame have been included in the Chiltern Hills.

where partible inheritance also prevailed and the peasants were also rather free of seigneurial control, but where settlement was predominantly in large, tightly knit villages that controlled the agrarian activities of their residents; and the woodland regions of the Weald of Kent* and the Forest of Arden,† where settlements were relatively recent and very scattered and the peasantry largely free from the control of lords. These divisions, following the boundaries of the medieval hundreds, are artificial to an extent. Social structure did not neatly coincide with administrative districts. Where the common-field region of Felden Warwickshire left off and the Forest of Arden began certainly did not correspond to the boundary between Kineton Hundred and the other hundreds in Warwickshire. The same is true of the seven other regions. Yet the social structure within the hundreds that have been grouped together to make up the eight regions was probably sufficiently homogeneous to warrant treating them as coherent entities. In dividing the counties in this fashion, however, certain regional differences have also been glossed over. No attempt has been made to consider the breckland or fenland areas of Norfolk as separate entities, or to consider Romney Marsh apart from the rest of Kent. The social history of these areas is as yet poorly known, and it therefore did not seem practicable to attempt an independent analysis of the patterns of homicide in them.

The first question that poses itself is that of the relative frequency of violence in these different areas. Unfortunately, this fundamental question is one that can be answered with very little precision. If population estimates made for an entire county are only vague approximations, the same is even more true of any estimate for a specific area within a county. Therefore, this problem must be approached on the county level. Murder appears to have been far more frequent in the counties

* The hundreds of Blackburn, Barkley, Cranbrook, Marden, East Barnfield, Rolvenden, Tenterden, and Selbrittenden have been included in the Weald.
† The hundreds of Barlichway, Hemlingford, Knightlow, and the Liberty of Pathlow have been included in the Forest of Arden.

of Kent and Warwick than anywhere else (see Table 2, p. 36). Warwick was clearly the most violent of the five counties. Kent was probably the next most violent.* The shire with the lowest homicide rate was Norfolk, which had a rate of only about 9/100,000 per annum. Bedford and Oxford came between these extremes. At first sight this pattern is surprising, since one would have expected the close-knit common-field villages of Oxford and Bedford to have produced higher homicide rates. One would have expected that the necessity for close economic cooperation and the restraints placed upon villagers by the community would have produced intense and bitter conflicts. Yet it appears that in these areas there were other factors at work that restrained violence.

One of these factors was the strength or weakness of lordship. Where lords were powerful, manors engulfed entire villages, and manorial courts existed—as in Oxford and Bedford— homicide rates tended to be low. It appears that in these areas manorial courts were among the most important mechanisms that facilitated peaceable settlement of conflict. The manorial court, although a seigneurial institution used as a means of disciplining and exploiting the peasantry, was nevertheless also an embodiment of community sentiment. More than just the unfree tenants of a manor attended the sessions of the court. Although the great surveys carried out by many abbeys in the thirteenth century do not list freeholders as owing suit of court, on most manors they regularly attended the court.[1] In the course of the century manorial courts also became more active. For example, on three manors belonging to the bishopric of Winchester, the fines levied by the courts for breaches of manorial discipline—infractions of the assize of bread and ale, damages to the lord's property, failure to perform services, etc.—increased greatly in number throughout the century. In 1210, 106 fines

---

* Although Table 2 does not indicate that Kent had homicide rates too noticeably higher than those of Oxford and Bedford, it should be remembered that those homicides committed in the Cinque Ports of Kent were not recorded in the eyre rolls. These additional killings, if their numbers were known, would push the homicide rates for Kent higher than those indicated in the table.

were levied at Downton, 31 at Farnham, and 96 at Waltham. In 1299, 225 fines were imposed at Farnham and 244 at Waltham; in 1330, 240 were levied at Downton.[2]

If people were willing to bring their quarrels to their lord's court, it appears that these courts could be efficient in settling disputes. For example, late in 1276 at Highworth in Wiltshire, Henry the miller and Walter the tailor quarreled about the sale of a cow by Henry to Walter. In May 1277 they both brought suit against one another in the court of their lord, Adam de Stratton, one of the most powerful of Edward I's officials, Henry alleging that he had been beaten by Walter. Both were ordered to wage their law, which usually seems to have required obtaining five oath-helpers. Walter appears to have succeeded in finding the requisite number of oath-helpers and Henry to have failed, for in September Walter made his law and Henry was amerced 6d. for a false plaint.[3] Had this dispute not taken place in an area where a seigneurial court existed, operated by a lord interested in bringing in as much business as possible so as to maximize his control over his men and his profits, the quarrel between Henry and Walter might never have been settled. What had begun as a relatively petty dispute would have been allowed to fester and perhaps ultimately to issue in a profound enmity and perhaps a deliberately murderous assault.

The extent to which a manorial court could become involved in settling day-to-day disputes is revealed by tracing the affairs of one man through the records of such a court. Richard Dalle was a tenant at Sevenhampton in Wiltshire, a manor that also belonged to Adam de Stratton. On February 18, 1281, Richard was amerced 6d. by the Sevenhampton court for raising the hue and cry. On April 14 he was again amerced 6d. for a trespass against William de Stretend. On September 20 he waged his law that he had not struck Thomas de Colecote with a rake on August 21. Although Richard was never again at loggerheads with his neighbors as frequently as in 1281, he was nevertheless often amerced in subsequent years. Between January 1282 and September 1288 he was amerced at least fourteen times for various assaults and trespasses committed against his fellow villagers.[4] Had there not been a seigneurial court at Sevenhampton, and had Richard's trespasses not been disciplined by it, things might have come to such a pass that some of his neighbors might have taken things into their own hands and administered a possibly fatal beating to him.

Another factor at work in reducing violence in these areas was the cohesion of the village community. This factor can be seen most readily if we turn our attention to the county of Norfolk. Although Norfolk was an area where lordship was weak and manors extremely small, with several often contained in one village, homicide rates tended to be very low. It appears that the highly integrated nature of the Norfolk villages, where peasants lived in large, nucleated settlements and where the community as a whole regulated the agrarian practices of the village, acted very effectively to contain conflict. Since everyone in the village was bound to almost everyone else by ties of friendship, blood, and economic cooperation, when conflict arose the pressures for a peaceful settlement could be very great and there were available a host of potential mediators and arbitrators to patch up the quarrel.* In Bedfordshire and Oxfordshire, where many people also lived in large nucleated villages practicing common-field husbandry, similar mechanisms must also have operated to restrain conflict, in addition to the workings of manorial courts.

But in Kent and the Forest of Arden, which embraced most of Warwickshire, neither lordship nor the village community was an effective means of resolving disputes. In both regions lords did not exert much control over the peasantry. And in both regions people lived in small, scattered hamlets and farmsteads. Therefore, disputes in these regions often could only be settled by violence.

Just as the level of violence varied from one region to another, so did the ways in which people became involved in it. For instance, the role of the family differed from one area to another. Family ties appear to have played a larger role in the commission of homicide in areas where lordship was weak and partible in-

* For a fuller discussion of this point, see Chapter 10.

heritance was practiced. According to Table 21, in Norfolk, of those people who were accused of having committed a murder with a partner, 22.4 percent did so with a relative. For Kent, outside of the Weald, this figure was 29.1 percent. And in the Weald of Kent, where admittedly the number of people involved was extremely small, the percentage was 31.3 percent. In the Chiltern Hills, 30.2 percent of those who killed with a partner did so with a relative. In Oxfordshire and Bedfordshire, however, where lordship was stronger and partible inheritance not practiced, relatives were less likely to help one another in committing homicide, the figures being 13.5 percent for Oxford, 18.5 percent for Bedford, and 12.8 percent for Felden Warwickshire.

It will be noted that the areas where relatives tended to aid one another more frequently were also, with the exception of Norfolk, the areas with high homicide rates. It is not surprising that high homicide rates, a high level of cooperation among relatives in the commission of violence, weak lordship, weak village communities, and the widespread practice of partible inheritance should coincide. The weak nature of lordship and the village community in these regions resulted in more conflicts being settled violently. Confronted by the need to resort more frequently to violence, people were compelled to search for allies to help them in such risky undertakings. One of the first groups they looked to for aid was that composed of relatives. And in regions where partible inheritance was practiced, family cohesion had not been weakened to the same extent as it had been in regions of impartible inheritance. Noninheriting heirs were not faced with the same necessity of having to emigrate from the village to seek a better livelihood. Therefore, there were more relatives available from whose ranks allies could be recruited.

The Forest of Arden, however, presents a striking exception to this pattern. The Forest was an area where both lordship and the village community were relatively weak in the thirteenth century. The homicide rate was also exceedingly high, being about

Table 21. *Nature of Accomplice with Whom Homicide Was Committed, by Region*

Region	Relative		Master/servant		Fellow villager		Different villager		Total committing homicide with partners	Total committing homicide
	Number	Percent	Number	Percent	Number	Percent	Number	Percent		
Rural Bedford	43	18.5%	13	5.6%	38	16.4%	23	9.9%	232	358
Rural Kent	102	29.1	4	1.1	70	20.0	60	17.1	350	532
Weald of Kent	10	31.3	0		11	34.4	3	9.4	32	45
Rural Norfolk	191	22.4	17	2.0	184	21.6	143	16.8	851	1,106
Oxford plains	18	13.5	2	1.5	22	16.5	32	24.1	133	214
Chiltern Hills	16	30.2	5	9.4	6	11.3	14	26.4	53	83
Forest of Arden	26	17.1	7	4.6	39	25.7	19	12.5	152	263
Felden Warwickshire	6	12.8	2	4.3	11	23.4	16	34.0	47	93
Large cities	41	10.7	49	12.8	56	14.7	55	14.4	382	542
Small cities	26	18.6	6	4.3	20	14.3	21	15.0	140	256
TOTAL	479	20.2%	105	4.4%	457	19.3%	386	16.3%	2,372	3,492

47/100,000 per annum. But the high proportion of relatives that one would expect aiding one another in committing murder is not found. Of all the rural areas, the Forest of Arden had one of the lowest percentages of people committing homicide with a relative, only 17.1 percent. This ranks it behind Bedfordshire and only slightly ahead of Oxfordshire and Felden Warwickshire. By contrast, the percentage in the other woodland region, the Weald of Kent, was 31.3 percent.

It is probable that this aberrant pattern is due to the fact that Warwick north of the Avon was still an area of active colonization in the thirteenth century. Thanks to the detailed work of local historians, the chronology of the settlement of the Forest of Arden is known with some precision. In the parish of Tanworth, for example, colonization took place in three stages. The first, which was over by about 1180, saw the initial settlement. The first pioneers settled in large villages surrounded by open fields in which their holdings were scattered in strips. In the second stage, from the 1180's onward, there was a determined attack on the surrounding wastes and woodlands. New farmsteads away from the original nuclei of settlement were created. Eventually people disposed of their holdings in the original villages and devoted all their efforts to their homesteads. In the third stage, which lasted into the first decades of the fourteenth century, yet more land was cleared, the dispersion of settlement became even more pronounced, and the strips in the fields of the original settlements were enclosed.[5] As is readily apparent, the colonization process entailed a great deal of physical mobility on the part of the settlers. This mobility disrupted family ties. Indeed, it seems to have impeded the formation of group ties of all sorts. For the Forest of Arden had one of the smallest percentages of accused killers who acted in cooperation with someone else, only 57.8 percent. The only other rural region with a lower percentage than this was Felden Warwickshire, with 50.5 percent.

In the Weald of Kent, on the other hand, the process of settlement had largely been completed by the beginning of the thirteenth century. The history of the area around Battle Abbey, just over the border in the Sussex Weald, is known in detail. In 1086 the country surrounding the abbey had been largely empty, the convent's demesne barely amounting to 100 acres. Thereafter, however, it appears that colonization proceeded very rapidly. By 1124 the abbey had about 600 acres in demesne and another 837 acres held by tenants. By the end of the twelfth century enough of the forest had been cleared so that cattle raising, which required large areas of cleared fields, could be undertaken on a large scale. By the thirteenth century the Weald had ceased to be a frontier region.[6] The inhabitants of the Weald had therefore been rooted on the land for some time, and family ties had had more of a chance to reestablish themselves than in the Forest of Arden.

Just as the importance of the family varied from region to region, so did the importance of different relatives within the family group. There appears to have been a greater tendency for parents and children to cooperate in homicide in areas where partible inheritance was practiced. The rural areas of Norfolk had the highest percentage of people committing homicide with a relative, cooperating with either parents or children, 81 (42.4 percent). The Oxford plains, an area of impartible inheritance, had the lowest, 11.1 percent. Partible inheritance, and free alienation *inter vivos*, which was generally found in association with it, allowed more children to remain in the village rather than forcing them to migrate in search of a better livelihood. Thus, in a village where partible inheritance was practiced, there were more people who had parents and children to turn to for aid than in a village where impartible inheritance was practiced.

In contrast to the variable importance of parents and children, in virtually all regions siblings formed the single most important group of relatives, with in every region at least 40 percent of all those who had a relative as a partner acting with a sibling.* This is what one would have expected in areas of parti-

* The figures are as follows: rural Bedford, 17 with brothers and 1 with a sister (39.5% and 2.3%); rural Kent, 40 with brothers and 9 with sisters (39.2% and 8.8%); Weald of Kent, 6 with brothers and 0 with sisters (60.0% and 0%); rural

ble inheritance. Here the fact that brothers did not have to leave the village resulted in the creation of lasting ties between siblings. On the other hand, one would have assumed that the opposite situation would have prevailed in the regions of impartible inheritance; that the ties between siblings would have been weakened, either by emigration of noninheriting children or jealousy between the heir and his other siblings. Yet it is in the Oxford plains that the highest proportion of siblings helping each other is found, 88.9 percent. Paradoxical as it may seem, the social structure of Midland villages strengthened the ties of dependence among siblings. To a large extent, the social position of a noninheriting child who chose to remain in his home village must have depended on the maintenance of good relations with the heir. Many brothers and sisters must have gotten much of their livelihood by working the land of their brother. In those regions where custom allowed some sort of gift of land to be made to noninheriting children, the exploitation of this small plot of land must have been closely linked to that of the larger patrimony. If the brothers and sisters of the heir lived in the same house with him, or in a satellite cottage in his curia, the bonds that a shared life of work and leisure created must have been very strong.

When one turns from the pattern of cooperation among family members to a consideration of the conflicts that divided them, the very small number of people involved makes it difficult to perceive any meaningful variations between the regions. Nevertheless, a few generalizations can be made. The number of people killed by siblings was 32, or 23.2 percent of the 138 persons killed by relatives for the entire rural population. In Kent outside of the Weald, however, this figure was 28.2 percent. This is surprising, for one would have anticipated that the tensions between siblings would have been reduced in a region where partible inheritance was practiced. Indeed, in Norfolk

---

Norfolk, 76 with brothers and 11 with sisters (39.8% and 5.8%); Oxford plains, 14 with brothers and 2 with sisters (77.8% and 11.1%); Chiltern Hills, 7 with brothers and 3 with sisters (43.8% and 18.8%); Forest of Arden, 16 with brothers and 1 with a sister (61.5% and 3.8%); Felden Warwickshire, 4 with brothers and 0 with sisters (66.7% and 0%).

only eight people were murdered by siblings, 19 percent of the total for that county. The explanation of this Kentish pattern may lie in the fact that, although all male heirs—or in their lack, all female heirs—received equal portions of their father's holding at his demise, the holding was at times worked in common. The number of inheritances held in common and the length of time such arrangements lasted may have been exaggerated by previous historians,[7] although it is clear that such practices did exist. But land held in common was usually divided up rather quickly. And the same tensions and disagreements that led to the dissolution of the joint management of the inheritance may have in part encouraged the high level of violence among siblings in Kent. In Norfolk, on the other hand, where the same practice of working inherited estates together does not seem to have existed, there were fewer occasions for dissensions among brothers.

Although Norfolk did not have the highest percentage of siblings killing one another, it did have the highest rate of homicide committed by parents against children and vice-versa. Three people (7.1 percent) were killed by their fathers, four by their mothers (9.5 percent), four (9.5 percent) by their sons, and one each (2.4 percent) by daughters, stepsons, and stepdaughters. This pattern may again reflect the practice of partible inheritance. For partible inheritance was generally accompanied by free alienation of land *inter vivos*. If a man did not hold his land in villeinage in Norfolk, he could sell or lease it to whom he would during his lifetime without impediment, thus disinheriting his heirs. The heir thus had a major stake in attempting to control the management and disposition of his father's tenements. At the same time, he had few legal means by which to prevent his parent from selling or leasing his land.* This situa-

---

* It appears that *retrait lignager* did not operate in England in the thirteenth century, except in some boroughs. This was the right of the heir apparent, or of some other kinsman, of a person who sells his tenement to buy back that tenement within a year and a day at the price given for it. (Pollock and Maitland, 1: 344, 647–48; 2: 308–15.) Although the royal courts favored freedom of alienation, the heir of a socage tenant may not have been completely at the mercy of

tion undoubtedly produced conflict, some of which resulted in death.*

Although family members played differing roles in one another's lives in the various rural regions of medieval England, the same does not seem to have been true of masters and servants. The percentage of people who were assisted by a master, servant, or fellow servant in killing someone varied from a high of 9.4 percent in the Chiltern Hills to zero in the Weald of Kent. Aside from these two extremes, the percentages ranged from 1.1 percent to 5.6 percent. There is even less variation if one looks at the percentage of victims who were killed by masters or servants. In Norfolk, the Weald, and the Chilterns no one was killed by his master, servant, or fellow servant. In the other regions, the high was 1.2 percent, shared by Felden Warwickshire and the Forest of Arden, and the low was 0.6 percent in the Oxford plains. It thus seems that the bonds that service created, together with the tensions that such relationships engendered, were similar in all the rural regions of thirteenth-century England.

Despite the importance of kindred and servants, these groupings were only two of the many solidarities that united medieval Englishmen. The people who were assisted in a killing by relatives, masters, or servants accounted for only 460 of 1,850 people (24.9 percent) who had a partner in their act.† Unfortunately, the eyre rolls provide only very imprecise information on the nature of the other social groupings involved. Only six people were referred to as the "companions" (*socii*) of the people whom they helped. Yet from other sources it is apparent that the

the tenant's desire to alienate some of the patrimony. Local custom, which no court enforced, may in many places have acted to restrict freedom of alienation although the common law did not.

* We should expect to find this pattern duplicated in Kent, where free alienation of land *inter vivos* was also prevalent. However, only 15.4 percent of the people killed by relatives there were killed by parents or children. This discrepancy may be the result of the extremely small size of the groups that are being studied.

† The apparent discrepancy between this figure and that which can be derived from Table 21 is due to the fact that two people acted with both a servant and a relative.

ties that bound friends together must have been exceedingly strong and effective. For example, in the early fourteenth century Andreas the vicar of Caldecote and Nicholas de Kymewell, both of Cambridgeshire, swore to "maintain and support each other in all quarrels, transgressions, and felonies whatever."[8] Occasionally the sources allow a glimpse of these associations of friends in action. One day in Oxfordshire Gilbert de la Hide came to the house of Walter Balle and asked Walter, Peter le Wainer, Andreas le Rus, Simon le Feure, Robert le Feure, and Thurston de Sikeby to go with him to seize one John of Wallop "so that he could avenge himself on him." In the ensuing struggle on the Petipont Bridge at Oxford, John was fatally wounded.[9] In 1272 Ralph, son of Ralph the vicar of Bromholm, ran afoul of another such band of companions. On the night of February 25, as he was making his way past the village church, he encountered Robert Bernard of Wootton, Robert of Shefford, Richard Norman, and Roger Brien. Robert Bernard asked him who he was. He replied, "A man, who are you?" Robert, who was drunk, thereupon hit him in the head with an axe. Ralph died of this wound the next day. What is interesting about this incident is not the fact that Ralph met his unfortunate end in a drunken row outside the local church, but that, as the local villagers testified at the coroner's inquest, Robert and his fellows had "consented to do any other misdeed and were waiting to do injury to someone else there."[10] On occasion friends also intervened to rescue one of their own from the clutches of the law, like the multitude of Thomas the chaplain's *socii* who freed him from the archbishop of Canterbury's prison at Lyminge in Kent.[11]

The bonds that united villagers to one another were also strong. When confronted by the outside world, in the form of peasants from other villages, the demands of lords, or the exactions of the king, villagers coalesced to defend themselves or to attack their antagonists. Riots between villages were common. On June 16, 1274, the prior of St. Neot's was crossing the fields of Little Barford in Bedfordshire with a monk, three servants, and Lawrence his squire. Since they were in the lady of Little Barford's corn, and probably causing damage, John le Messer tried to take a surety from them. Lawrence refused to give any, and John finally raised the hue. As the villagers of Little Barford turned out in answer, the prior went on toward Croydon. In the melée that developed in the field, Lawrence was struck on the arm with a bow. One of the prior's servants got away and raced back to St. Neot's, where he reported that the men of Little Barford had wounded the prior and his men. The people of St. Neot's armed themselves[12] and invaded Little Barford. In the battle, Aytrop Stalun of Little Barford was fatally wounded.[13]

Similarly, sometime around 1305 some men from the land of Roger Mortimer came to the town of Bridgnorth in Shropshire to participate in some games. They quarreled with the local men. The fight escalated until finally the men of Bridgnorth blockaded themselves in the town while their opponents fired arrows into it. Eventually, one of the besiegers, William de Balbeneye, was killed by Walter son of William de Phanes, constable of the town and bailiff of the hundred of Stottesdon.[14] During the yearly Whitsun procession in the borough of Leicester in 1313, the men of Wigston Magna and another village fought each other with swords and sticks.*

If an attempt is made to assess statistically how often villagers cooperated with each other in committing homicide, the problem of determining whether two killers were from the same village is encountered. If the eyre rolls state that two or more men belonged to the same frankpledge, this is a sure indication that they were from the same village. However, most frequently the only information the rolls provide is whether or not the men had names with a similar place-name element in them. In 1,159

* Hoskins, *Midland Peasant,* p. 79. It was customary on the feast day of a saint for any daughter churches that had split off from a mother church to go in procession to the original church. These were occasions for battles among the parishioners. In 1236 Robert Grosseteste ordered his archdeacon to forbid "that in the procession in the yearly visit and honoring of the mother church any parish fight to go before another parish with its banners, since thereof are accustomed to arise not brawls only, but cruel bloodshed." (Robert Grosseteste, *Epistolae,* Cited in Homans, *English Villagers,* p. 373.)

cases it was impossible to establish whether two or more killers came from the same village. In 691 cases, however, there was some indication of whether they were fellow villagers: 381 of these (55.1 percent) acted with a fellow villager, and 310 (44.9 percent) did not. This last figure may be artificially inflated. The fact that two killers had different place-name elements in their names did not necessarily mean they were from different villages. It is possible that someone with a name indicating his origin in a different village had emigrated and lived for some years in the same village as that of the person with whom he committed a murder. If the available information were more complete, a higher percentage of people killing in company with their fellow villagers would probably be found.

Given the unreliable nature of the information in the eyre rolls, it is unfortunately not possible to discern any meaningful regional variations in the extent of cooperation among fellow villagers. The Chiltern Hills had the lowest percentage of killers cooperating with partners drawn from the same village as themselves, 11.3 percent, whereas the Weald of Kent had the highest, 34.4 percent. Perhaps an analysis of a larger number of cases would enable us to perceive some coherent patterns. But it is possible that the eyre rolls are simply too imprecise to provide a reliable measure of village solidarity.

Although the eyre rolls cannot be used to measure exactly the extent of cooperation between fellow villagers, they do show that a considerable number of people killed in company with people who were neither members of their family or household nor fellow villagers. It is obvious that the web of interrelationships that united peasants reached outside the boundaries of the village and the parish. In thirteenth-century England there was a great deal of physical mobility among the population. People tended to marry outside their villages. The survey of bondmen made by Spalding Priory in the Lincolnshire Fens in 1259–60 shows that 33 of 86 young adult women (38.4 percent) in the village of Weston had married outside of the village. Many adult males had also emigrated from their home village. At Weston 26 of 68 grown sons (38.2 percent) had emigrated, and at Moulton 14 of 60 (23.3 percent) had left their homes.[15] Not only did landless sons and daughters emigrate; so did leading members of the community, at least for part of their lives. On Ramsey Abbey's estates in the early fourteenth century, it was common for members of this group to leave their villages for periods of several years.[16] With so many people moving back and forth between villages, many strong ties were created that reached into several villages. One of these intervillage solidarities can be discerned in an incident that occurred in Oxfordshire. On July 24, 1271, William Preg and Philip the thresher of Steeple Aston went to the neighboring village of Somerton to watch a wrestling match. Emma, the widow of Gilbert Barel of Steeple Aston, was also there. During the games she approached Richard Vnwyne and his brothers Hugh and Roger, and said to them, " 'Those are the two who made me lose my house.' And they replied and said that they would meet their death before they left the vill." Richard and his brothers chased William and Philip to Somerton's mill, killed them, and threw them into the millpond.*

Answering the question of how often people killed their fellow villagers is also made difficult by the problem of determining whether the victim and the killer were from the same village. It is even more difficult to determine this than it was to determine if two fellow killers were from the same village. Since victims' frankpledges were never specified, only similar place-name elements in the names of killers and victims give any clue of their respective places of origin. In only 475 cases can it be determined if a victim was killed by someone from the same vil-

---

* PRO, J.I.2/261, m. 1r. Unfortunately the records do not tell us of the reason for Emma's desire for revenge. Emma's hatred of William and Philip may well have grown out of a dispute over a widow's portion. The two men may have been Gilbert Barel's relatives, who had successfully ejected Emma from her dead husband's house. Or they may have been the suitors of a court in which Emma had failed to prove her claim to the house.

Table 22. *Victims and Their Killers by Region*

Region	Killed by relatives		Killed by master/servant		Killed by fellow villager		Killed by nonfellow villager		Total victims
	Number	Percent	Number	Percent	Number	Percent	Number	Percent	
Rural Bedford	16	5.9%	2	0.7%	17	6.2%	42	15.4%	273
Rural Kent	39	8.7	5	1.1	13	2.9	86	19.2	448
Weald of Kent	2	7.7	0		2	7.7	9	34.6	26
Rural Norfolk	42	6.6	0		57	9.0	119	18.8	634
Oxford plains	19	12.3	1	0.6	10	6.5	37	24.0	154
Chiltern Hills	4	4.9	0		2	2.5	15	18.5	81
Forest of Arden	11	4.3	3	1.2	18	7.0	36	14.1	256
Felden Warwickshire	5	6.0	1	1.2	7	8.4	5	6.0	83
Large cities	8	2.9	5	1.8	16	5.8	49	17.7	277
Small cities	13	6.4	4	2.0	7	3.5	26	12.9	202
TOTAL	159	6.5%	21	0.9%	149	6.1%	424	17.4%	2,434

lage:126 (26.5 percent) were, whereas 349 (73.5 percent) were not. Considering the large number of people about whom there is no information concerning their place of origin, it is obvious that these figures should be interpreted cautiously. Yet it does appear that more homicidal attacks were directed against people outside the village community than against those within it. Again, no clear regional differences emerge. One would have expected those areas with the highest percentage of people killed by fellow villagers to be those where lordship was weak and institutionalized means of settling disputes between neighbors few. However, the patterns that the eyre rolls display show no consistency (see Table 22). Although an area of weak lordship and weak village communities like the Weald of Kent had the third highest percentage, 7.7 percent, the two highest percentages occurred in Norfolk (9.0 percent), where it appears that the tightly knit village communities were usually able to regulate successfully most conflict, and in Felden Warwickshire (8.4 percent), where manorial courts were common. Two of the lowest percentages also occurred in areas where the village community was loosely structured and lordship was not very important—in Kent outside the Weald, where 2.9 percent were killed by their fellow villagers, and in the Chiltern Hills, where 2.5 percent were killed by people from the same village. Despite the lack of any readily explicable variations between the regions, it is nevertheless clear that relations within the village community, no matter whether that community were a hamlet in Kent or a common-field village in Oxfordshire, were, if not tranquil, at least not as marred by murder as were relations between people from different villages.

Just as the involvement of relatives, friends, neighbors, and people from different home villages in homicidal conflict varied from one region to another, so did the involvement of the sexes. Women formed 20.5 percent of all victims in rural areas (see Table 16, p. 135). In Kent, however, they made up 27.5 percent of the total; in the Weald 23.1 percent; in the Chiltern Hills 29.6 percent; and in the Forest of Arden they accounted for 20.7 percent of the victims.* In the case of the Chiltern Hills and Kent, the high proportion of female victims may be explained in part by the high incidence in these areas of homicide committed in the course of robbery. As has been shown above, bandits had a propensity to seek out women as victims. This, however, does not account for the entire discrepancy. If those people killed by bandits are excluded from the analysis, the percentage of women who were killed in these areas becomes 24.3 percent for Kent, 13.6 percent for the Weald, 19 percent for the Chiltern Hills, and 19.8 percent for the Forest of Arden. Although these figures are reduced, they are nevertheless, with the exception of the Weald, still higher than those for the other regions.

Another explanation of these differences in the involvement of the sexes that comes to mind is that conflicts between male and female relatives, the type of conflict in which women tended to become involved, may have been more common in these regions. But this does not seem to have been the case. Of the 400 female victims killed in rural areas, 67 or 16.8 percent were killed by relatives. However, of the regions with a high proportion of female victims, only Kent outside the Weald surpassed this figure, with 17.9 percent. Elsewhere the percentage fell below 16.8. In the Weald no women were killed by relatives. In the Chilterns, women killed by relatives formed only 12.5 percent of the total and in the Forest of Arden only 11.3 percent.†

The explanation for the high proportion of female victims in

* If one considers the estimated homicide rates that have been calculated for men and women, Kent and Warwick have the highest rates for women, 6.2/100,000 and 8.3/100,000 respectively (using the author's population estimates).

† The complete breakdown on the number of males and females slain by relatives is as follows: rural Bedford, 10 males and 6 females (4.2% and 18.2%); rural Kent, 17 males and 22 females (5.2% and 17.9%); Weald of Kent, 2 males and 0 females (10.0% and 0%); rural Norfolk, 25 males and 17 females (4.9% and 13.5%); Oxford plains, 7 males and 12 females (5.4% and 50.0%); Chiltern Hills, 1 male and 3 females (1.8% and 12.5%); Forest of Arden, 5 males and 6 females (2.5% and 11.3%); Felden Warwickshire, 4 males and 1 female (5.6% and 9.1%); large urban, 2 males and 6 females (0.9% and 13.6%); small urban, 6 males and 7 females (3.5% and 22.6%). Total slain by relatives: 79 males and 80 females (4.0% and 16.8%).

these regions probably lies in the fact that, with the exception of the Forest of Arden, the most important network uniting people with one another in Kent, the Weald, and the Chilterns was the family. (See Table 21.) The wider networks of the village, the manor, and the parish did not serve to integrate people in these regions as much as they did in the common-field regions. Therefore, the basic cells between which conflict occurred in these regions were families, rather than other groups. People turned more readily to their kin for aid in these regions, and conflict tended to involve one family against another. Since the family was the only network in which women played an active role, they were more frequently sought out as victims by their male relatives' enemies. Thus they were killed more frequently in these regions than in those where conflict occurred more frequently between competing allegiance groups other than families. Since women played a less important role in these other groups, they were less likely to be involved in a conflict between these sets of allies.

It is more difficult to understand the significance of the varying proportions of women who were involved in homicide as killers. In all the rural areas, women constituted 8.4 percent of the accused killers. Kent and the Chilterns again show a higher-than-average involvement for women (see Table 16). In Kent and the Weald they formed 11.1 percent of the total. In the Chilterns they made up 12 percent of the killers. By contrast, the common-field regions had a much lower ratio of women involved in homicide as killers. In Bedford, the Oxford plains, and Felden Warwickshire they made up 6.7 percent, 5.1 percent, and 4.3 percent of the killers. This difference, like the difference in the number of women killed in these areas, can be explained by the fact that conflict in the non-common-field areas tended to be primarily between families, whereas in the common-field areas it involved other groups of allies. Just as women were more likely to be killed in the non-common-field areas, they were more likely to kill someone in those same areas in the course of a dispute between two sets of kin.

The Forest of Arden appears to present a striking contrast to this pattern. The Forest possessed many aspects of social organization to be found in Kent, Norfolk, and the Chiltern Hills: weak lordship, scattered settlement, and weak village organization. Yet instead of having a high proportion of women involved in conflict as killers, it had the lowest percentage of all the regions, only 2.3 percent. This very low figure for the Forest of Arden may reflect the fact not that women there were more pacific but that men were more violent. It will be recalled that Warwickshire, which was largely composed of the Forest, had extremely high homicide rates, around 47/100,000. As a frontier area, it possessed fewer institutionalized means of solving conflicts. Men were accordingly compelled to resort to violence in larger numbers than elsewhere. Therefore, although women may have been more prone to use violence in the forest areas of Warwickshire than elsewhere, the actual level of their violent behavior may be masked by the extremely high level of male violence.

Determining the economic status of killers in the different areas of rural England is made difficult by the fact that next to nothing is known of the relative distribution of wealth in those areas. A man with movable property worth 20s. who lived in a relatively impoverished area might have occupied a more important place in his community than a man with the same amount of chattels but living in a more prosperous region. Nevertheless, a consideration of the confiscated chattels of outlawed or condemned felons reveals some interesting contrasts between regions. (See Table 23.) Murderers who lived in areas marked by weak lordship, weak village communities, partible inheritance, scattered settlement, or high homicide rates such as Norfolk, Kent, and the Forest of Arden, tended to have more property than their counterparts from areas of strong lordship, strong village communities, nucleated settlement, and impartible inheritance, i.e. the Oxford plains, Bedfordshire, and Felden Warwickshire. If it is remembered that Kent and Norfolk were also areas peopled by a substantial number of near-landless

Table 23. *Mean Value of Confiscated Chattels by Region*

Region	Number of accused	Mean value of chattels (pence)	Percent of accused with no chattels	Excluding accused with no chattels	
				Number of accused	Mean value of chattels (pence)
Rural Bedford	200	63.6	54.5%	91	139.7
Rural Kent	250	85.6	52.4	119	179.8
Weald of Kent	16	36.9	37.5	10	59.1
Rural Norfolk	525	106.0	60.2	209	266.2
Oxford plains	115	57.9	66.1	39	170.8
Chiltern Hills	45	42.2	60.0	18	105.6
Forest of Arden	139	70.9	63.3	51	193.3
Felden Warwickshire	56	43.7	57.1	24	102.0
Large cities	243	204.6	72.4	67	742.0
Small cities	135	141.3	61.5	52	366.8
Entire population	1,724	104.4	60.6	680	264.7

and therefore impoverished peasants, it is clear that killers in the non-common-field regions were recruited from wealthier levels of the population than in the common-field regions. This is once again what one would expect in areas where formal means of settling conflicts were not as numerous as elsewhere. A quarrel between two wealthy peasants in northern Oxfordshire would most likely have been resolved in a manorial court. But in the settlements of the Forest of Arden or in the hamlets of Kent there was no such body to which men could take a dispute for settlement or arbitration. Therefore, some of these disputes among substantial members of the community could have become sufficiently exacerbated to result in a fatal assault. In areas where such institutionalized means of settling disputes existed, the use of violence was largely restricted to the poorer members of society, people whose poverty and consequent marginal position in society made them less amenable to the standard means of mediating disputes.

The county of Norfolk, however, is an exception to this general pattern. Here a high mean value of confiscated chattels is found in conjunction with low homicide rates and relatively weak lordship. As has been pointed out above, it appears that, despite the weakness of lordship, the Norfolk village community was cohesive enough to regulate most conflicts that arose between neighbors. One would therefore have expected that what homicide was committed would have been the work of the poorer members of the society. But this seems to be contradicted by the evidence of the eyre rolls. A close examination of the rolls, however, shows that to a very large extent homicide was indeed the work of the poorer members of society. Although Norfolk had the highest mean value of confiscated chattels, a very large number of the accused killers, 60.2 percent, had no movable property at all. This figure was exceeded only by those for the Forest of Arden, 63.3 percent, and the Oxford plains, 66.1 percent. Although most murder appears to have been the work of the very poor, the very wealthy in Norfolk were also willing to turn to violence as a last resort when the village community failed to arbitrate a dispute successfully.

From this consideration of the nature of homicide in the eight regions studied here, certain broad patterns emerge. Areas of weak lordship, weak village communities, partible inheritance, and scattered settlement tended to have high homicide rates, probably because other means of settling conflicts than by force were largely lacking. As a result, wealthier members of society were forced to use violence against one another more often than in other areas. Since the practice of partible inheritance allowed more members of a family to remain on the land, allies in the prosecution of violence were recruited frequently among relatives. Conflict thus tended to take the form of competition between family groups. As a result, women were more frequently involved.

In the common-field areas of England, however, where lordship and community were strong, where impartible inheritance was practiced, and where settlement tended to be nucleated, violence was less common. Killers tended to come primarily from the poorer elements in society. Relatives were recruited less often as allies, largely because the practice of impartible inheritance forced many family members to emigrate from their home villages. Conflict thus tended to occur between competing allegiance groups other than the family. And, as a result, women were less often involved. Lordship and strong village communities thus appear to have been something of mixed blessings. A person who lived under such a regime had to put up with economic exploitation by his lord and constant meddling in his affairs by his neighbors. But his lord and his neighbors provided effective mechanisms by which his disputes could be resolved peacefully. People who did not live in the common-field regions were undoubtedly much freer of the constraints of both lordship and the village community. But with fewer means of settling conflicts available, life in these regions was darkened by the greater frequency of murder.

9. Homicide and the Urban Community

The development of cities and of an urban life based on trade and manufacture was one of the major features of medieval social history. Despite the importance of medieval cities and the flood of books written about them, little is known of the social arrangements that existed within them. Although this deficiency is being rectified for Italian cities,[1] the serious study of medieval urban society north of the Alps is only beginning. The thirteenth-century English eyre rolls can be used to sketch certain aspects of life in the new urban centers of northern Europe.

Although thirteenth-century England was not heavily urbanized, it did contain one major city, London. Following London in size and importance were towns like Bristol, Norwich, and Great Yarmouth, each with between 10,000 and 20,000 inhabitants, and each an important shipping, manufacturing, or administrative center. These four centers have been analyzed together. England also contained numerous market towns and boroughs. Thirty-one of these (see footnote, p. 25) have been selected for analysis as a separate group. This group admittedly is very heterogeneous, including places like King's Lynn, an important North Sea grain-exporting and fishing port in Norfolk; Warwick, a sleepy county town; and Banbury, a small regional market in Oxfordshire. Yet grouping the towns and cities into these two broad categories permits an analysis that will take account not only of differences in patterns of homicide between rural and urban areas but of differences between the patterns of large urban centers and small towns.

One of the most striking aspects of homicide in medieval English urban areas is that it seems to have occurred much less commonly than in rural areas. The difficulty of making population estimates precludes the possibility of making any estimates of the frequency of homicide in the small market towns. But in the cases of London, Bristol, and Norwich, homicide rates that are probably not too inaccurate can be derived. The homicide rate in Norwich appears to have been about 16.1/100,000 per annum (see above, p. 84). The rates for London in the periods covered by the 1244 and 1276 eyres were about 8/100,000 and 15/100,000 per annum. And the rate in Bristol in the period covered by the 1227 and 1248 eyres was only 4/100,000 per annum. These rates are consistently lower than those in the rural areas, with the exception of Norfolk (see Table 2, p. 36).

This is at first sight a puzzling finding, since one would have expected just the opposite. Medieval English cities, like other preindustrial cities, had a very unstable population. The birthrate was seldom high enough to make good the losses from death. Therefore, the people required to keep the urban populations from shrinking and to make them grow, as they did rapidly in the twelfth and thirteenth centuries, had to be supplied by immigration. One would have thought that this great mass of immigrants, removed from their home communities, confronted by a new environment, and often forced to eke out a living as poorly paid laborers, would have been readily involved in violence.[2] But this was not the case. Paradoxically, it seems that this very social fragmentation contributed to a low level of violence. It will be recalled that one of the most pronounced characteristics of medieval English homicide was its collective nature. Almost two-thirds of all accused killers had a partner in the commission of their crime. This was true in both urban areas, where 65.4 percent had partners, and rural areas, where 68.7 percent had partners.* It appears that immigrants from the countryside brought with them a group of behavioral patterns that included collective assault. But in the cities and towns the groups from whose ranks people normally recruited allies—family, friends, neighbors, parishioners—were largely absent. When confronted by a situation in which they would have reacted violently had they been in their home villages, these new immigrants were unable to find the allies they felt necessary to support a violent confrontation. And therefore they let the injury or insult pass unavenged. When they could find allies, they did react with violence. But the only people who were in a position to do this were those who were native to the town or had had sufficient time to become established in it. Thus, homicide rates in England's urban areas tended to be lower than in the countryside.

The fragmented social networks that existed in urban areas are illustrated by the fact that the involvement of family members in homicide differed markedly from that found in the countryside. In the rural areas, 22.3 percent of those who had an accomplice had as their partner a relative. In the cities and towns, only 12.8 percent had as their ally a relative. In the four large cities, the figure was even lower, being only 10.7 percent. However, the disparity was not as marked between the rural areas and the small towns as between the rural areas and the large towns. In the small towns, 18.6 percent of the killers had a relative as their accomplice. Life in the smaller towns was still in many ways rural. People tilled fields, kept animals, and undoubtedly maintained many intimate ties with the inhabitants of the surrounding countryside.[3] Therefore, the family was not as fragmented as in the larger towns, and family members accordingly played a larger role in homicide.

The similarity in behavioral patterns between the small towns and the countryside is also revealed by the fact that people in

* In the country, 844 (31.3 percent) did not have partners. In the cities this figure was 276 (34.6 percent). For this distribution, Yates's chi-square = 2.85 with 1 degree of freedom; $p = 0.09$. This indicates that the null hypothesis that there is no relationship between urbanism and the number of accomplices in the commission of a homicide should be accepted.

both areas turned to the same types of relatives for aid. Siblings, parents, and children were the most important relatives, with 14, or 53.8 percent, of the accused killers acting with a sibling and 10, or 38.5 percent, acting with a parent or child. Ties between spouses were less important, with only 8, or 30.8 percent, acting with a husband or wife. However, in the large cities of London, Bristol, Norwich, and Great Yarmouth, where a more thoroughly urban form of life prevailed, a markedly different pattern of cooperation among relatives existed. Whereas in the countryside the ties between man and wife had not been as important as those between siblings, here they had become the most important, 22, or 53.7 percent, of everyone committing murder with a relative in a major urban area doing so with a spouse. Siblings, however, remained important, with 17, or 41.5 percent, acting with a brother or sister. But the ties that united parent and child, which in many places in the countryside had been extremely strong, were considerably reduced in the large cities. If all the towns, large and small, are considered together, only 10, or 14.9 percent, of the accused killers who killed someone with a relative did so with a parent or child. In the four major urban areas, no one committed a murder with a parent or a child. This phenomenon can probably be explained by the low fertility rates in the cities and the greater infant mortality, and by the fact that children were separated at an early age from their parents, to be brought up in other households as servants or apprentices.

The urban environment also affected the patterns of violent strife within the family. Whereas in the rural areas conflict between husband and wife accounted for the largest amount of intrafamilial homicide, it was only one part of an entire spectrum of violence that often involved siblings, parents, and children. But in the urban areas intrafamilial homicide involved virtually only spouses. Of the 21 people killed by relatives in the towns, seventeen were murdered by their spouses (81 percent). In the cities of London, Bristol, Great Yarmouth, and Norwich, everyone who was killed by a relative was slain by a spouse or lover. The fact that people were not murdered by other types of relative is also a reflection of the fragmented nature of the urban family. In many cases relatives other than spouses may simply not have been around to be killed. Since many city dwellers were immigrants, they had left behind parents, siblings, and in-laws when they left their homes. The practice of apprenticing out children, coupled with low fertility rates and high infant mortality, removed children rapidly from the urban household. Therefore, the only relative with whom one was likely to be in prolonged contact in the city and hence with whom one might come into deadly conflict was one's spouse.

The role of the other component of the medieval household, servants, also differed in towns and rural areas. In the countryside the proportion of people who chose to commit homicide with a master, servant, or fellow servant was low, being only 1.1 percent in Kent, 2 percent in Norfolk, 1.5 percent in the Oxford plains, 9.4 percent in the Chiltern Hills, 5.6 percent in Bedfordshire, 4.6 percent in the Forest of Arden, and 4.3 percent in Felden Warwickshire. In all, only 2.7 percent of the killers from rural areas who had a partner had as that partner a master, servant, or fellow servant. This low figure reflects the low demand for regular wage laborers on peasant farmsteads in the countryside. Probably only the richest peasants had permanent servants. On the majority of peasant farms most of the necessary tasks could be performed by the tenant's family or with help from neighbors. Wage labor was needed only seasonally, during periods like harvest when very heavy work was required in the fields. Lords, of course, employed large numbers of servants to work their manorial demesnes. But the situation of these laborers, who did not live in close association with their employers, was more analogous to that of modern wage laborers than to that of their contemporaries who worked on a peasant farmstead or in an artisan's shop. Accordingly, the demesne servant was unlikely to form the close, personal ties with his master that would lead him to help his master in the event of a violent conflict. In the small towns the importance of ties between masters and servants does not seem to have been too much greater than in the countryside. In the 31 small towns included in this study, only six of the 140 killers (4.3 percent) who had a partner chose a master, servant, or fellow servant as their partner.

In the large cities, however, servants were a far more important part of domestic arrangements. Servants constituted a larger proportion of the urban population.[4] The greater availability of cash and the more constant demand for labor required and enabled city dwellers to hire more servants. Since family ties were weaker in the cities than in the countryside, the role of the artificial family composed of retainers and servants was also correspondingly greater. Therefore, in London, Bristol, Norwich, and Great Yarmouth, 12.8 percent, almost three times the percentage for the entire population, of those who killed with an accomplice did so with a master, servant, or fellow servant.* In fact, more people acted with a master or servant in the large cities than with a kinsman.

Just as the urban environment caused a change in the way family members behaved toward one another, it also affected the ways in which the sexes behaved. Urban women in particular engaged in violence in ways very different from those of rural women. Women made up a slightly smaller proportion of the victims in urban areas than in rural ones, 15.7 percent as opposed to 20.5 percent. Similarly, they formed only a slightly higher percentage of killers, 9 percent as opposed to 8.4 percent. However, these figures may be deceptive. It is possible that urban populations were disproportionately male, composed as they were of a large number of immigrants.[5] Therefore, it is conceivable that although women constituted a somewhat

---

* In the cities 522 people committed murder with a partner. Of these, 55 (10.5 percent) acted with a servant; 467 (89.5 percent) did not. In the rural areas, 1,850 people acted with a partner. Of these, 50 (2.7 percent) acted with a servant or master; 1,800 (97.3 percent) did not. For this distribution, Yates's chi-square = 57.22 with 1 degree of freedom; $0.001 > p$; phi = 0.16. Contingency coefficient = 0.16. Lambda (asymmetric) = 0.0 with master/servant as the dependent variable; 0.01 with urban/rural as the dependent variable. Uncertainty coefficient (asymmetric) = 0.06 with master/servant as the dependent variable; 0.02 with urban/rural as the dependent variable.

smaller proportion of all victims and killers in the cities, they were nevertheless far more likely to engage in homicidal activity than their rural counterparts. Until demographers better understand the distribution of the sexes in thirteenth-century Europe, however, this must remain speculation.

Whether or not women were more inclined to become involved in homicide in urban areas, the ways in which they were involved were different. Although the overwhelming majority of women, 68.8 percent, were killed in houses in the towns, a larger proportion were killed in places where social interaction with nonfamily members occurred. Three (9.4 percent) were killed in the streets of a city, as opposed to only 0.4 percent who were killed in village streets. And in London one woman was killed in a brothel, institutions that do not seem to have existed in rural districts.

Women were also more likely to be killed alone in the cities. In the rural districts 36.3 percent of all women were killed with a companion (145 of 400). In the towns, however, only 14.7 percent were killed in company with someone else (eleven of 75).* And in contrast to the situation in the countryside, when women were killed with someone else, it was very rare for them to be killed with a relative. In rural areas 26 percent (104 of 400) of the female victims were killed with a relative. In the cities only 10.7 percent (eight of 75) were killed with relatives.† Similarly, in urban areas women killed someone in company with a relative less frequently. In rural areas 56.8 percent (108 of 190) of the women who committed homicide with a companion did so with a

---

* For this distribution, Yates's chi-square = 12.38 with 1 degree of freedom; $p = 0.0004$; phi = 0.17. Contingency coefficient = 0.17. Lambda (asymmetric) = 0.0 with the number of companions as the dependent variable; 0.0 with urban/rural as the dependent variable. Uncertainty coefficient (asymmetric) = 0.02 with the number of companions as the dependent variable; 0.04 with urban/rural as the dependent variable.

† For this distribution, Yates's chi-square = 7.41 with 1 degree of freedom; $p = 0.0341$; phi = 0.04. Contingency coefficient = 0.04. Lambda (asymmetric) = 0.0 with relative/nonrelative as the dependent variable; 0.0 with urban/rural as the dependent variable. Uncertainty coefficient (asymmetric) = 0.01 with relative/nonrelative as the dependent variable; 0.02 with urban/rural as the dependent variable.

relative. In the towns, on the other hand, only 42.4 percent of the women (25 of 59) who committed homicide with a partner did so with a relative.* In the towns both men and women also killed members of their own families much less frequently. In rural areas 4.3 percent of the men (106 of 2,467) killed members of their families. In the cities 2.5 percent (eighteen of 726) did so.† Similarly, 21.6 percent of the women (49 of 227) in the rural districts killed their relatives, whereas only 9.7 percent of the urban women (seven of 72) did so.‡

From a consideration of these figures it appears that in many ways the role of women was more assimilated to that of men in medieval urban areas than in the country, a fact that has been noted by other observers. Women played a more active role in medieval English cities. For example, they had a great deal more initiative in economic matters than their rural counterparts, a fact that legal custom recognized. In rural areas women were subject to the common law, which more than any other medieval European legal system deprived them of effective rights over property.[6] If a married woman were herself the tenant in fee of an estate, her husband could alienate it without her consent, as long as he did not try to confer an estate that would endure after the end of the marriage. At the same time the woman could not alienate any of her estate without her husband's consent. All of the movable goods that a wife had were considered her husband's property, and he could sell or give all of them away, except for her necessary clothes, without her consent. And a mar-

---

* For this distribution, Yates's chi-square = 3.23 with 1 degree of freedom; $p = 0.0724$. This is not a statistically significant distribution.

† For this distribution, Yates's chi-square = 4.5 with 1 degree of freedom; $p = 0.0341$; phi = 0.04. Contingency coefficient = 0.04. Lambda (asymmetric) = 0.0 with relative/nonrelative as the dependent variable; 0.0 with urban/rural as the dependent variable. Uncertainty coefficient (asymmetric) = 0.01 with relative/nonrelative as the dependent variable; 0.0 with urban/rural as the dependent variable.

‡ For this distribution, Yates's chi-square = 4.31 with 1 degree of freedom; $p = 0.038$; phi = 0.13. Contingency coefficient = 0.13. Lambda (asymmetric) = 0.0 with relative/nonrelative as the dependent variable; 0.0 with urban/rural as the dependent variable. Uncertainty coefficient (assymetric) = 0.02 with relative/nonrelative as the dependent variable; 0.02 with urban/rural as the dependent variable.

ried woman could not enter into contracts, except as her husband's agent.[7] But in many English towns there existed legal customs that allowed a married woman to have a legal personality and to carry on a trade of her own as a *femme sole,* with the full legal rights and responsibilities of a citizen.[8] These customs recognized the fact that women played a much more active role in life in the towns than in the country. Women in urban areas interacted, independently of males, with a much wider number of people. As traders in their own right, and as women who were perhaps less tightly controlled by males, women participated in networks of allegiances and dependencies that were more widespread than those of country women and more analogous to male networks. Hence, there was a greater possibility that urban women would be drawn into conflict as active participants in their own right rather than as adjuncts to males.

Women in the towns participated in conflicts over money and power in a way that would have been most unexpected in the countryside. In 1263 or 1264 Richard Valet was walking by a brothel in Bishopsgate in London. Three of the whores, Beatrice of Winchester, Isabella de Stanford, and Margery de Karl, came out, dragged him into the house, and tried to take some of his property. Richard stabbed and killed Margery while defending himself.[9] In 1241 Christine, the widow of Joce le Espicer, became involved in a quarrel with Simon FitzMary, who at various times during the mid-thirteenth century was an alderman, sheriff, and chamberlain of London. As the leader of the royalist faction within the city, FitzMary had been engaged in various affrays with several of the leading families in London. At the 1244 eyre Christine charged that on May 4, 1241, Simon and Robert de Herbinton had seized her ward, William son of William, in All Hallows Church in Bread Street. William's wardship was apparently a lucrative one, involving six marks and 4s. worth of rent every year for his upkeep. Christine alleged that the two had carried him off and kept him imprisoned until December 13, when he died. She demanded £200 in damages. Although Simon and John admitted that they had had custody of William, they denied any wrongdoing and maintained that William had died a "lawful" death, and not in prison. Dealing as they were with rich and powerful people, the justices temporized, and it appears from the eyre roll that they never came to any decision about the case.[10]

This dispute between Christine and FitzMary is also indicative of another unusual aspect of violence in urban areas—the propensity of leading members of the community to become involved in violent assaults. In the four major cities of London, Bristol, Norwich, and Great Yarmouth, the mean value of confiscated chattels was the highest of any region, being approximately 17s. 1d. (204.6 pence). In the lesser market towns the value of chattels was less, being about 11s. 9d. (141.3 pence). For all urban areas, the mean value of confiscated chattels was 15s. 2d. (182 pence), whereas in the rural areas it was only 6s. 11d. (82.6 pence). To be sure, the impoverished masses committed homicide in the towns as well as in the country. Indeed, London, Bristol, Norwich, and Great Yarmouth had the highest proportion of totally impoverished killers, 72.4 percent of all the accused having no movable property at all. In the smaller urban centers, fully 61.5 percent had no property. When these figures are considered, the high mean value of confiscated chattels of urban killers becomes even more striking (see Table 23, p. 171). If a man committed murder in a town, he was likely to be either a marginal figure in society or a substantial member of the community.

That the wealthier ranks of urban society should have been drawn into violent conflict is not surprising. In many ways English cities in the thirteenth century were, like the Forest of Arden, frontier areas. In the two hundred years following the Norman Conquest, the structure of power and authority had been fairly well settled in the countryside. But in the cities these questions had not yet been resolved. Social and political hierarchies had not completely solidified, and lines of authority were still vague and disputed in the thirteenth century. As a result, the cities and towns of England were agitated by struggles for

power and authority. The only English city in which these conflicts have been thoroughly studied is London. Although the
struggle for power did not reach the heights of violence that
were attained in northern Italy or Flanders,[11] London experienced much unrest. As in many other medieval cities, the struggle was one between the old ruling oligarchy, which monopo-
lized the positions of power and privilege, and the newly wealthy
who wished a greater voice in the direction of affairs.[12]

The participants in these quarrels were often ready to resort
to physical violence. In 1196 when the justiciar Hubert Walter
was trying to raise King Richard's ransom, he made heavy financial demands on the city of London. The ruling oligarchs tried
to shift the bulk of this burden to the poorer elements. William
FitzOsbert made himself the champion of the poor, and demanded that everyone should contribute according to his
wealth. His activities enraged Hubert Walter as well as the rulers
of the city. Eventually Hubert tried to arrest William. William
killed the man who had been sent to take him, however, and fled
to the church of St. Mary le Bow. When he refused to surrender,
the church was set on fire. As William fled from the burning
building, he was stabbed by the son of the man whom he had
killed. Wounded, he was taken to the Tower, where he was condemned to death and taken thence to Tyburn, where he was
hanged with several of his companions.[13]

In 1228, as part of the struggle between the factions composed of the Bukerel, Bat, and Tovy families on the one side,
and the Juvenal, Lambert, and FitzMary families on the other,
Ralph Eswy II was killed, the Juvenals and Lamberts being accused of the murder by Ralph's children. Several years later, in
1243, Simon FitzMary himself, the leader of the royalist faction
in the city, was attacked by a group of young patricians, including Matthew Bukerel and Peter FitzRobert, both sons of former
mayors, and Peter and Robert de Basing.[14]

If the account of the alderman FitzThedmar can be believed,
in 1265 Thomas FitzThomas, the mayor, and Thomas de Piwels-
don laid a plot to kill approximately 50 of the "more lawful" men

of the city because they were faithful to Henry III and the Lord Edward in their struggle against Simon de Montfort. According to FitzThedmar, the plotters planned to take their enemies during a meeting at the Guildhall and put them to death. The conspirators came to the assembly with weapons concealed under their clothes, but the rumors of Simon's defeat and death at Evesham, which arrived shortly before they could carry out their scheme, caused them to abandon their plans.[15]

A scandalous, indeed sacrilegious, murder in the late thirteenth century involved some of the most prominent men in London. Ralph Crepyn, the "first recognizable Common Clerk" of the city and at times an alderman, had been locked in a long vendetta with Laurence Duket, a goldsmith of prominent family. The bad feelings between the two may have grown out of the fact that Duket had killed a Master William de Leffrement and Crepyn had, in helping him to secure a royal pardon, cheated him out of some of his property. Their relations may have been further embittered by differences over Duket's sister's sale of some buildings to Crepyn in 1273. No matter what the exact cause of their enmity, in July 1284 Duket attacked and seriously wounded Crepyn. He fled to the church of St. Mary le Bow. Crepyn's supporters broke into the church by night, tortured Duket, and hung him from a beam in the roof. For this outrage, seven men were drawn and hanged. Crepyn's mistress, Alice atte Bow, was burnt, and Crepyn himself and three others were only saved from execution by their clerical status.[16]

Politics and the vendettas that they engendered were not the only reasons why the London bourgeoisie turned against itself in violent assaults. In 1257 or 1258 William Assheboef, a silk merchant, came to the house of Master Adam of Lynton, clerk to the Master of the Temple, to sell some silk to Adam's wife Matilda. When Adam and his servant William le Waleys returned home, Matilda, for reasons that are not specified but that are easy to surmise, hid the merchant. Adam and his servant searched him out and killed him. William le Waleys fled across the sea, but Adam himself was pardoned by the king. His chattels, however, were confiscated. They were valued at 20 marks and his house was held to be worth two marks a year.[17]

Although the internal history of other English towns is less well known, their leading citizens also appear to have willingly indulged in violence. In 1272 Norwich was the site of a spectacularly violent outburst. On the last day of the Feast of the Holy Trinity in June 1272, a quintain was erected in a place called the Tombland outside the priory of Norwich. Eventually, the townspeople and the priory's servants quarreled over the broken spears that piled up during the tilting. A fight started and the priory's servants were driven into the priory. From within the walls William le Messer fired a crossbow bolt at the townsmen and killed Adam de Newenton. The city coroners held an inquest and subsequently arrested two of the priory's servants. The prior, William de Burnham, retaliated by excommunicating the citizens. Relations deteriorated, and by August the prior's men had barricaded the priory's gates and were sniping at passing citizens with bows and arrows. The prior also imported three barges full of armed men from Great Yarmouth. With these reinforcements the priory's servants made a sally into the town, killed and wounded several people, broke into taverns, looted, and burned down three houses.

The townspeople held a public meeting and wrote a letter of complaint to Henry III. They also resolved to rid themselves of the malefactors who had made "an illegal castle" in their city. On August 9 they attacked the priory by the Ethelbert gate. The gate was fired, the parish church of St. Ethelbert just inside the gate was seized and also burned. The bell tower of the main church caught fire and was consumed by flame. Thirteen of the priory's defenders were killed. Some of those who died were apparently captured, taken into Norwich, tried in the city courts, and executed. The day following the assault, the prior himself killed a man named John Casmus. On the 15th the king dispatched three of his men to take charge of the city.

On September 14 the aged king himself arrived in Norwich and took over the administration of both the priory and the city.

In the inquests that followed, 173 of Norwich's citizens, including fourteen men who had at one time been bailiffs of the city, were named as participants in the attack. Twenty-nine people were hanged. After Henry III's death, however, the new king, Edward I, ordered a further inquest. This inquest placed most of the blame on the prior. It found that the priory church had been burned accidentally by a fire set by the prior's own smiths, that the prior had intended to burn the entire city, and that he was guilty of robbery and murder. Edward I had William arrested and delivered to his bishop. He was allowed to purge himself, but died soon afterward.[18]

The cities of the high Middle Ages were new features in what had hitherto been an almost exclusively agrarian society. At once the products and, in part, the agents of the process by which the basic cells of village, seigneurie, and castellany were reorganized into larger regional units, they possessed a social structure very different from that of the countryside. Men and women were grouped together differently and interacted in different ways. In the cities of thirteenth-century England, and to a lesser extent in the towns, this affected the incidence and the type of violence. The fragmentation of traditional social groupings and the necessity of creating new ones resulted in a lowering of the overall level of violence; altered patterns of cooperation and conflict, especially within the family; gave women a more active role in violence; and drew leading members of the urban communities into frequent and bloody struggle for power and authority.

10. Violence and Its Control

But is it not allowed me to become angry, since anger is an attribute
of the soul, and a natural power? For what is permitted to me by
nature does not seem illicit: by nature I am a son of wrath; therefore why should I not grow angry. God himself shows anger.

—HENRY II

Thirteenth-century England was a violent society.* The threat
of violence and the effects of violence were, if not a common
part of the average Englishman's day, something that he could
expect to experience, if only as a spectator, at some time in his
life. Although in the previous discussion of the specific patterns
of social behavior involved in homicide, certain of the factors
that promoted or inhibited violent conflict have been referred
to, in this section the problems of the social or cultural origins of
violence and the mechanisms for its control will be addressed directly. The streets and lanes of medieval England may not have
run with blood, but the level of violence was sufficiently greater
than that known in other agrarian societies to require an explanation.

The ubiquitous presence of weapons in medieval England
possibly rendered fatal many quarrels that would otherwise have
resulted only in bruises. Although medieval Englishmen did not
have available such efficient means of destruction as firearms
and explosives, they nevertheless habitually carried weapons. In

---

* The above statement is at least that which Peter of Blois put into Henry's
mouth in the "Dialogus inter Regum Henricum II et abbatem Bonaevallensem,"
in *Patrologia cursus completus . . . series latina,* ed. by Jacques Paul Migne (224
vols.; Paris, 1844–1907), 207, cols. 978–79.

a society where most people made their living from agriculture, virtually everyone had on his person a knife, for cutting bread[1] and for the innumerable other tasks that required a cutting edge. The accounts of accidental deaths that the records contain graphically picture the ubiquitous presence of knives in medieval life. In Kent, Roger de Teldenne and Walter le Paumer of Aldington were digging one day in Aldington's meadow. They got into some good-natured roughhousing, in the course of which Walter's knife cut through its scabbard and wounded Roger. He died the next day.[2] At a Bedfordshire party in 1265 Richard Muriweder accidentally fell on the knife of Gerard Motun, a clerk, and died of the wound he received.[3] Even small children carried knives, like the eleven-year old William Palfrey, who stabbed to death the nine-year old William Geyser outside the village of Whittlesford in Cambridgeshire,[4] or the girl named Matilda who accidentally cut off her playmate William's finger.[5]

Thus, when people quarreled, there was always the possibility that the participants might resort to knives, with lethal consequences. For 455 of the 2,434 victims listed in the eyre rolls, information is given on the way in which they were murdered. Of these, 136, or 29.9 percent of the total, died of knife wounds. Should knives not be available, the common tools of agricultural life offered potentially lethal weapons. Axes (64 cases), forks (seven), spades (two), mattocks (one), and scythes (four) were all used to kill people. Even if there was no sharp-edged tool at hand, people were ready to resort to whatever they could lay hold of. After knives, the most popular murder weapon was a stick of some sort, which accounted for 100 victims. Stones (fifteen cases), trivets (one), stools (one), and pieces of firewood (one) were all pressed into service at some time. Forty people were simply beaten or strangled to death, presumably with only hands and feet.

Medieval Englishmen had available not only knives, tools, pieces of furniture, fists, and teeth, but also more sophisticated weapons. By Henry II's Assize of Arms all free men were required to be sworn to possess arms in accordance with their

wealth. Early in the thirteenth century the provisions of the Assize were extended to include villeins.[6] Englishmen possessed
not only the useful bow, which was needed for the hunting
required to supplement their low protein diet, and which accounted for almost 6 percent of all the fatalities, but also swords,
maces, and crossbows. It was not uncommon for people to go
about heavily armed, especially at night. To look for a cartload
of his corn, one Bedfordshire peasant went out one night
equipped with helmet, haqueton, and lance.[7] Scholars at Oxford
went about armed.[8] The ruling secular elite, which defined itself
in large part as a warrior class, spent much time exercising itself
in the use of these and more elaborate weapons. But a passion
for proficiency with weapons was not limited to the knightly
classes. Englishmen of lower ranks also devoted time to perfect-
ing martial skills. Aside from the informal training available to
all, such as shooting at marks with bow and arrow, there were
also, at least in London, professional schools of fence, or, in the
language of the time, "buckler play" (*eskirmer de bokeler*). In 1280,
under pain of 40 days' imprisonment, such schools were forbid-
den in London.[9] This prohibition was repeated in 1286. Yet
such regulations failed to end the popularity of these schools. In
1311 Master Roger le Skirmisour was prosecuted in the Mayor's
Court "for keeping a fencing school for divers men, and for en-
ticing thither the sons of respectable persons so as to waste and
spend the property of their fathers and mothers upon bad practices." [10] The burghers had good reason to dislike the "bad practices" that these schools encouraged, for the devotees of dueling
were prone to disorderly conduct. In 1300 Richard Tripaty and
Laurence de Shirebourne came to William Marisone's house in
London. There they asked his wife to let them into a room to
engage in buckler play. When she refused, they assaulted her
with their swords. The beadle of the ward, Richard de Barber,
was summoned. Richard and Laurence proceeded to attack him
also, wounding him in the brawl that developed.[11]

But the mere availability of weapons does not guarantee their
use. The predominantly rural African societies referred to ear-

lier also provide their members with a host of potentially deadly weapons similar to those possessed by thirteenth-century Englishmen. Yet many modern Africans do not seem to slaughter each other with the same frequency as did the people of medieval England. Although the widespread diffusion of weapons in medieval society provided the means, why medieval Englishmen were so frequently moved to attack each other with fatal consequences has still to be explained.

The sociologists, psychologists, and psychiatrists who have studied the problem of homicide in modern societies have yet to offer any overwhelmingly compelling explanations of homicidal behavior. Some of their insights may nonetheless help the historian to understand better the phenomenon in medieval England. The discussions in the medical literature that have attempted to find correlations between violent behavior and physical states such as mental deficiency, brain lesions, and hypoglycemia[12] are not of much use to the medievalist, for it is difficult to apply such insights to a medieval society. Aside from the general realization that the health of the average medieval peasant must have been poorer than that of modern Englishmen, almost nothing is known about the health of medieval people. Excavations of village cemeteries may eventually add to our knowledge,[13] but at the moment the effect of ill health on the behavior of medieval individuals is totally unknown.

The work of psychiatrists has indicated that inability to think about the future is a contributing factor in violent behavior.[14] A person who is unable to think beyond the short-range outcome of his immediate plans either may not realize the consequences of his actions or may find any interference so intolerable that he will react violently. Without too much distortion this insight can be applied to medieval England. Medieval Europeans did have a concept of time, but it was not the carefully calibrated and rigidly delimited time of the industrial world. Mechanized clocks only came into use in the early fourteenth century. Before then time was generally measured either in terms of the seasonal occupations of the agrarian year or by the church calendar. The only instruments available for measuring its passage were highly imprecise, such as sundials, water clocks, and hourglasses.[15] As a result, medieval people had difficulty in determining what "time" it was. When a judicial duel was scheduled at Mons in Hainault in 1188 and one of the participants failed to appear, a conference of the assembled clergy was required to determine if the hour of the liturgical day which had been appointed for the meeting had indeed passed and the absentee thus defaulted.[16] Lacking the ability to measure the passage of time which modern societies possess, the men of the thirteenth century may well have found it more difficult to think about the future. Quarrels may have escalated into deadly affairs before the participants were able to realize the potential consequences of their actions.

The consumption of alcohol also seems to contribute to violent behavior. A study of 588 criminal homicides in Philadelphia between 1948 and 1952 found that in 63.6 percent of the cases either the victim or his killer had been drinking immediately before the slaying.[17] Alcohol appears to have a twofold effect in promoting homicidal behavior, altering the behavior of both the victim and the killer. The habitual heavy drinker, even when he is not drinking, is not able to assess the consequences of his actions,[18] and is thus more likely to engage in assaultive behavior. Alcohol affects the victim in a similar fashion. His ability to perceive warning cues that he is dangerously frustrating someone's expectations is lessened. And, if he is attacked, his ability to defend himself is markedly impaired.[19]

Medieval Englishmen were prodigious drinkers. Alcohol, beer for the lower classes and wine for the upper, was a staple of the diet, and an indispensable adjunct to many recreational activities. In 1309 there were 354 taverns in London and 1,334 brewshops.[20] Every conceivable social occasion, from weddings and christenings to the inception of a master in theology at a university, was celebrated with drink. By the beginning of the thirteenth century English beer was already famous throughout Europe. In 1206 Pope Innocent III chided an English lawyer for opinions on a point of law with the comment that "Surely both you and your masters had drunk a lot of English beer when you maintained this." [21]

The records abound with stories of people who, in essence, drank themselves to death, like Simon of Coughton who fell dead from his horse in the high street of Alcester in Warwickshire "through drunkenness," [22] or the unidentified man who, in a drunken stupor, fell out of a window during a party at Alan Cissor's house in Durham.[23] The 1250 eyre of Norfolk has left an almost burlesque tale of the evils of drink. Benedict Lithere, together with his brother Roger and Alan son of Elena were at a tavern in Henstead. Benedict got so drunk that "he could neither walk nor ride nor barely even stand up." His brother decided to take him home, and put him on a horse. Benedict promptly fell off. Roger put him back on. Again he fell off. The third time Roger tied him to the horse, but Benedict fell off again and died instantaneously.[24]

Medieval clerics, at least, were convinced of the potential dangers of drink as a cause of homicide. The tavern was denounced as the "deuylys knyfe." [25] Alcohol was regarded as a poison that produced cursing and the shedding of blood.[26] Although it can never be determined with certainty from the eyre rolls if alcohol was involved in a particular killing (of 1,368 homicides whose location can be determined, only 26, or 1.9 percent, were associated with taverns), it is possible that heavy drinking contributed to many homicides.

The ready availability of weapons, ill health, a confused sense of time, and excessive indulgence in the pleasures of drink may help to explain, in part, the high incidence of homicide in thirteenth-century England. But all these conditions are present in many African and Asian agricultural societies that have low homicide rates. It is apparent that some other factor is at work. Sociologists and anthropologists have recently attempted to explain high levels of violence by arguing that certain cultures or subcultures regard violence as a normal, and indeed often normative, way of dealing with life.[27] Violence is regarded as a learned response, a cultural trait.

Albert Bandura has recently given a cogent explanation of how this works.[28] People inevitably undergo what Bandura terms "aversive experiences," i.e. they are angered, frustrated, or depressed by people or events. They can respond to these situations with any of a wide range of possible behavior: dependency, achievement, withdrawal and resignation, psychosomatization, self-anesthetization with drugs and alcohol, "constructive problem solving," and aggression. How a person will react to a given situation depends on his learning experiences and hence on his cultural background. Bandura's theory purports to explain not only aggression evoked by "aversive experiences," but also aggression prompted by its anticipated benefits. Just as violence may be one of several ways of coping with people who cause frustration or anger, so it can also be a normal means of getting what one wants, even if the target of aggression is not an agent that causes frustration or anger in his killer.

According to this theory, violent behavior is learned in a large variety of ways: from parents, peer or reference groups, and social or political leaders.[29] The practice of physical discipline is regarded by this school of interpretation as a peculiarly important mechanism by which the validity and utility of violent behavior are taught by one generation to the next. By the very act of physical aggression the parent or adult who inflicts corporal punishment on a child provides a model for the child of approved adult behavior. "The punishing parent serves as a model whom the child imitates and whose behavior instructs the moral conscience—the super-ego." [30] Studies of child brutality have tended to support this view of violence as a learned trait. One study of child abuse over three generations found that children who themselves had suffered harsh physical treatment at the hands of their parents were inclined to treat their own children in the same fashion.[31]

Medieval Europe believed firmly in the use of the rod and the staff as a means of moral correction and improvement. Thomas of Chobham in his *Summa* on penitence wrote that physical violence as a means of punishment and correction was permissible according to canon law and could be used by both laity and clergy. Parents were allowed to beat their children, masters their servants, teachers their pupils, and confessors their penitents. Adulterers, people who stole from churches, slanderers, inveterate drunkards, false witnesses, and defaulting debtors were all to be whipped publicly through the streets of the city.[32] Physical discipline was regarded as particularly salubrious for the sins caused by the appetites of the flesh, such as gluttony and lust.[33] Should someone accidently die as the result of such correction, canon law held that the killer was not culpable of homicide, provided that he had not exceeded the customary measure in administering a beating.[34]

The use of corporal punishment was widespread within the medieval family. Men beat their wives and children. Indeed, the village community would on occasion punish women who had violated one of its regulations by ordering the errant woman's husband to beat her. For example, at Chalgrave, in Bedfordshire, the manorial court found Margery Hingeleys to be a "malefactor in others' corn" and ordered her husband to beat her.[35] On occasion these familial chastisements proved fatal. In 1247 John Blecheliche was presented for homicide by the jury of Stodden Hundred in Bedfordshire. The jurors reported that he had wished to beat his wife with a stick. She ran away from him, and he threw the stick at her. It hit a mattock hanging on a post. The mattock fell off the post into the cradle of John's infant son Richard and struck him on the head. Richard died two days later. The jury held that John had killed through misadventure, but no formal judgment of him was rendered.[36] Fourteen years later at the 1261 eyre of Oxford, Robert le Blunt, an inhabitant of the borough of Oxford, was presented for a similar crime. He had been beating his wife and had accidentally struck his half-year-old daughter Isolda and killed her. Robert had fled and his outlawry was ordered.[37]

The received wisdom of the Middle Ages held that children, like all men after Adam's fall, were inherently prone to evil. Vincent of Beauvais in his tract on education wrote that "the feelings and thoughts of the human heart are prone to evil from youth. Therefore it is necessary to prevent the flowering of this evil in children, and to fight it and resist it with discipline." [38] The punishment meted out to children could reach spectacular levels of brutality. Ralph, the son of Augustine the chaplain of Taynton in Oxfordshire, refused to learn his lessons. As a punishment, his father and his father's clerk tied him to the tail of a horse. Unfortunately, the horse escaped and dragged Ralph to his death. At the 1241 eyre Augustine was reported to have fled into Buckinghamshire. [39]

The rod was an indispensable instrument of education in medieval schools. The best opinion held that those who learned readily were not to be handled roughly. But those who were like "unbroken young colts" were to be taught good manners against their will by discipline. [40] In 1301 the wife of John de Neushom found him drowned in the river Cherwell. John was a clerk and a teacher of schoolboys in Oxford. Having gone to gather twigs with which to beat his pupils, he had climbed up into a willow tree next to a millpond and fallen from it into the river. [41] Schoolboys were beaten regularly. The saintly bishop of Lincoln, Hugh of Avalon, who was not averse to cuffing his servants when they displeased him, remembered his childhood in a Burgundian monastery as a long string of beatings. [42] Not only were pupils liable to be beaten; so on occasion were their masters. In grammar schools it appears that if the *magnus magister* found at one of his weekly examinations that the boys under the *parvi magistri* did not know their lessons, both the boys and their masters were to be whipped. [43]

Children and errant wives were not the only people likely to experience a beating. Physical punishment, administered publicly, was an integral part of the medieval church's penitential system. The church regularly imposed flogging as a penance for sexual derelictions. On February 25, 1299, for example, John le Cuppere of Nottingham was found guilty of adultery in the court of the archdiocese of York. He was reconciled to his wife Agatha. But Archbishop Henry of Newark prescribed that if he treated her badly in the future he was to pay the extremely heavy fine of £10 or be flogged round the marketplace of Nottingham for five days.[44] In a period of one and a half to two months in May and June 1300, the court of the rural deanery of Droitwich ordered the beating of 78 people, 37 men and 41 women, almost all accused of either adultery or fornication. It appears that this sentence was actually carried out on 32 people, fourteen men and eighteen women.[45] Within the monastic cloister physical discipline was also customary.[46] Bearing in mind the injunction *"Probate si ex Deo est spiritus,"* the monks undertook to beat their novices even more severely than those who had made their profession. "For it is better that one depart beaten before his profession . . . than that after his profession, through lack of patience, he flee to his damnation." [47]

At times these penitential beatings provided mass spectacles. Sometime in the late twelfth century at Bury St. Edmunds the abbey's servants and the townspeople met for games on the day after Christmas in the cemetery. Things got out of hand and there was a major riot in the churchyard. The abbot of Bury, Samson, excommunicated those involved for sacrilege. To beg his forgiveness, about 100 men, naked except for their drawers, prostrated themselves before the abbey church. As they lay before the church door, they were scourged and absolved.[48]

In even more dramatic fashion, Bishop Hugh of Lincoln exacted a gruesome penance from some of his flock. A thief had taken refuge in the parish church at Brackley. According to church law and the common law of England, he was entitled to remain there in safety for 40 days or until he abjured the realm. The servants of the earl of Leicester, however, lured him out of the church by a ruse and hanged him. Hugh, outraged by this violation of the right of sanctuary, excommunicated all those responsible. To be reconciled to the church, they presented themselves naked except for their breeches at the place where the man had been executed. There they dug up the putrefying body of the thief, put it on a bier, and carried it to the church in which he had taken refuge. From there they had to carry the rotting corpse around all the churches of the district. Outside of each they were beaten by all the priests of the Lincoln cathedral chapter. At last they buried the thief with their own hands in the cemetery of the church from which they had lured him. Then they had to walk barefoot to Lincoln where they were whipped round all the churches of the city. All of this took place during the winter, which, as Hugh's biographer was careful to point out, made the penance "particularly severe." [49]

A model for brutal and violent behavior was held out to thirteenth-century Englishmen not only by the practice of corporal punishment but also by the most popular forms of recreation. Many of the games of thirteenth-century England consisted of the slightly refined and orderly bashing of one's neighbors. The aristocracy had the tournament, which in the thirteenth century was still a rough and dangerous exercise hardly to be distinguished from war. Common Englishmen had their own games of violence. These may not have reached the extremes known in some Italian cities like Siena, where every year the various quarters of the city fought a free-for-all in the *piazza*,[50] but they did provide a great deal of gouging and battering. FitzStephen in his panegyric on twelfth-century London devoted a rapturous passage to the description of the violent exercises of the London youth. Like the children of the nobility, they whiled away their time practicing the martial skills of fighting on horseback. In the Easter season they turned to jousting from boats, endeavoring to knock their opponents off the prows of their ships. In winter, when the river froze over, skaters would try to knock each other over with lances.[51]

The most popular sport of the common man, however, appears to have been wrestling. Several villages would often turn out for a match.[52] These contests were so popular that the author of a treatise on estate management felt it necessary to write, "No good shepherd ought to leave his sheep to go to fairs, markets, and wrestling matches or to spend the evenings with friends or go to the tavern without asking for leave." [53] Villages often took sides against each other, and the match then might turn into a small battle. On September 4, 1261, Richard de Borham and other Londoners went to Bermondsey priory, where they wrestled with the local men. A fight broke out, and the Londoners pursued the locals into the priory. Some of the monks climbed up into a room above the gate and began throwing stones down on the Londoners. One of the monks, Arnulph by name, wounded Richard so seriously that he subsequently died.[54] Similarly, a great wrestling match held on July 22, 1289, in Staffordshire ended fatally. After a day of wrestling, a quarrel erupted in the evening. William Smith of Hales, hard pressed by the other side, drew his knife. He was wounded with swords and sticks and knocked to the ground. His servant, Alice Witfax, threw herself on top of him to keep him from being killed. She was accidentally wounded by William's knife, and later died.[55]

Women were not averse to taking a try at wrestling. On May 25, 1267, William de Stanesgate was walking down a road in Sussex carrying a crossbow and a poisoned arrow. He encountered Desiderata, the wife of Roger le Champeneys. Desiderata had been godmother to one of William's children and was a particular friend of his. To tease him, she asked if he were one of the men going about to capture malefactors and robbers on the king's order. She said that she could handle two or three like him. She tripped him and fell on top of him. She was struck in the side by the poisoned arrow and died.[56]

Thirteenth-century Englishmen were thus well schooled in violence. From childhood subjected to physical punishment by their parents and teachers, the witnesses of beatings administered to wives by husbands and to servants by masters, onlookers at the ritualistic floggings of penitents, they learned that a ready recourse to violence and the infliction of pain were a common, and necessary, part of adult life. These impressions were reinforced, and their skills at violence honed, by the popularity of violent games, from the exalted tournament to the lowly village wrestling match. A readiness to resort to aggression and violence was therefore a common character trait among thirteenth-century English peasants.

But to state that the culture of thirteenth-century England was one in which violence was regarded as a normal, indeed normative, way of dealing with certain problems still does not explain why violence and murder were so common. In sixteenth- and seventeenth-century England many of the same cultural factors were at work. People still beat their wives, children, and servants, and corporal punishment—both capital and noncapital—was publicly inflicted on those who had been convicted of deviant behavior. Yet the homicide rate appears to have been much lower (see Table 3, p. 39). Child-rearing practices and other social-psychological factors may have been responsible for much of the homicidal activity in thirteenth-century England, especially that involving relatives, neighbors, and others in close daily contact. But such cultural factors alone did not produce the high level of violence found in England in the central Middle Ages. The structure of society itself promoted certain types of homicide, by producing ever larger numbers of people who were pushed into a marginal position in society and by bringing all members of the old local communities into ever more frequent contact with people who were not from that community and with whom often uneasy relations were entertained.

How this came about will become clearer if we consider violence, not as a cultural trait, but as a mechanism of conflict resolution. Violence is only one means of settling disputes, and not a terribly effective one at that, since it is risky and involves dire and often incalculable consequences. But it was one which was possibly resorted to ever more frequently in the late twelfth and thirteenth centuries as people became involved in relationships and quarrels that could not be mediated peacefully by the old mechanisms that society provided.

A brief survey of these mechanisms and how they worked is in order. The first impulse of a modern American or European is to look to the state and its courts as the ultimate arbiter of disputes. But in England in the thirteenth century, the formal, institutionalized mechanisms of state power and seigneurial control were of only secondary importance in the mediation and resolution of most conflicts. The rapid development of royal courts and royal law in the twelfth and thirteenth centuries provided an effective means of resolving disputes for only a limited number of Englishmen. In civil matters, the king's courts interested themselves only in affairs involving property held freely, a restriction that excluded the bulk of the population. And of freeholders, only the well-to-do could sustain the expenses, the traveling, and the delays that were involved in all but the least complicated cases. The royal courts may have sold good justice, a better article than was to be found anywhere else, but, like all luxury items, it was beyond the reach of the ordinary person.

Manorial courts, where they existed, were, for the average person, undoubtedly a more effective means of controlling violent conflict and settling disputes. Although the manorial court was a seigneurial institution used to discipline and exploit the peasantry, it was nevertheless also an embodiment of community sentiment. As has been argued above, in certain regions of England the manorial courts were instrumental in reducing the level of violence. Especially in the common-field regions, they provided peaceful means of settling disputes. But the effectiveness of manorial courts should not be exaggerated. They did not exist everywhere. In large areas of England manor courts either were nonexistent or possessed insignificant powers. Even in the common-field regions they could vary greatly in importance. The court of a large manor embracing several villages, like Halesowen in Worcestershire[57] or Wakefield in Yorkshire,[58] was undoubtedly a far more effective means of conflict resolution than a court held by a lord who had to share control of a village with two or three other lords.

In medieval England the most effective means of settling disputes were informal. The mediation of friends, relatives, and neighbors was undoubtedly far more effective than the activities of royal and manorial courts. Unfortunately, the very informality of these mechanisms makes them difficult to know. Often their existence and the ways they operated can only be surmised from the barest hints in the records. And all too often they become visible only because they failed and a man or a woman was killed.

Although the records never say so explicitly, it appears that women played a role in the containment of violence. As has been shown above, women, by comparison with men, were seldom involved in homicide. Being unlikely to resort to violence or to be its targets, they occupied a special position in a violent society. Although what role, if any, they played in the resolution of the fundamental causes of disputes between men is unknown, there is evidence that they often interposed themselves between two combatants in an effort to prevent disputes from turning into fatal brawls. The example of Alice Witfax, who threw herself on top of her master during a riot to keep him from being killed, will be recalled.

A similar event occurred in the borough of Oxford late in the thirteenth century. A clerk, Robert of Acton Burnell, had been living on the alms of Master William Burnell. One day in 1297 he quarreled with William de Wydintone, the master's doorkeeper. Robert was so angered that he struck William twice with an ash-wood staff. One Matilda de Crickelade leapt between them to stop the fight, and Robert hit her in the head with the staff. She died the next day.[59] Similarly, on September 10, 1301, in Bedfordshire, William the son of Peter of Bromham, Stephen de Rivers, William the Cobbler, and Margery le Wyte were going from a tavern in Bedford toward Wootton when they fell to arguing. For a reason left unclear in the records, William shot an arrow at John Hokerynge, who was following them. Margery had stepped between the two to prevent their quarrel. She was killed instantly when the arrow hit her in the throat.[60] The women in these three examples all failed to stop a fight, and, indeed, died as a result of their actions. But for every woman who failed to prevent a fatal quarrel, there must have been many who succeeded. The passive role of women in thirteenth-century English society, a role that made them something of outsiders, thus paradoxically enabled them to function as a means by which the peaceful functioning of that society could in part be furthered.

Although women's special role in medieval English society served to stop some physical violence short of murder, the mechanisms by which the original grounds of disputes were resolved were very different. The crosscutting and interpenetration of the different allegiance groups to which a man belonged were the chief factors that made for a peaceful settlement of conflicts.[61] An individual in medieval England, as in every society, belonged to a host of solidarity groupings and had many different kinds of bonds with many different people. If he became involved in a quarrel with someone, these bonds provided allies with whom he could prosecute his dispute, even to the point of murder. Yet these bonds also served as a means of limiting and containing conflict. The people to whom a man turned for aid either might not wish to be drawn into a quarrel for pragmatic reasons of their own, or might themselves have competing ties of allegiance with the enemy. In the latter situation, caught in a painful moral and social dilemma, a man's allies felt a strong impulse to bring the parties to a peaceful agreement.

Given the nature of the court records, the efforts at mediation made by relatives, friends, and neighbors only become apparent if they have failed. Nevertheless, the efforts are in themselves interesting. For every group of people who tried unsuccessfully to stave off violent conflict, many undoubtedly succeeded. Although the records of the royal courts have apparently left no trace of family members who tried to dissuade one another from committing a violent assault, it is probable that kinsmen often played a very great role in moderating and composing disputes. Relatives were the group to whom one turned first and most readily for aid in prosecuting a quarrel; of those who committed a homicide with a partner, 20.2 percent did so with a relative. Should relatives be unwilling to provide aid, a man or a woman undoubtedly often thought twice before launching on a potentially homicidal assault.

The records are more explicit about the mediating role that friends, masters, and retainers were expected to play. It was a recognized fact that friends often intervened to restrain their compatriots from acting rashly. In his discussion of the form of an appeal to be used against someone accused of being an accessory to a murder, Bracton wrote that the appellor should state specifically that the accused had held the victim "wickedly and feloniously" while he was killed. This precision was necessary, Bracton went on, because "very often those who are killed or slain feloniously, are held back by their friends with good intentions and not maliciously. And therefore it is prudent and honest to inquire diligently about intent (*animo*) and will." [62]

Masters and lords probably often acted in the same fashion to restrain their servants or retainers. For example, the London Mayor's Court recorded an incident in which a master tried to arrange a formal concord between a former servant of his and someone else. On August 7, 1305, Robert de Wedon brought a plea of trespass against John Goys, a smith. According to Robert, he had asked Geoffrey de Blyd, Master James the king's smith, Henry le poter, Michael de Wymbys, Robert de Alegate, Geoffrey le poter, Salamon le poter, Gilbert atte Herst, and Gilbert de la Marche and his brother to make an agreement and peace between John Goys and William de Northampton, formerly Robert's servant. Fittingly enough for this solemn occasion, the group had assembled in St. Mary Woolchurch. John Goys, however, apparently wanted nothing of a peaceful settlement: he came to the church with a band of unknown accomplices armed with swords and bucklers, assaulted Robert, seized him by the nose, tried to drag him out of the church, and threatened to kill him. [63]

Members of a village community also intervened in efforts to keep their fellows from committing a homicide. The records contain frequent references to peasants who attempted to halt quarrels. In Northamptonshire, when Roger Gylot and Robert the son of Richard were fighting with one another in Arthingworth, Hugh Wade attempted to separate them. Roger, who was trying to hit Robert with an axe, missed and struck Hugh instead, who died the next day. [64] Similarly, in the Cambridgeshire village of Grantchester, when William the son of John Stonelere and Aubrey Bonvalet of Haselingfeld got into a fight, John the son of William de Scalars tried to stop it. He was killed by William, who hit him with a rake.[65]

People were even willing to intervene in family quarrels, although it was generally recognized that a man had the right to beat an errant wife. In Northamptonshire a man named John and his wife Agnes quarreled, and John began beating Agnes with a stick. At this point a man named William came up, seized the stick from John, and stepped between the two. John drew his sword and struck William in the head, killing him.[66] Similarly, when Robert de Fengers and his wife were going home from a party in Coventry, they began to quarrel. Robert eventually drew his knife. At this point, a servant named Walter son of Pain came up. Fearing that Robert was going to stab his wife, he stepped between the two. According to the jurors of the borough of Coventry, he did this in such a way that he accidentally wounded himself on Robert's knife. The wound became infected, and he died three weeks later.[67]

On occasion the village community probably intervened in a more corporate fashion to regulate conflict among fellow villagers. As a collective unit the village could exert considerable influence on the behavior of its members. A person who contradicted the community's wishes might be socially ostracized. Not only would this be an emotional hardship; it could also be a heavy economic sanction. Only the richest peasants had the resources in equipment, animals, and labor to work their land alone. Virtually everyone in the village required assistance from his fellows in plowing and harvesting.*

* This argument is rather speculative. Although what we know of the structure of medieval villages, especially common-field ones, would indicate that such mechanisms of social control must have existed, I have been unable to find any direct evidence of such mechanisms. In the *Rotuli hundredorum* (cited in Ault, "Open-Field Husbandry," p. 31), I, 341, however, there is the story of a man from Belton in Lincolnshire who complained that he was unable "to find a single neighbor who dared yoke an ox to a plough with him because of the bailiff's forbiddance and power." Although in this instance it was the fear of a seigneurial official that had led to the man's ostracism, in many cases villagers must have taken similar action on their own initiative.

Thus, when the villagers as a whole decided that a quarrel ought to be composed peacefully, it must have been difficult for the men at odds to resist their will. For example, on September 15, 1280, Richard le Bonde came to Woburn Chapel in Bedfordshire and violently insulted and defamed John son of Ralf Ordwy. When John's brother Ralf protested, Richard abused him also and struck him with his fist. Ralf brought suit on November 9, 1280, in the manorial court at Chalgrave, claiming damages of 10s. Richard denied all of Ralf's allegations. He was ordered by the court to prove his innocence with six oath-helpers. However, before he could do this, the neighbors intervened to impose a settlement, which apparently required a great deal of negotiation, for the agreement was only recorded by the court on May 10, 1281. At the time it was stated that Richard and Ralf had come to an agreement "through the neighbors" (*per vicinos*). Richard admitted that he had laid violent hands on Ralf and gave him 4d. In return, Ralf, "in accordance with the opinion of the neighbors" (*per consideracionem vicinorum*), withdrew his suit, for which he was fined 6d. by the court.[68]

Possibly one of the more effective ways in which conflict was diminished in thirteenth-century English villages was by emigration. The survey made in 1258–59 by Spalding Priory, referred to above, reveals that this emigration was substantial. At Weston, in the Lincolnshire Fens, fully 38.2 percent of the adult sons of the villagers had emigrated (26 of 68). Of the 86 young adult women in the village, 46 (53.5 percent) had also left.[69] This constant outflow of people probably served to prevent many hatreds from being worked out violently, as the aggrieved, malcontented, and quarrelsome sought opportunities elsewhere.

If all the sanctions against violence failed and a quarrel resulted in a killing, it appears that emigration, in the form of flight, was a means by which the potential consequences of the murder were lessened. Flight was, of course, a necessity for the accused.* Although royal agents may have been inefficient in

---

* Although flight after the commission of a murder may have been common in medieval England, it is not a universal pattern of behavior. Among the Maria

capturing criminals, murder was still very much against the law and uniformly punishable only by death, except under very narrow sets of circumstances. A killer also had to fear the wrath of his victim's kin. But if flight was necessary to preserve a killer's safety, it also served to remove a source of further conflict from the community. A victim's kin and friends were spared the necessity of having to take direct revenge on his killer or killers. Similarly, the killer's family and friends did not have to defend them. Thus, the flight of the murderer or murderers kept the quarrel from involving more people than it already had.

Fully 1,758 of the 3,492 accused killers (50.3 percent) listed in the eyre rolls had taken to flight and not been apprehended by the time the justices in eyre held their sessions. Indeed, so deeply ingrained was flight as a common behavioral pattern after a violent death that many people who were in no way culpable also fled. When Felicia the widow of Hugh le Caretar was crushed by a cart which overturned at Herlingdon in Bedfordshire, Gilbert Thorald, who had been driving the cart, fled.[70] Similarly, when three Jews fell out of a cart crossing the Ketelbridge at Stagsden in Bedfordshire and drowned, the cart's driver, William the miller, a servant of the Hospital of St. John in Bedford, fled.[71]

Certain of the people who fled after committing a murder even managed to obtain the protection of the church. These were the abjurors of the realm of whom 258 (7.4 percent) were listed in the eyre rolls. According to English law, an accused felon had the right to take refuge in a church. For 40 days he could remain there and be supplied with food and drink. At the end of the 40 days he could either surrender to the king's peace or abjure the realm. If he refused to do either, he still could not be taken forcibly from the church, but he could then be starved into submission. If he chose to abjure, he had solemnly to

---

of India, flight after the commission of a homicide is the exception. Although, when India was a British colony, killers who remained in the village were very likely to be apprehended by the authorities, only ten of 117 killers studied by Elwin tried to run away. *Maria Murder,* p. 174.

confess his felony to the county coroner. He was then assigned a
port from which to leave England, never to return. Dressed as a
pilgrim, barefoot, wearing only a shirt and carrying a wooden
cross, the abjuror was required to proceed directly to the port
and quit the realm. If he turned aside and tried to leave the
road, he could be taken and executed immediately as an outlaw.

A cynical view would hold that few of the thousands of people
who must have abjured the realm in the thirteenth century ever
actually left England, the vast majority availing themselves of the
first stretch of deserted, wooded road to flee. Certainly some of
those who abjured the realm for homicide must eventually have
returned home, like Walter Albe, who abjured in Somerset for
the death of Robert le Corbiller but who later returned to his
home, to be left undisturbed by his fellow villagers.[72]

Some were perhaps killed in turn by the friends and relatives
of their victims. But virtually all the abjuring felons whom the
records state to have been killed were thieves, like John of Ireland and John le Conreny. Confessed thieves who had been
imprisoned at Winchester, they had managed to break out of
their prison and flee into the great church of St. Swithun's,
where they stayed for their allotted 40 days. On the fortieth day
they abjured. However, as they set out on the road from Winchester, they were waylaid by twelve men and beheaded.[73] Similarly, an unknown man who had been imprisoned at Southoe
but who had escaped and abjured in the county of Huntingdon
was overtaken by pursuers on October 5, 1267, at Sudbury in
Bedfordshire and beheaded.[74]

Despite these stories and the repeated complaints of the English clergy about secular violations of the right of sanctuary,[75] it
is unlikely that many homicides perished in this fashion. Unlike
thieves, common murderers did not pose a threat to the entire
community. And although allowing criminals to abjure was tan-
tamount to letting them escape, it does appear to have been a
practice that for the most part was scrupulously respected. The
violation of one petty thief's rights even led to the fall of the
sheriff of Northampton, Hugh de Manneby, in 1262. A thief by

the name of Richard de Glaston had been caught and imprisoned in Northampton. He admitted his guilt and turned approver. Subsequently, however, he managed to escape from the prison and flee to the church of St. Gregory in Northampton. There he abjured the realm and set out for Dover. Hugh, however, sent four men after him. They caught up with him on the road between Northampton and Newport Pagnell. There they seized him as "he lay prostrate on the ground, biting the earth with his teeth and clinging to the spokes of a cartwheel with his hands." They dragged him by his feet out of the high road, beat him with bows and sticks, took him to a nearby mill and there raised the hue on him as though he had voluntarily left the king's highway. The beatings he received caused all the flesh on his back and arms to putrefy, and the jurors who reported these events to the justices doubted that he would survive. The justices ruled that, if he recovered, the mayor and bailiffs of Northampton were personally to escort him to the place where he had been seized and see him on his way toward Dover. Whether Richard lived or not is something the records do not reveal. The sheriff, however, was arrested. At his trial at Westminster, he claimed clerical privilege and was released to the bishop elect of Lincoln as one convicted.[76]

Even if a killer had not taken refuge in a church, the local country people seem to have been more than willing to let the culprit slip away unmolested. For example, in 1259 or 1260 a group of five men were returning from a party that had been held in North Aston in Oxfordshire. Between Somerton and North Aston they began quarreling on a bridge next to the house of Roger Gambun, who was disturbed by their uproar. Gambun came out of his house brandishing an axe. Accidentally, he struck John le Hoppere, whom the jurors stated to be his *"amicus specialis,"* and killed him. After this deed, no one made any effort to arrest Roger, who was allowed to depart.[77]

This killing was clearly accidental. But even in cases where a killing had been committed purposefully, the local community was often willing to let the killer leave without hindrance. The ten people who were in Richard Iring's house in Depwade Hundred in Norfolk when Walter the son of Ivo of Gising killed William of Smallburgh[78] or the six people in Robert the chaplain's curia in South Erpingham Hundred in the same county when Robert the son of Matilda of Birmingham killed William of Erpingham[79] made no efforts to apprehend the slayers. References to the failure of witnesses to a killing to apprehend the offender and to villages that had failed to answer the hue and cry are so numerous in the eyre rolls as to make it clear that people were reluctant to apprehend a murderer.[80]

As can be seen, the mechanisms available for solving conflict peacefully were not numerous in thirteenth-century England. And, with the exception of emigration, the ones that existed required small, tightly knit communities to be effective. In a small community, where most social interactions occurred among a limited number of people, an individual was likely to be tightly bound to almost everyone else by some important tie—of blood, friendship, or economic cooperation. A conflict between two or more people inevitably involved whole networks of overlapping allegiances. In such conditions, the pressures for a peaceful, if not amicable, settlement became intense.

In the thirteenth century, however, English society was evolving in such a way as to produce new groups of people who were often beyond the reach of these mechanisms of dispute settlement. The rapid development of the economy in the central Middle Ages enriched many, but it also pushed many others into a marginal position in society. From around the year 1000 there appears to have been steady improvement in agricultural practices, which produced a corresponding increase in grain yields. In large part these new, improved practices consisted of better plowing techniques—in the development of heavy-wheeled plows, stronger animals to pull the plows, and better methods of harnessing the beasts to the plow. As a result, the importance of plowing increased compared to other agricultural pursuits. This produced increased social differentiation within the village. Those peasants who were not rich enough to own plows or plow beasts, the *manouvriers* who had to work their land by hand, found their position vis-à-vis the plow and animal-owning peasants, the *laboureurs,* deteriorating. Their productivity declined relative to that of the richer peasants.[81] And, as production for the market became ever more important in the thirteenth century, in large part because of the increased demands of lords and kings for money dues from the peasants, their ability to compete in this new mercantile framework declined. As a result, more and more peasants became impoverished. And, as we have seen, it was the poorer elements of medieval agrarian society that were primarily responsible for homicide. Furthermore, it was probably from this group, and on occasion from the ranks of the lesser gentry, who also found their economic and social position threatened in the thirteenth century, that the bandit groups that plagued England and accounted for much homicide recruited much of their membership.

At the same time as large numbers of peasants were forced into a marginal role in society and became less amenable to the traditional forms of social control, even those peasants whose social position did not deteriorate or who even prospered in these new conditions found themselves involved in novel relationships that could not be managed by the old communal methods of dispute settlement. In the thirteenth century English villages and hamlets were being rapidly integrated into the new and wider networks of a national monarchy and an international economy. As the century wore on, the peddler, the grain merchant, the out-of-work agricultural laborer, the moneylender, the tax collector, the military recruiter, and the professional estate manager became ever more common figures in rural England, along with a host of other people who had found their vocations in serving as the links between the old local networks of village and parish and the new overarching networks of the state and the economy. And the success or failure of many peasants came to depend on how well they could cope with and manipulate these new figures.

In such an environment, the restraining and mediating forces of family, friends, and neighbors could not operate with the same effectiveness as when the social horizon had been largely bounded by village, parish, and seigneurie. The disagreements that arose in the context of these new and ever expanding relationships in which the English peasantry found itself all too often could be resolved only by violence. In time, as these new relationships took root, new, mutually balanced networks of dependence and allegiance evolved that could resolve these disputes without resort to violence. But until that time, if a disagreement arose in the context of these new networks, the old networks of family and village provided allies with whom to prosecute a quarrel but no mediators to settle it.* A heightened level of violence in thirteenth-century England was thus a consequence of the transformation of European society from one based on the intensely local groups of the early Middle Ages— the village, seigneurie, and castellany—to the larger regional units of the high and late Middle Ages, based on national monarchies, powerful duchies, and a continental network of commercial exchanges.

We have attempted to analyze some of the intricacies of interpersonal behavior in a medieval society as these were manifested in homicide. By intention and by necessity this investigation has been predominantly quantitative. Much of the discussion has been rather abstract, cast in terms of numbers and percentages. But for the men and women of thirteenth-century England, who suffered through it, homicide was a very real matter of anger, pain, fear, guilt, and grief.

To us, some of the impulses that led one person to murder another in the thirteenth century are easily comprehensible. Although the structure of the European family and the nature of the conflicts within it have evolved since the Middle Ages, the

---

* It will be recalled that 424 people (17.4 percent) are definitely known to have been killed by someone from a different village. At the same time, only 149 (6.1 percent) are known to have been killed by someone definitely from the same village as themselves.

tensions that the intimate bonds of shared domestic life generated in medieval England are not too alien to our sensibilities.
What is much more difficult to come to terms with is the
apparently cold-blooded and calculating nature of much
thirteenth-century murder. Although in the twentieth century
the products of European civilization and culture have shown
themselves ready to kill on a scale unimaginable in the Middle
Ages, they have done so in the context of the operations of the
bureaucratic, industrial state. To the overwhelming majority of
people, violence is not an acceptable means of dealing with the
day-to-day problems of life.

That a medieval peasant should murder a friend or a realtive
in anger is readily comprehensible to the modern mind. But the
largely instrumental nature of much medieval homicide is
strange and repellent. For the people of thirteenth-century England, murder and violence were tools, often employed only
reluctantly but still used with great frequency, for the settling of
grievances and the gratification of desires. From the thief who
slew his victims, to the servants who fought for their masters, to
the villagers who ganged up on an obstreperous member of the
community, violence was regarded as an acceptable, and often
necessary, facet of life. The leniency with which accused killers
were treated in court was symptomatic of the prevailing belief
that violence often served a need within society and should be
tolerated. Since the old communal mechanisms for mediating
disputes were rapidly becoming outmoded and new means of
resolving conflict had not yet been devised, this was perhaps inevitable. But the human toll of such a development was very
great.

Appendix. Statistical Tests Used

Chi-square. Chi-square is used to determine if a relationship exists between two or more variables. The first step in performing this test is to construct a joint frequency distribution table. Then the cell frequencies that are to be expected if *no* relationship existed between the variables, given the existing row and column totals, are calculated. The discrepancies between the expected and the observed cell frequencies are then measured. The greater the discrepancy, the larger the value of chi-square. The probability (p) that a particular chi-square score might be obtained by chance is then determined, given the degrees of freedom involved (a measure that takes into account the number of rows and columns in the table). If the probability is less than or equal to a predetermined significance level (commonly used significance levels are 0.05, 0.01, and 0.001), the null hypothesis that there is no relationship between the variables is rejected (in this essay for two-by-two tables with more than 21 cases, Yates's corrected chi-square has been used). Chi-square indicates only whether a relationship exists between variables. It does not provide any information about the strength of that relationship. Certain other tests that are based on chi-square are designed to measure the strength of the association between two variables.

Phi. Phi is used as a measure of association for a two-by-two table. It corrects for the fact that the value of chi-square is directly proportional to the number of cases by adjusting the chi-square value. If there is no relationship between the variables, phi = 0. If the variables are perfectly related, phi = +1.

Cramer's V. This is a modified version of phi that is used for larger tables, since phi has no upper limit when it is calculated for tables that have more than two rows and two columns. Its values also range from 0 to +1.

Contingency coefficient. This is another measure of association. Its minimum value is 0, but its maximum value depends on the size of the table. Therefore it should be used only to compare tables having the same number of rows and columns.

Lambda. Asymmetric lambda measures the percentage of improvement in the ability to predict the value of the dependent variable, once the value of the independent variable is known.

Uncertainty coefficient. The asymmetric uncertainty coefficient measures the proportion by which the uncertainty in the dependent variable is reduced by knowledge of the value of the independent variable.

Notes

CHAPTER 1

1. Bolland, p. 27.
2. *Ibid.*, p. 32.
3. Meekings, p. 34.
4. Latham and Meekings, eds., p. 58.
5. *Ibid.*, p. 55.
6. Stenton, *Rolls . . . Warwickshire*, p. 335.
7. Veale, pp. 144–45.
8. Hall, p. 174.
9. *Beds. Cor. Rolls*, p. xi.
10. For a description of the appeal process, see Henry de Bracton, 2: 399–435.
11. Pollock and Maitland, 2: 509–10.
12. On the functioning of the frankpledge system, see William Morris, pp. 72–83.
13. *Beds. Cor. Rolls*, p. v.
14. See the complaints about the conduct of Bedford borough and Buckinghamshire coroners made in 1278–79 in PRO, J.I.2/255/1b.
15. Hunnisett, *The Medieval Coroner*, pp. 9–36.
16. Bolland, pp. 38–41, 53–54.
17. Green, pp. 687–94.
18. Latham and Meekings, p. 64.
19. Among other works, see J. A. Raftis, *Tenure and Mobility* and *Warboys: Two Hundred Years in the Life of an English Medieval Village* (Toronto, 1974); DeWindt; Homans, *English Villagers;* Hoskins, *The Midland Peasant;* and Ault, "Open-Field Husbandry and the Village Community."
20. Kosminsky, *Studies in the Agrarian History,* pp. 90–91.
21. *Ibid.*, p. 206.

22. *Ibid.*, pp. 90–91.
23. Kosminsky, "Services and Money Rents," p. 30.
24. Beresford, p. 339.
25. Kosminsky, *Studies in the Agrarian History*, p. 125.
26. *Ibid.*, pp. 90–91.
27. Kosminsky, "Services and Money Rents," p. 30.
28. Kosminsky, *Studies in the Agrarian History*, p. 206.
29. Homans, *English Villagers*, p. 118.
30. Baker and Butlin, p. 328.
31. *Ibid.*, p. 329.
32. Roden, "Demesne Farming," p. 10.
33. Roden and Baker, p. 74.
34. Baker and Butlin, p. 333.
35. Roden and Baker, p. 74.
36. Roden, "Fragmentation of Farms and Fields in the Chiltern Hills," pp. 228–29.
37. *Ibid.*, p. 237.
38. Baker and Butlin, p. 356.
39. Kosminsky, *Studies in the Agrarian History*, pp. 90–91.
40. Baker, "Field Systems in the Vale of Homesdale," pp. 22–23.
41. *Ibid.*
42. Baker and Butlin, p. 402.
43. DuBoulay, *The Lordship of Canterbury*, pp. 181–82.
44. Jolliffe, p. 37.
45. DuBoulay, *The Lordship of Canterbury*, p. 145.
46. Roden and Baker, p. 75.
47. *Ibid.*, pp. 80–81.
48. Baker and Butlin, p. 413.
49. Thirsk, p. 9.
50. Homans, *English Villagers*, p. 110.
51. DuBoulay, *The Lordship of Canterbury*, pp. 146–47.
52. Blake, p. 236.
53. Douglas, p. 169.
54. *Ibid.*, pp. 127–28.
55. Baker and Butlin, p. 307.
56. Faith, p. 81.
57. Dodwell, "Holdings and Inheritance," pp. 61–62.
58. Thirsk, p. 45.
59. Douglas, pp. 164–65.
60. Baker and Butlin, pp. 294, 312–13.
61. Hilton, *Social Structure*, p. 16.
62. *Ibid.*, p. 17.
63. Roberts, p. 109.
64. Hilton, *Social Structure*, p. 15.
65. *Ibid.*, p. 17.
66. See the discussion in E. A. Wrigley, *Population and History* (New York 1969), pp. 96–98.

67. Ekwall, pp. xiv–xv, lxi.
68. Williams, *Medieval London*, contains a detailed discussion of London politics in this period.
69. On this point see the discussion, based on nineteenth-century Russian experience, in A. V. Chayanov, *The Theory of Peasant Economy* (ed. by Daniel Thorner, Basile Kerblay, and R. E. F. Smith; Homewood, Ill., 1966), pp. 120–26.
70. Various village studies have suggested much continuity in family landholding patterns among the peasantry. See, for example, DeWindt, p. 66; Harvey, p. 123; and Hoskins, *The Midland Peasant*, pp. 34–49.
71. Thrupp, pp. 118–30.
72. See Georges Duby's discussion of the volatile nature of the fortunes of the twelfth-century bourgeoisie in the Maconnais in *La Société aux xie et xiie siècles dans la région mâconnaise* (Paris, 1971), pp. 310–11. Colin Platt has also found that there was a rapid turnover among the leading burgess families in Southampton. In part this was due to the failure of heirs, bankruptcies, and so forth, but in large part it was also due to the fact that burgesses who had made their fortune tended to abandon the town, buy up property in the countryside, and turn themselves into members of the gentry. For this, see his *Medieval Southampton: The Port and Trading Community, A.D. 1000–1600* (London, 1973), pp. 62–64.
73. R. E. Glasscock, ed., *The Lay Subsidy of 1334* (London, 1975), pp. 1, 140, 192, 235, 319.
74. Glasscock in various of his works (*The Distribution of Lay Wealth in South-East England in the Early Fourteenth Century*, "The Distribution of Lay Wealth in Kent, Surrey and Sussex in the Early Fourteenth Century," and "The Distribution of Wealth in East Anglia in the Early Fourteenth Century") has tried to deal with this problem by calculating the amount of assessed wealth per square mile. Unfortunately, although this is a suggestive procedure, it is not a complete solution to the problem. People, not land, possess wealth. Until we know how wealth was distributed among the population, we will not be able to gauge the relative prosperity of the different regions of medieval England with any accuracy.
75. Homans, *English Villagers*, pp. 112–13.
76. DuBoulay, *Medieval Bexley*, p. 22.
77. Great Britain, PRO, *Inquisitions and Assessments Relating to Feudal Aids*, 1: 16–22; 3: 9–19, 449–83; 4: 161–72; 5: 174–80.
78. J. K. Wallenberg, *The Place-Names of Kent* (Uppsala, 1934). The reader will note that the figure of 698 settlements given for Norfolk differs from the 695 villages mentioned by Blake in his "Norfolk Manorial Lords in 1316" (cited above, note 52). This discrepancy is due to the fact that Blake excluded the three places listed as boroughs in the county from his enumeration.
79. Williams, p. 317.
80. Hilton, *A Medieval Society*, p. 168.

81. Translations of the Domesday Book surveys for these counties, and the county of Kent, can be found in the following: *The Victoria History of the County of Bedford*, 1: 221–66; *Kent*, 3: 203–52; *Norfolk*, 2: 39–203; *Oxford*, 1: 396–428; and *Warwick*, 1: 299–344. For the figures on which the Kentish population estimate is based, see Hanley and Chalkin.

82. This is the multiplier suggested by H. C. Darby in *A New Historical Geography of England* (Cambridge, Eng., 1973), p. 45.

83. Russell, *British Medieval Population*, pp. 132–33. The figures that Russell gives are as follows: Bedford, 30,508; Kent, 89,551; Norfolk, 146,726; Oxford, 41,008; and Warwick, 45,396. These figures are regarded by many historians as far too low. For a recent statement of the most common criticisms of Russell's calculations, see Titow, *English Rural Society*, pp. 66–73, 83–89.

84. Great Britain, Parliament, *Parliamentary Papers (Commons)*, *1852–53*, vol. 85 (*Accounts and Papers*, vol. 29), Cmnd. 1631, "Population of Great Britain: Volume I," p. ccviii. Since the 1801 census was the first governmental census carried out in Great Britain, it is not very accurate and underrepresents the size of the population. On some of the problems involved in the use of the early censuses, see D. V. Glass, *Numbering the People: The Eighteenth-Century Population Controversy and the Development of Census and Vital Statistics in Britain* (Farnborough, 1973), pp. 90–95.

85. See, among others, Russell, *British Medieval Population* and "Demographic Limitations of the Spalding Serf Lists"; Hallam, "Some Thirteenth-Century Censuses" and "Further Observations on the Spalding Serf Lists"; J. Krause, "The Medieval Household: Large or Small?," *Economic History Review*, 2d ser., 9 (1957): 420–32; and Titow, *English Rural Society*, pp. 66–73, 83–89.

86. For the differing population growth rates of Felden Warwickshire and the Forest of Arden, see Harley, "Population Trends and Agricultural Developments," p. 13. For an area where population increased phenomenally between 1086 and the late thirteenth century, see H. E. Hallam's work on the Lincolnshire Fens in "Population Density in the Medieval Fenland," *Economic History Review*, 2d ser., 14 (1961): 78, and in *Settlement and Society: A Study of the Early Agrarian History of South Lincolnshire* (Cambridge, Eng., 1965), pp. 198–200.

CHAPTER 2

1. Johann Huizinga, *The Waning of the Middle Ages: A Study of the Forms of Life, Thought and Art in France and the Netherlands in the XIVth and XVth Centuries* (London, 1937), p. 18.

2. Achille Luchaire, *Social France at the Time of Philip Augustus* (New York, 1912), p. 8.

3. Tout, p. 5.

4. Bloch, p. 411.

5. *Ibid.*, p. 73.
6. Georges Duby and Robert Mandrou, *Histoire de la civilisation française* (2 vols.; Paris, 1958), 1: 57–58.
7. Lorcin, p. 284.
8. Vaultier, p. vii.
9. Williams, pp. 21–22.
10. Hilton, *A Medieval Society,* p. 55.
11. *Ibid.*, p. 218.
12. Daniels et al., pp. 249–50.

CHAPTER 3

1. Letter of Pope Clement V, dated June 9, 1343, in Heinrich Denifle, ed., *Chartularium universitatis Parisiensis* (4 vols.; Paris, 1891–99), 2: 538–39.
2. This pattern has been noticed by other historians, especially Yvonne Lanhers in her "Crimes et criminels au xive siècle," pp. 325–28, which is a study of the criminal sessions of the Parlement of Paris in the early fourteenth century. She attributes the tendency of medieval Frenchmen to gang up on one another to a "vie personnel inconsistante."
3. Colin Morris, *The Discovery of the Individual, 1050–1200* (New York, 1972), pp. 14–15, 55, 98, 100–101, 104–6.
4. PRO, J.I.1/569a, m. 30r.
5. Meekings, p. 191.
6. PRO, J.I. 2/120, m. 17r.
7. Maitland et al., *Year Books,* 1: 64–65.
8. In an area like Kent, where tenements may have been worked jointly for a time by the heirs (for examples of this practice, see Homans, *English Villagers,* pp. 111–12), the interest of the siblings in preserving the economic viability of their joint holding is obvious. Even in areas where impartible inheritance was the rule, arrangements were at times made for noninheriting children which gave them a stake in the family patrimony. For example, in the early fourteenth century on the abbot of Crowland's manors of Oakington, Cottenham, and Drayton, noninheriting children were given a small plot of land to hold until they married, left the village, or died, at which time the land returned to the heir. (See F. M. Page.) Page believes this to have been a unique practice, but it is possible that similar arrangements existed elsewhere.
9. *Cal. Inq. Misc.,* p. 579.
10. See the tables in Russell, *British Medieval Population,* pp. 180–81. However, in the Huntingdonshire village of Holywell-cum-Needingworth, DeWindt (p. 188) has found that in the fourteenth and fifteenth centuries men who survived infancy tended to live into middle age. He calculates that of some 117 men resident in Holywell between the second half of the fourteenth and the second half of the fifteenth century, 32 percent lived less than 40 years, 31 percent survived into

their forties, 15 percent into their fifties, 16 percent into their sixties, and 6 percent into their seventies. Altogether, 79 men, or 68 percent, lived to middle age.

11. See Pearson, pp. 68–80.

12. Sheehan, p. 251. Of the marriage cases heard by the bishop of Ely's consistory court between March 1374 and March 1384, more than 40 percent concerned bigamy.

13. I am indebted to Paul Seaver of the Stanford University History Department for this insight.

14. Hallam, "Some Thirteenth-Century Censuses," pp. 356–57.

15. Hilton, *A Medieval Society*, p. 25.

16. Raftis, "The Concentration of Responsibility in Five Villages," pp. 116–17. From an examination of much later evidence, the poll-tax returns of 1380–81, R. H. Hilton has estimated that in 80 Cotswold villages there might have been one household in eight with a servant or servants, usually not more than two. (*English Peasantry*, pp. 32–34.)

17. Vaultier, pp. 141–42. Marion la Blondelle, eleven years old, who refused to go to sleep when she was first apprenticed because she was afraid, was taken into her master and mistress's bed. This practice became habitual and Marion was eventually impregnated by her master, the 68-year-old Jehan Nyvelon.

18. On the social milieu that produced these ballads, see the interesting but inconclusive debate in *Past and Present:* R. H. Hilton, "The Origins of Robin Hood"; J. C. Holt, "The Origins and Audience of the Ballads of Robin Hood" and "Robin Hood: Some Comments"; and Maurice Keen, "Robin Hood—Peasant or Gentleman?"

19. Child, 3: 97–99.
20. *AM* (Waverly), 2: 257.
21. PRO, J.I. 1/700, m. 12r.
22. BM, Add. Ch. 5153, m. 3r.
23. *Beds. Cor. Rolls*, p. 16.
24. A. H. Thomas, p. 219.
25. Stenton, *Rolls . . . Warwickshire*, pp. 368–69.

26. Thomas of Monmouth, *The Life and Miracles of St. William of Norwich*, ed. by Augustus Jessop and Montague Rhodes James (Cambridge, Eng., 1896), pp. 97–110.

27. *CRR*, 6: 152–53.

28. *Cal. Inq. Misc.*, p. 342.

29. *AM* (Dunstable), 3: 273.

30. PRO, J.I.1/700, m. 9r. English bishops in the thirteenth century could secure a writ from the royal chancery directed to the local sheriff to capture and imprison, until such time as he was absolved, any person who had remained excommunicate for more than 40 days. For a discussion of the operation of this system, see F. Donald Logan, *Excommunication and the Secular Arm in Mediaeval England: A Study in Legal Procedure from the Thirteenth to the Sixteenth Century* (Toronto, 1968).

31. *Beds. Cor. Rolls*, pp. 25–26.

32. PRO, J.I.1/10, m. 37d.

33. Riley, *Memorials of London*, pp. 9–11; see also Sharpe, *Letter-Book B*, pp. 263–65.

34. Svalastoga, p. 40.
35. Wolfgang, pp. 206–7.
36. Bohannan, p. 37.
37. *Ibid.*, p. 106.
38. Elwin, p. 105.
39. Wolfgang, p. 25.
40. *Ibid.*, p. 207.

41. Barbara Hanawalt has found in her study of gaol delivery rolls from the first half of the fourteenth century that 55.5 percent of the intrafamilial homicides tried at goal deliveries involved spouses, 31.6 percent involved parents and children, and 11.4 percent involved siblings. See "The Peasant Family and Crime," p. 5.

42. Thomas of Chobham, pp. 458–59.

43. *CRR*, 5: 64–65. I owe this reference to Paul Hyams of Pembroke College, Oxford.

44. PRO, J.I.1/358, m. 22r.

45. Adam of Eynsham, 2: 31–32.

46. *Beds. Cor. Rolls*, p. 11.
47. *Ibid.*, pp. 13–14.
48. Amphlett et al., 1: 5–6.
49. *Beds. Cor. Rolls*, p. 10.
50. Dale, p. 40.
51. Amphlett et al., 1: 67.

52. PRO, J.I.1/569a, m. 15r.

53. Fowler, *Calendar of the Roll of the Justices in Eyre, 1247*, p. 159.

54. PRO, J.I.1/701, m. 29r.

55. PRO, J.I.1/695, m. 25d.

56. Meyer, 1: 19–20, lines 512–16.

57. Vaultier, pp. 1–4.
58. *Beds. Cor. Rolls*, p. 93.
59. Mannyng, pp. 231–33.
60. Meekings, p. 189.
61. PRO, J.I.1/568, m. 4d.

62. Stevenson, p. 91. Miracula multa et magna apud sanctum Aedmundum per beatum puerum Robertum quem quidam Judeus occulter crudeliter neci tradidit. Similiter apud Huntodinam de alio puero Herbert nomine nova contigerunt, quem proprius pater ad stipitem impie ligavit et in aquam que juxta ipsam villam decurrit miserabiliter extinxit. I am indebted to Gavin Langmuir of the Stanford University History Department for this reference.

63. *Cal. Inq. Misc.*, p. 395. Barbara Hanawalt has found that, in the early fourteenth-century gaol delivery rolls, about a third of all intrafamilial homicide cases involved killers believed to be insane, and that the majority of these killings involved the murder of children by parents. See "The Peasant Family and Crime," p. 11.

64. Eric R. Wolf, *Peasants* (Englewood Cliffs, N.J., 1966), pp. 67–70.

65. Amphlett et al., 1: 31–32.

66. PRO, J.I.1/10, m. 33r.

67. Titow, "Some Differences Between Manors," pp. 6–8.

68. Hoskins, "Murder and Sudden Death" and *Midland Peasant*, pp. 77–78.

69. Chadwyck-Healey and Landon, 1: 285.

70. PRO, J.I.1/701, m. 19d.

71. Latham and Meekings, pp. 77–78. Robert de Cruce appears to have been a well-off peasant, since his chattels were valued at £5.

72. Chew and Weinbaum, pp. 61–62. In one case where a servant killed his master the murderer seems to have exhibited signs of a pathological mental state. Sometime in late November 1276, Simon of Winchester, a London taverner, hired Roger of Westminster. On the evening of December 5 the neighbors heard the two quarreling. On the following day they again heard the two arguing and abusing one another. That night, as Simon slept, Roger cut his head off with a knife and hid his body amongst the coal. The next day he opened the shop and sold wine, telling everyone that Simon had gone to Westminster to recover some debts owed to him. This he did for three days. On the evening of the third day, he left, saying he was going to look for his master. He took with him a silver cup, a robe, some bedclothes, and apparently Simon's head. On the first of January, John Doget, another taverner, came with Gilbert de Colchester to recover some money that Simon owed him for wine. They took away a tun and half a vat of wine worth 50s., and other goods worth 2s. Finally, on the Tuesday before Palm Sunday, Master Robert le Sarigien, who owned the building, came, broke in, and enfeoffed it to Michael le Oynter. On Saturday of Easter Week, Michael was examining the premises to see what needed to be cleaned when he discovered the body. (Sharpe, *Letter-Book B*, pp. 265–66; Riley, *Memorials of London*, pp. 11–13.)

CHAPTER 4

1. For an effort to define a subculture of violence, see Wolfgang and Ferracuti.

2. Hilton, *A Medieval Society*, p. 5.

3. Farmer, "Some Grain Price Movements," p. 212.

4. Pollock and Maitland, 1: 553.

5. *Beds. Cor. Rolls*, pp. 52–54.

6. Hill, 3: xl–xli; 4: 104–5, 107–8, 150–56.

7. *Dictionary of National Biography*, 20: 822–23.

8. Guy Devailly, *Le Berry du xe siècle au milieu du xiiie: étude politique, religieuse, sociale et économique* (Paris, 1973), p. 524 and 524 note 3.

9. Indeed, a religious order, the Cavalieri Gaudenti, was founded with the specific task of promoting peace between warring factions. See John Larner, "Order and Disorder in Romagna, 1450–1500," in *Violence and Civil Disorder in Italian Cities, 1200–1500*, ed. by Lauro Martines (Berkeley, Calif., 1972), pp. 65–66.

10. Otto Brunner, *Land und Herrschaft: Grundfragen der territorialen Verfassungsgeschichte Südostdeutschlands im Mittelalter*, 3d ed. (Brünn, 1943), pp. 15–16.

11. P. Hume Brown, "The Scottish Nobility and Their Part in National History," *Scottish Historical Review*, 3 (1906): 161, and I. F. Grant, *The Social and Economic Development of Scotland Before 1603* (Edinburgh, 1930), pp. 193–94.

12. J. E. Morris, *The Welsh Wars of Edward I* (Oxford, 1901), pp. 224–35.

13. *Dictionary of National Biography*, 20:822, and Henry Richards Luard, ed., *Flores historiarum* (3 vols.; RS, London, 1890), 3: 17–18.

14. It should be noted that the events described by F. M. Powicke in "The Murder of Henry Clement and the Pirates of Lundy Island," *Ways of Medieval Life and Thought* (London, 1950), pp. 38–68—the murder of Clement, a clerk and messenger of the justiciar of Ireland, by William de Marisco, the son of a former justiciar of Ireland, and William's subsequent career as an outlaw and pirate—although they took place in England, involved members of the Anglo-Irish ruling groups and grew out of the complexities of Irish politics. For an example of a murderous assault that did grow out of English politics, however, see Powicke's essay in the same volume, "Guy de Montfort (1265–71)," pp. 69–88, which deals with the murder of Henry of Almain, the son of Earl Richard of Cornwall, by Guy de Montfort in Viterbo on March 13, 1271.

15. Jocelin de Brakelond, p. 119.

16. Paris, 3: 416–18; *AM* (Dunstable), 3: 146–47.

17. Macray, pp. 127, 144–45.

18. *Beds. Cor. Rolls*, pp. 93, 96, 101.

19. Paris, 5: 634, 676–77.

20. *Ibid.*, 5: 223–24.

21. PRO, J.I.1/569a, m. 39d, 33r–33d.

22. PRO, J.I.1/873, m. 14r.

23. Walsingham, 1: 316–18.

24. PRO, J.I.1/358, m. 19d, 20d.

25. PRO, J.I.1/361, m. 57r.

26. The best descriptions of tournaments, as they were held in northern France in the last half of the twelfth century, are to be found in Meyer. See also Denholm-Young, pp. 241–43.

27. Denholm-Young, pp. 245–46.

28. *AM* (Dunstable), 3: 45; also Walter de Coventria, 2: 234.

29. *AM* (Waverly), 2:328; Paris, 4: 135–36; Trivet, p. 230.

30. *AM* (Tewkesbury), 1: 150; Paris, 5: 318–19.

31. Gransden, p. 87; John de Oxenedes, p. 258; Florence of Worcester, 2: 237.

32. Bateson and Chinnery, 1: 368.

33. Paris, 5: 83.   34. *Ibid.*, 5: 265.

35. Denholm-Young, p. 252.   36. Paris, 4: 135.

37. *Ibid.*, 5: 318–19.

38. Gransden, p. 87; John de Oxenedes, p. 268; Florence of Worcester, 2: 237.

39. Hilton, *A Medieval Society*, p. 65. Hilton has also found that clerics formed almost 10 percent of those accused of poaching deer at the Feckenham Forest Assizes of 1270 and 1280. Hilton attributes the clergy's predilection for disorderly behavior to their idleness.

40. *Ibid.*, pp. 62–64.

41. Richardson, p. 118.

42. Arnold J. Taylor, pp. 17, 19, 21, 30, 33, 41.

43. Russell, *British Medieval Population,* p. 285.
44. Salter, *Records of Mediaeval Oxford,* p. 3.
45. *Ibid.,* p. 8.   46. Anstey, 1: 20–25.
47. Rogers, pp. 150–51.   48. Rishanger, p. 167.
49. Salter, *Records of Mediaeval Oxford,* pp. 6–7; Rogers, pp. 174–75. For a brief survey of town-gown disturbances in medieval Oxford, see W. A. Pantin, *Oxford Life in Oxford Archives* (Oxford, 1972), pp. 68–75, 99–104.
50. Marc Bloch, *Land and Work in Medieval Europe: Select Papers* (Berkeley, Calif., 1967), p. 141.
51. *Ibid.,* pp. 157–58, for one such struggle between the abbot of St. Alban's and his tenants. For other disputes involving mills and millers, see the cases cited in C. H. S. Fifoot, *History and Sources of the Common Law: Tort and Contract* (London, 1949), pp. 80, 96–97.
52. PRO, J.I.1/951a, m. 4d.
53. R. H. Hilton, "Peasant Movements in England Before 1381," *Economic History Review,* 2d ser. 2 (1949): 117–36. See also his *Bond Men Made Free: Medieval Peasant Movements and the English Rising of 1381* (New York, 1973).
54. Searle, pp. 163–64.
55. Great Britain, PRO, *Calendar of the Patent Rolls . . . Edward I, A.D. 1301–1307,* p. 352.
56. *Beds. Cor. Rolls,* pp. 82–83.
57. Great Britain, PRO, *Calendar of the Patent Rolls . . . Edward I, A.D. 1301–1307,* pp. 197–98; see also pp. 274–75, 403–4.
58. PRO, J.I.1/778, m. 62r.
59. *Beds Cor. Rolls,* pp. 109–10.
60. PRO, J.I.1/755, m. 1r; Chadwyck-Healey and Landon, 1: 30–31.

CHAPTER 5

1. Gluckman, *Politics, Law and Ritual in Tribal Society,* p. 7.
2. Wolfgang, pp. 295 note 1, 381.
3. PRO, J.I.1/361, m. 50r. See also J.I.1/569a, m. 13d, an instance where the justices expressed similar disapproval when they learned that John Cully had been hanged in the liberty of Ausing in Norfolk for having murdered Margaret, daughter of William the smith of Ausing.
4. Pollock and Maitland, 2: 647–48.
5. See F. W. Maitland, "The Murder of Henry Clement," in *Collected Papers* (3 vols.; Cambridge, Eng., 1911), 3: 11–16, for a transcript of one of the rare criminal trials in which witnesses were carefully examined by the justices.
6. In discussing criminal trials, the author of the legal treatise known as *Britton* wrote, "Et si il [the jurors] dient sur lour sermentz qe il ne sevent riens del fet, soint mis autres qi en sevent . . ." Francis Morgan Nichols, ed., *Britton* (2 vols.; Oxford, Eng., 1845), 1: 31. See also 2: 87, where, in speaking of civil trials, the author puts these words into the king's mouth: "Issint qe chescun juror distingtement soit garni en touz

pointz, sur quel point il se deit aviser avaunt soen vener en nostre court."

7. For examples of the ways in which some African judges use the concept of the "reasonable incumbent of a social position" to aid them in arriving at decisions, see Max Gluckman, *The Judicial Process Among the Barotse of Northern Rhodesia,* 2d ed. (Manchester, 1967), pp. 82–162. The evidence I have accumulated tends to support Thomas A. Green's critique (pp. 683–86) of Naomi Hurnard's belief that jurors' excusable homicide verdicts were relatively truthful.

8. Elizabethan juries showed a similar reluctance to condemn people accused of homicide. Of those people tried between 1558 and 1603 for homicide at the Sussex and Essex county assizes, 24 percent and 13 percent, respectively, were executed. For this see Thomas A. Green, "The Jury and the English Law of Homicide, 1200–1600," *Michigan Law Review,* 74 (1976): 493.

9. See Hurnard, *The King's Pardon,* for a full discussion of the medieval pardoning system. The eyre rolls do not accurately reflect the number of pardons actually granted. Many people who obtained pardons never bothered to appear before the justices in eyre as the letter of the law required them to do. I owe this information to Mr. Thomas A. Green of the University of Michigan Law School.

10. Stenton, *Rolls . . . Warwickshire,* p. 381.

11. PRO, J.I.1/358, m. 16r.

12. PRO, J.I.1/569a, m. 6r.

13. PRO, J.I.1/361, m. 62r.

14. See, for example, Great Britain, Record Commission, *Rotuli hundredorum,* 1: 200, where the jurors of Bleangate Hundred in Kent report that John Baudifer, cleric and escheator, had taken 10s. from John Gervase le Taillur by falsely accusing him of killing his wife. Baudifer, according to the jurors, had also extorted 40s. from Daniel the merchant by falsely claiming that Daniel's wife had killed their child.

15. PRO, J.I.1/951a, m. 1d.

16. PRO, J.I.1/10, m. 33d.

CHAPTER 6

1. This contrasts with the opinion of John Bellamy: "Homicide for money was less in evidence [as a gang activity] and, in general, killings were the result of personal quarrels or of the necessity to escape from pursuers." *Crime and Public Order,* p. 81.

2. Fowler, *Calendar of the Roll of the Justices in Eyre, 1247,* p. 151.

3. PRO, J.I.1/361, m. 55r.

4. *Beds. Cor. Rolls,* p. 116.

5. *Ibid.,* p. 78.

6. Stenton, *Rolls . . . Warwickshire,* pp. 393–94.

7. Stones, "The Folvilles of Ashby-Folville," and Bellamy, "The Coterel Gang."

8. Norman Scot Brien Gras, *The Evolution of the English Corn Market*

from the Twelfth to the Eighteenth Century (Cambridge, Mass., 1915), pp. 62–63.

9. Hilton, *A Medieval Society*, pp. 196–97 and plate 4.
10. Michel, p. 39.
11. *AM* (Oseney and Thomas Wykes), 4: 315; Rishanger, p. 117; Walter of Guisborough, pp. 224–25.
12. Rishanger, p. 117.
13. Paris, 5: 56–60; Meekings, p. 6; Cam, *The Hundred and the Hundred Rolls*, pp. 30–31.
14. PRO, J.I.1/361, m. 36r.
15. Beresford and Hurst, p. 107.
16. Stenton, *Rolls . . . Warwickshire*, p. 378; PRO, J.I.1/10, m. 29d.
17. Beresford and Hurst, pp. 104–13.
18. *Beds. Cor. Rolls*, p. 116.
19. Stenton, *Rolls . . . Warwickshire*, p. 393.
20. Beresford and Hurst, pp. 94–95.
21. *Beds. Cor. Rolls*, p. 92. Cf. pp. 22, 45.
22. Ault, "Open-Field Husbandry," pp. 16–17.
23. *Beds. Cor. Rolls*, p. 12.
24. PRO, J.I.1/361, m. 56d.
25. Stenton, *Rolls . . . Warwickshire*, p. 380.
26. Chew and Weinbaum, p. 42.
27. Bateson and Chinnery, 1: 368–69.
28. PRO, J.I.1/710, m. 57r.
29. PRO, J.I.1/710, m. 57r–57d.
30. Chew and Weinbaum, p. 51.
31. *Ibid.*, p. 59.
32. BM, Add. Ch. 5153, m. 2r, 2d, 3r, 3d, 6d, 9d, 13r.
33. Ault, "The Village Church," p. 199.
34. Meekings has found some instances where the clerks who drew up the eyre rolls conflated two separate incidents in which people were killed by unknown thieves. (Latham and Meekings, p. 108.) Although this would affect the figures given here, I doubt that it would seriously alter the impression that emerges from them.
35. PRO, J.I.1/710, m. 42r.
36. *Beds. Cor. Rolls*, pp. 7–8. In 1297 ten people were assessed for the king's ninth in Honeydon (A. T. Gaydon, ed., *The Taxation of 1297: A Translation of the Local Rolls of Assessment for Barford, Biggleswade and Flitt Hundreds, and for Bedford, Dunstable, Leighton Buzzard and Luton* [Bedfordshire Historical Record Society, 39, Aspley Guise, 1958], pp. 24–25). Although it is difficult to make any population estimate from this figure, Honeydon's population was probably not much greater than 300. Thus the four people killed during the raid constituted a not insignificant portion of the entire village population.
37. *Beds. Cor. Rolls*, p. 22.
38. *Ibid.*, pp. 12–13.
39. Bellamy, *Crime and Public Order*, p. 88.

40. Hilton, *A Medieval Society*, p. 254.
41. Blok, "The Peasant and the Brigand," pp. 498–99.
42. Kosminsky, *Studies*, pp. 258–78. See also Edmund King, "Large and Small Landowners in Thirteenth-Century England," *Past and Present*, 47 (1970): 29–30. For the story of a family of wealthy peasants who tried, ultimately with no success, to turn themselves into the lords of the village of Canley in Warwickshire, see Hilton, *The Stoneleigh Leger Book*, pp. 30–34.

43. Searle, pp. 159–60.   44. Paris, 3: 370.
45. *Ibid.*, 5: 234.   46. AM (Dunstable), 3: 377.
47. PRO, J.I.1/710, m. 47d.   48. PRO, J.I.1/954, m. 48r.
49. This may well be the same Robert Chandos whom Matthew Paris referred to as a bandit.
50. *VCH Warwick*, 3: 82.
51. *Ibid.*, 3: 79.
52. Great Britain, PRO, *Liber feodorum*, p. 1275.
53. *Ibid.*, p. 824.
54. Raine, pp. 39–40.
55. *The Victoria History of the County of York*, 3: 37.
56. York Cathedral Library, Melton i Register, folio 489v. I am indebted to Professor Rosalind M. T. Hill of the University of London for a transcript of this passage.
57. PRO, J.I.1/10, m. 40r.
58. This is slightly lower than the figure of 20.2 percent for the entire population of 3,492, which might indicate that Barbara Hanawalt and John Bellamy have exaggerated the role that family members played in the organization of bandit groups. See Hanawalt, "Peasant Family," p. 13, and Bellamy, *Crime*, p. 69.
59. *Beds. Cor. Rolls*, p. 1.
60. *Ibid.*, pp. 48–49. Cf. PRO, J.I.1/10, m. 29r.
61. Stenton, *Rolls . . . Warwickshire*, pp. 384–85.
62. *Beds. Cor. Rolls*, pp. 45–46.
63. Chadwyck-Healey and Landon, 1: 33–34.
64. PRO, J.I.1/361, m. 35r.   65. *Cal. Inq. Misc.*, p. 573.
66. PRO, J.I.1/703, m. 5d.   67. AM (Worcester), 4: 487.
68. AM (Dunstable), 3: 165.   69. *Beds. Cor. Rolls*, pp. 5–6.
70. Richard FitzNeale, *Dialogus de Scaccario, The Course of the Exchequer; and Constitutio Domus Regis, The King's Household*, ed. and trans. by Charles Johnson (New York, 1950), p. 87.
71. Shirley, 1: 167.   72. AM (Burton), 1: 281.
73. Livett, p. 57.   74. *Beds. Cor. Rolls*, p. 48.
75. Hoskins, "Murder and Sudden Death," p. 176.
76. Amphlett et al., 1: 25.
77. Ault, "Open-Field Husbandry," p. 59.
78. Bracton, 2: 198–99.
79. *VCH Bedford*, 3: 49.
80. Chadwyck-Healey and Landon, 1: 42.

81. Robert of Flamborough, p. 278.
82. *Beds. Cor. Rolls*, p. 64.
83. Hilton, *The Stoneleigh Leger Book*, p. 99.
84. *CRR*, 5: 246.
85. *Cal. Inq. Misc.*, pp. 572–73.
86. *AM* (Dunstable), 3: 95.
87. Great Britain, PRO, *Calendar of the Patent Rolls: Henry III, A.D. 1216–1225*, p. 364.
88. *Ibid.*, p. 446.
89. Stenton, *Pleas Before the King*, 2: 68–69.
90. *Beds. Cor. Rolls*, pp. 42–43
91. PRO, J.I.2/120, m. 17r.

CHAPTER 7

1. For a recent bibliography of work on women in medieval Europe, see Carolly Erickson and Kathleen Casey, "Women in the Middle Ages: A Working Bibliography," *Mediaeval Studies*, 37 (1975): 340–59.
2. In Philadelphia between 1948 and 1952, 23.6 percent of the victims of homicide were women. Women also made up 17.6 percent of the killers. (Wolfgang, p. 32.) Thirteenth-century women thus appear to have been involved in homicide somewhat less often than twentieth-century women. However, they appear to have been involved in homicide, at least as victims, in about the same proportion as women in some modern agricultural societies. For example, among the Tiv of central Nigeria, women comprised 13.1 percent (16) of the 122 homicide victims recorded between 1931 and 1949. Of the 114 homicide victims recorded among the BaLuyia of Kenya between 1949 and 1954, women made up 16.7 percent (19). (Bohannan, pp. 36–37, 169.)
3. Vaultier, pp. 40–41.
4. E. P. Thompson, " 'Rough Music,' " p. 294.
5. Many of the miracles attributed to the Virgin turned on the salvation of a sinner whose only possible claim to grace was his devotion to the Mother of God. For some examples, see Edward H. Weatherley, ed., *Speculum sacerdotale* (Early English Text Society, 200, London, 1936), pp. 42–45.
6. Guilelmus Alvernus, "De universo creaturarum," Part 3, c. xii, xxiv, in *Opera omnia* (2 vols.; Frankfurt-am-Main, 1963; reprint of 1674 Orléans edition), 1: 1036, 1066. For other examples of these beliefs about female spirits, see Norman Cohn, *Europe's Inner Demons: An Inquiry Inspired by the Great Witch Hunt* (London, 1975), pp. 213–14.
7. Alan Macfarlane, *Witchcraft in Tudor and Stuart England: A Regional and Comparative Study* (New York, 1970), pp. 160–61.
8. *CRR*, 1: 108.
9. William Page, pp. 343–44.
10. Philippe de Novarre, *Les Quatre ages de l'homme*, ed. by Marcel de Fréville (Société des Anciens Textes Français, 1888), p. 20, as translated by Eileen Power, "The Position of Women," p. 404.

11. PRO, J.I.1/361, m. 40d.
12. *Beds. Cor. Rolls*, p. 27; PRO, J.I.1/10, m. 33r.
13. PRO, J.I.1/755, m. 3r.
14. PRO, J.I.1/10, m. 40d.

CHAPTER 8

1. Ault, "Open-Field Husbandry," p. 42.
2. May, p. 390.
3. Pugh, ed., *Court Rolls*, pp. 117, 119.
4. *Ibid.*, pp. 63–64, 66–67, 70, 75–76, 80, 82–83, 87, 90, 93, 98–100, 102, 107, 110.
5. Roberts, pp. 103–10.
6. Searle, pp. 59, 65–66.
7. Notably George Homans in *English Villagers*, pp. 111–16.
8. Mary Margaret Taylor, p. 9.   9. PRO, J.I.1/700, m. 4r.
10. *Beds. Cor. Rolls*, pp. 55–56.   11. PRO, J.I.1/361, m. 48r.
12. Fifty-two people were eventually named in the appeal in PRO, J.I.1/10, m. 30r.
13. *Beds. Cor. Rolls*, pp. 60–62.
14. *Cal. Inq. Misc.*, p. 643.
15. Hallam, "Some Thirteenth-Century Censuses," pp. 356–57.
16. Raftis, "Concentration of Responsibility," p. 117.

CHAPTER 9

1. See, among recent works, Jacques Heers, *Le Clan familial au moyen âge: étude sur les structures politiques et sociales des milieux urbains* (Paris, 1974).
2. See the discussion in Lewis Yablonsky, *The Violent Gang* (New York, 1962), pp. 170–84.
3. For a different view of the nature of small market towns, see Hilton, *English Peasantry*, pp. 76–85.
4. David Herlihy has found that in the city of Verona, servants made up about 8 percent of the population in 1425, with an average of 0.37 per household. In 1502 servants made up about 12 percent of the population, with an average of 0.72 per household. "The Population of Verona in the First Century of Venetian Rule," in *Renaissance Venice*, ed. by J. R. Hale (Totowa, N.J., 1973), pp. 109, 112.
5. In the fourteenth and fifteenth centuries some German towns took censuses from which it appears that women outnumbered men. For every 1,000 men in Frankfurt in 1385 there were 1,100 women. Similarly, for every 1,000 men there were 1,207 women in Nuremberg in 1449, and 1,247 women for every 1,000 men in Basel in 1454. (Power, p. 411.) However, the situation of these cities, in a period of population contraction and economic stagnation, may have been very different from that of thirteenth-century English towns.
6. Longrais, p. 140.
7. Pollock and Maitland, 2: 403–10. See also Longrais, pp. 141–43.

8. Power, p. 407, and Thrupp, pp. 169–74.

9. BM, Add. Ch. 5153, m. 7r.

10. Chew and Weinbaum, pp. 73–74, 85–86, 117; Williams, pp. 202–7.

11. For violent conflict in the city of Ghent, see Nicholas, pp. 1173–76.

12. Williams, pp. 196–202, 230.

13. Roger de Houeden, 4: 5–6; Gervase of Canterbury, 1: 532–34; Diceto, 2: 143; William of Newburgh, "Historia Rerum Anglicarum," in Howlett, 2: 466–71.

14. Williams, pp. 202–6.

15. FitzThedmar, pp. 114–15; Sharpe, London and the Kingdom, 1: 98–99.

16. Williams, pp. 248–54; Great Britain, Record Commission, Rotuli hundredorum, 1: 407; Thornley, p. 298; John de Oxenedes, p. 264; Florence of Worcester, 2: 233; AM (Worcester), 4: 489–90; Bartholomew de Cotton, p. 166; Gransden, p. 82; Stubbs, 1: 92–93; Aungier, pp. 18–19.

17. BM, Add. Chr. 5153, m. 4d; Great Britain, PRO, Calendar of the Patent Rolls: Henry III, A.D. 1247–1258, p. 548.

18. In describing these events I have followed Walter Rye's brilliant reconstruction in "The Riot Between the Monks and Citizens of Norwich in 1272."

CHAPTER 10

1. Vaultier, p. vi.

2. PRO, J.I.1/361, m. 42r.

3. PRO, J.I.1/10, m. 28r.

4. Palmer, p. 36.

5. PRO, J.I.1/358, m. 25r.

6. H. G. Richardson and G. O. Sayles, Law and Legislation from Aethelbert to Magna Carta (Edinburgh, 1966), pp. 99–102, 136–38.

7. Beds. Cor. Rolls, p. 48.

8. PRO, J.I.1/710, m. 53d.

9. Williams, p. 249; Riley, Munimenta Gildhallae Londoniensis, vol. 2, pt. 1, pp. 282–83.

10. Castle, pp. 23–24.

11. A. H. Thomas, pp. 86–87.

12. For a brief summary of this literature, see Wolfgang and Ferracuti, pp. 197–206.

13. Beresford and Hurst, pp. 134–35.

14. Daniels et al., p. 117.

15. Jacques Le Goff, "The Town as an Agent of Civilisation, c. 1200–c. 1500," in The Fontana Economic History of Europe: Vol. I, The Middle Ages, ed. by Carlo M. Cipolla (London, 1972), pp. 86–88. See also Le Goff's La Civilisation de l'occident médiéval (Paris, 1964), pp. 221–24.

16. Bloch, p. 74.

17. Wolfgang, p. 136.

18. Daniels et al., p. 346.

19. Ibid., p. 347.

20. Williams, pp. 21–22.

21. Macray, p. 189.

22. Stenton, *Rolls . . . Warwickshire*, pp. 344–45.
23. Bayley, p. 55.
24. PRO, J.I.1/565, m. 9d.
25. Mannyng, p. 37.
26. Powicke and Cheney, p. 220; Giraldus Cambrensis, 4: 55–56.
27. For a detailed theoretical discussion, see Wolfgang and Ferracuti.
28. Bandura, pp. 53–57. 29. Daniels et al., pp. 80–81.
30. Gold, p. 654. 31. Bandura, p. 93.
32. Thomas of Chobham, pp. 420–21.
33. Powicke and Cheney, p. 1074; Morey, p. 190.
34. Raymond de Peñaforte, vol. 2, tit. 1, chap. 3, p. 150.
35. Dale, p. 47.
36. Fowler, *Calendar of the Roll of the Justices in Eyre, 1247*, p. 159.
37. PRO, J.I.1/701, m. 29r. 38. Vincent of Beauvais, p. 89.
39. PRO, J.I.1/695, m. 25d. 40. Vincent of Beauvais, p. 89.
41. Rogers, pp. 161–62.
42. Adam of Eynsham, 1: 128, 6.
43. Robert de Sorbon, *De conscientia*, cited by Hastings Rashdall, *The Universities of Europe in the Middle Ages*, 2d ed., ed. by F. M. Powicke and A. B. Emden (3 vols.; Oxford, 1936), 3: 358 note 2.
44. William Brown, ed., *The Registers of John le Romeyn, Lord Archbishop of York, 1286–1296, and of Henry of Newark, Lord Archbishop of York, 1296–1299* (2 vols.; Surtees Society, 123, 128; Durham, 1913–16), 2: 279.
45. Pearson, pp. 69–80.
46. Edward Maunde Thompson, 1: 232–33; 2: 191–92; and Knowles, pp. 100–102, 104, 116–17.
47. Edward Maunde Thompson, 1: 259; 2: 223–24.
48. Jocelin de Brakelond, pp. 92–94.
49. Adam of Eynsham, 2: 157–58.
50. Ferdinand Schevill, *Siena: The Story of a Mediaeval Commune* (New York, 1909), 341–44.
51. James Craigie Robertson and J. Brigstocke Sheppard, eds., *Materials for the History of Thomas Becket, Archbishop of Canterbury (Canonized by Pope Alexander III, A.D. 1173)* (7 vols.; RS, London, 1875–85), 3: 8–12.
52. PRO, J.I.1/700, m. 5r; Fowler, *Calendar of the Roll of the Justices in Eyre, 1247*, p. 148.
53. Oschinsky, p. 287.
54. BM, Add. Ch. 5153, m. 6r.
55. *Cal. Inq. Misc.*, p. 618.
56. *Ibid.*, p. 570. Football, which today provides a popular opportunity for riot and disorderly conduct in England, is mentioned for the first time in that country in 1314. Nicholas of Farndon, the mayor of London, charged by Edward II who was departing for a campaign in Scotland with maintaining the peace, prohibited the playing of football within the city limits because of the "great uproar" and "tumults" that

the game had provoked. (Francis Peabody Magoun, Jr., *History of Football from the Beginnings to 1871* [Kölner Anglistische Arbeiten, 31; Bochum-Langendreer, 1938], p. 5.) Sir Thomas Elyot in the early sixteenth century included an attack on football in his *Boke of the Governour*. Football, in his opinion, was "nothyng but beastely fury and extreme violence, whereof procedeth hurte, and consequently rancour and malice do remayn with thym that be wounded." (Cited in Joseph Strutt, *The Sports and Pastimes of the People of England*, new ed., enlarged and corrected by J. Charles Cox [London, 1903], p. 96.)

57. See Amphlett et al.

58. See Baildon et al.

59. Salter, *Records of Mediaeval Oxford*, p. 4.

60. *Beds. Cor. Rolls*, p. 107.

61. On this concept, see the seminal essay, which first appeared in 1926, of Bronislaw Malinowski, *Crime and Custom in Savage Society*. The ideas expressed in it have been considerably elaborated in the works of Max Gluckman; see especially "The Peace in the Feud," pp. 1–14, which has been reprinted as a chapter (pp. 1–26) of *Custom and Conflict in Africa* (Oxford, 1965), and *Politics, Law and Ritual in Tribal Society*, pp. 138–45. See also P. H. Gulliver, "Dispute Settlement Without Courts: The Ndendeuli of Southern Tanzania," in *Law in Culture and Society*, ed. by Laura Nader (Chicago, 1969), pp. 24–68.

62. Bracton, *Laws and Customs*, 2: 390.

63. A. H. Thomas, pp. 210–11. 64. PRO, J.I.1/640, m. 1r.

65. Palmer, pp. 34–35. 66. PRO, J.I.2/107, m. 12d.

67. PRO, J.I.1/952, m. 43r. 68. Dale, pp. 12–16.

69. Hallam, "Some Thirteenth-Century Censuses," pp. 356–57.

70. Fowler, *Calendar of the Roll of the Justices in Eyre, 1247*, p. 181.

71. Fowler, *Roll of the Justices in Eyre at Bedford, 1227*, pp. 172–73.

72. PRO, J.I.1/755, m. 2d.

73. PRO, J.I.2/262.

74. *Beds. Cor. Rolls*, p. 8.

75. Great Britain, Record Commission, *The Statutes of the Realm*, 1: 172–73; and Powicke and Cheney, pp. 534, 580–81, 679–80, 884–85, 1142.

76. PRO, J.I.1/1187, m. 14d. 77. PRO, J.I.1/701, m. 21d.

78. PRO, J.I.1/568, m. 12r. 79. PRO, J.I.1/568, m. 27d.

80. Examples are too numerous to cite, but see PRO, J.I.1/568, m. 11d, m. 13r, m. 13d, m. 22r, m. 22d, m. 26r, m. 26d, m. 27r, m. 27d, m. 34r.

81. Georges Duby, *Rural Economy and Country Life in the Medieval West* (Columbia, S.C., 1968), pp. 115–16.

Selected Bibliography

AM	Luard, Annales monastici
BM	British Museum, London
Beds. Cor. Rolls	Hunnisett, Bedfordshire Coroners' Rolls
Cal. Inq. Misc.	Great Britain, PRO, Calendar of Inquisitions Miscellaneous
CRR	Great Britain, PRO, Curia Regis Rolls
PRO	Public Record Office, London
RS (Rolls Series)	Rerum Britannicarum medii aevi scriptores (Chronicles and Memorials of Great Britain and Ireland During the Middle Ages) London
VCH Bedford	The Victoria History of the County of Bedford
VCH Warwick	The Victoria History of the County of Warwickshire

MANUSCRIPTS

British Museum, London. Additional Charter Roll 5153. The 1276 London eyre roll.
Corporation of London Records Office, London. Miscellaneous Roll AA. Late thirteenth-century copy of the 1244 London eyre roll.
Public Record Office, London:

J.I.1/1	1202 Bedford eyre roll	J.I.1/60	1272 Buckinghamshire eyre roll
J.I.1/2	1227–28 Bedford eyre roll	J.I.1/271	1221 Gloucestershire eyre roll
J.I.1/4	1247 Bedford eyre roll	J.I.1/272	1221 Gloucestershire eyre roll
J.I.1/7	1276 Bedford eyre roll		
J.I.1/8	1276 Bedford eyre roll	J.I.1/274	1248 Gloucestershire eyre roll
J.I.1/9	1276 Bedford eyre roll		
J.I.1/10	1276 Bedford eyre roll, main roll	J.I.1/358	1227 Kent eyre roll

J.I.1/359   1241 Kent eyre roll
J.I.1/361   1255 Kent eyre roll
J.I.1/559   1198–99 Norfolk eyre
             roll
J.I.1/562   1250 Norfolk eyre roll
J.I.1/563   1250 Norfolk eyre roll
J.I.1/564   1250 Norfolk eyre roll
J.I.1/565   1250 Norfolk eyre roll,
             main roll
J.I.1/568   1257 Norfolk eyre roll
J.I.1/569a   1268–69 Norfolk eyre
             roll
J.I.1/640   Northamptonshire
             coroners' roll, 29 Ed-
             ward I–9 Edward II
J.I.1/695   1241 Oxfordshire eyre
             roll
J.I.1/696   1241 Oxfordshire eyre
             roll
J.I.1/700   1247 Oxfordshire eyre
             roll
J.I.1/701   1261 Oxfordshire eyre
             roll
J.I.1/703   1268 Oxfordshire eyre
             roll
J.I.1/705   1285 Oxfordshire eyre
             roll
J.I.1/707   1285 Oxfordshire eyre
             roll
J.I.1/708   1285 Oxfordshire eyre
             roll
J.I.1/709   1285 Oxfordshire eyre
             roll
J.I.1/710   1285 Oxfordshire eyre
             roll
J.I.1/755   1225 Somersetshire gen-
             eral sessions for
             novel disseisin and
             gaol delivery
J.I.1/778   1256 Hampshire eyre
             roll
J.I.1/873   1259 Guildford gaol de-
             livery
J.I.1/950   1221–22 Warwick eyre
             roll
J.I.1/951a   1232 Warwick eyre roll
J.I.1/952   1247 Warwickshire eyre
             roll
J.I.1/954   1247 Warwick eyre roll
J.I.1/1187   1258–59 pleas and as-
             sizes held by Hugh le
             Bigod and his fellow
             justices

J.I.2/1   Bedford coroners' rolls,
             53–56 Henry III
J.I.2/2   Bedford coroners' rolls,
             53–56 Henry III
J.I.2/3   Bedford coroners' rolls,
             1–3 Edward I
J.I.2/4   Bedford coroners' rolls,
             4 Edward I
J.I.2/46   Bedford coroners' rolls,
             49–56 Henry III
J.I.2/106   Northamptonshire
             coroners' rolls, 27
             Edward I–20 Ed-
             ward II
J.I.2/107   Northamptonshire
             coroners' rolls, 21
             Edward I–9 Ed-
             ward II
J.I.2/120   Northamptonshire
             coroners' rolls, 25 Ed-
             ward I–5 Edward II
J.I.2/128   Oxfordshire coroners'
             rolls, 25–26 Edward I
J.I.2/255/- Bedford coroners' rolls,
  1a   4 Edward I
J.I.2/255/- Misdeeds of Bedford
  1b   borough and Buck-
             inghamshire coron-
             ers, 6 Edward I
J.I.2/258   Worcestershire coron-
             ers' rolls, 45–48 Hen-
             ry III
J.I.2/259   Devon coroners' rolls,
             13 Henry III
J.I.2/260   Hertfordshire coroners'
             rolls, 13–14 Edward I
J.I.2/261   Oxfordshire coroners'
             rolls, 52–56 Henry
             III
J.I.2/262   Hampshire coroners'
             rolls, 1–2 Edward I
J.I.2/263   Norfolk coroners' rolls,
             53 Henry III–2 Ed-
             ward I
J.I.2/264   Norfolk coroners' rolls,
             12–13 Edward I
J.I.2/265   Bedford coroners' rolls,
             4 Edward I
J.I.2/266   Norfolk coroners' rolls,
             53 Henry III–10 Ed-
             ward I
J.I.2/267   Essex coroners' rolls, 9
             Edward I

PRINTED WORKS

Abbiateci, André. "Les Incendiaires devant le Parlement de Paris: essai de typologie criminell (xviiie siècle)," in Crimes et criminalités en France 17e–18e siècles. Cahiers des Annales, 33. Paris, 1971.

Adam of Eynsham, Magna vita sancti Hugonis. Ed. and trans. by Decima L. Douie and Hugh Farmer. 2 vols. London, 1961–62.

Africa, Thomas W. "Urban Violence in Imperial Rome," *Journal of Interdisciplinary History*, 11 (1971):3–21.

Alexander, Nora. "The Raid on Beaumes Manor, Shinfield, Berks., Good Friday, 1347," *Berkshire Archaeological Journal*, 35 (1935): 144–53.

Amphlett, John, Sidney Graves Hamilton, and Rowland Alyn Wilson, eds. Court Rolls of the Manor of Hales, 1270–1307. 3 vols. Worcestershire Historical Record Society. Oxford, 1910–33.

Anchel, Robert. Crime et chatiments au xviiie siècle. Paris, 1933.

Anstey, Henry, ed. Munimenta academica, or Documents Illustrative of Academical Life and Studies at Oxford. 2 vols. RS, London, 1868.

Aston, T. H. "Robin Hood," *Past and Present*, 20 (1961):7–9.

Ault, Warren O. "Open-Field Husbandry and the Village Community: A Study of Agrarian By-Laws in Medieval England," *Transactions of the American Philosophical Society*, n.s., 55 (1965), pt. 7.

———. Private Jurisdiction in England. New Haven, 1923.

———. "The Village Church and the Village Community in Mediaeval England," *Speculum*, 45 (1970), 197–215.

Ault, Warren O., ed. Court Rolls of the Abbey of Ramsey and of the Manor of Clare. New Haven, 1928.

Aungier, G. J., ed. Croniques de London depuis l'an 44 Hen. III jusqu'à l'an 17 Edw. III. Camden Society, 28. London, 1844.

Bacon, Margaret K., Irwin L. Child, and Herbert Barry III. "A Cross-Cultural Study of Correlates of Crime," *Journal of Abnormal and Social Psychology*, 66 (1963): 291–300.

Baildon, William Paley, John Lister, and J. W. Walker, eds. Court Rolls of the Manor of Wakefield. 5 vols. Yorkshire Archaeological Society, Record Series 29, 36, 57, 78, 109. Leeds, 1901–45.

Baker, Alan R. H. "The Field System of an East Kent Parish (Deal)," *Archaeologia Cantiana*, 78 (1963): 96–117.

———. "Field Systems in the Vale of Holmesdale," *Agricultural History Review*, 14 (1966): 1–24.

———. "Open Fields and Partible Inheritance on a Kent Manor," *Economic History Review*, 2d ser., 17 (1964): 1–23.

———. "Some Fields and Farms in Medieval Kent," *Archaeologia Cantiana*, 80 (1965): 152–74.

Baker, Alan R. H., and Robin A. Butlin, eds. Studies of Field Systems in the British Isles. Cambridge, Eng., 1973.

Bandura, Albert. Aggression: A Social Learning Analysis. Englewood Cliffs, N.J., 1973.

Bartholomew de Cotton. Historia Anglicana (A.D. 449–1298) necnon ejusdem liber de archiepiscopis et episcopis Angliae. Ed. by Henry Richards Luard. RS, London, 1859.

Bateson, Mary, and G. A. Chinnery, eds. Records of the Borough of Leicester. 6 vols. London and Leicester, 1899–1967.

Bayley, K. C., ed. "Two Thirteenth Century Assize Rolls for the County of Durham," in Miscellanea vol. 2. Surtees Society, 127. Durham, 1916.

Bellamy, John G. "The Coterel Gang: An Anatomy of a Band of Fourteenth-Century Criminals," English Historical Review, 79 (1964): 698–717.

———. Crime and Public Order in England in the Later Middle Ages. London and Toronto, 1973.

Bercé, Yves. "Aspects de la criminalité au xviie siècle," Revue historique, 239 (1968): 33–42.

Beresford, Maurice. The Lost Villages of England. London, 1954.

Beresford, Maurice, and H. P. R. Finberg. English Medieval Boroughs: A Hand-List. Newton Abbot, 1973.

Beresford, Maurice, and John G. Hurst, eds. Deserted Medieval Villages: Studies. London, 1971.

Bill, P. A. The Warwickshire Parish Clergy in the Later Middle Ages. Dugdale Society Occasional Papers, No. 17. Stratford-upon-Avon, 1967.

Billacois, François. "Le Parlement de Paris et les duels au xviiie siècle," in Crimes et criminalités en France 17e–18e siécles. Cahiers des Annales, 33. Paris, 1971.

———. "Pour une enquête sur la criminalité dans la France d'Ancien Régime," Annales: Économies, Sociétés, Civilisations, 22 (1967): 340–49.

Birrell, Jean. "Peasant Craftsmen in the Medieval Forest," Agricultural History Review, 17 (1969): 91–107.

Blake, William J. "Norfolk Manorial Lords in 1316," Norfolk Archaeology, 30 (1952): 235–86.

Bloch, Marc. Feudal Society. 2 vols. Chicago, 1962.

Blok, Anton. The Mafia of a Sicilian Village, 1860–1960: A Study of Violent Peasant Entrepreneurs. New York, 1975.

———. "The Peasant and the Brigand: Social Banditry Reconsidered," Comparative Studies in Society and History, 14 (1972): 494–503.

Bohannan, Paul, ed. African Homicide and Suicide. Princeton, N.J., 1960.

Bolland, William Craddock. The General Eyre: Lectures Delivered in the University of London at the Request of the Faculty of Laws. Cambridge, Eng., 1922.

Boutelet, Bernadette. "Etude par sondage de la criminalité dans le bailliage du Pont-de-l'Arche (xviie–xviiie siècles): de la violence au vol: en marche vers l'escroquerie," Annales de Normandie, 12 (1962):235–62.

Bowsky, William M. "The Medieval Commune and Internal Violence: Police Power and Public Safety in Siena, 1287–1355," American Historical Review, 73 (1967): 1–17.

Bracton, Henry de. On the Laws and Customs of England. Ed. by George E. Woodbine and trans. by Samuel E. Thorne. 2 vols. Cambridge, Mass., 1968–.

Cam, Helen Maud. The Hundred and the Hundred Rolls: An Outline of Local Government in Medieval England. New York, 1930.

———. Studies in the Hundred Rolls: Some Aspects of Thirteenth-Century Administration. Oxford, 1921.

Cam, Helen Maud, ed. The Eyre of London, 14 Edward II, A.D. 1321. 2 vols. Publications of the Selden Society, 85, 86. London, 1968–69.

Carus-Wilson, E. M. "The First Half-Century of Stratford-upon-Avon," *Economic History Review*, 2d ser., 18 (1965): 46–63.

Castle, Egerton. Schools and Masters of Fence: From the Middle Ages to the End of the Eighteenth Century. London, 1893.

Celier, Léonce. "Les Moeurs rurales au xvᵉ siècle d'après les lettres de rémission," *Bulletin philologique et historique (jusqu'à 1715) du Comité des Travaux Historiques et Scientifiques*, 1958, pp. 411–19.

Chadwyck-Healey, Charles E. H., and Lionel Landon, eds. Somersetshire Pleas, Civil and Criminal, from the Rolls of the Itinerant Justices. 4 vols. Somerset Record Society, 11, 36, 41, 44. London, 1897–1930.

Champin, Marie-Madeleine. "Un Cas typique du justice bailliagère: la criminalité dans le bailliage d'Alençon de 1715 à 1745," *Annales de Normandie*, 22 (1972): 47–84.

Chew, Helena M., and Martin Weinbaum, eds. The London Eyre of 1244. London Record Society, 6. London, 1970.

Child, Francis James, ed. The English and Scottish Popular Ballads. 5 vols. Boston, 1898.

Clanchy, M. T., ed. The Roll and Writ File of the Berkshire Eyre of 1248. Publications of the Selden Society, 90. London, 1973.

Clay, Charles Travis, ed. Three Yorkshire Assize Rolls for the Reigns of King John and King Henry III. Yorkshire Archaeological Society, Record Series, 44. Leeds, 1911.

Coleman, Emily R. "L'Infanticide dans le haut moyen âge," *Annales: Economies, Sociétés, Civilisations*, 29 (1974): 315–35.

Coser, Lewis A. Continuities in the Study of Social Conflict. New York, 1967.

Cox, J. Charles. The Sanctuaries and Sanctuary Seekers of Medieval England. London, 1911.

Cronne, H. A. The Borough of Warwick in the Middle Ages. Dugdale Society Occasional Papers, No. 10. Oxford, 1951.

Curtis, Evelyn. Crime in Bedfordshire, 1600–1688. Elstow Moot Hall Leaflet, No. 4. Elstow, 1957.

Dale, Marian K., ed. Court Roll of Chalgrave Manor, 1278–1313. Bedfordshire Historical Record Society, 28. Streatley, 1950.

Daniels, David N., Marshall F. Gilula, and Frank M. Ochberg, eds. Violence and the Struggle for Existence, Boston, 1970.

Darby, H. C. The Medieval Fenland. Cambridge, Eng., 1940.

Davenport, Frances Gardiner. The Economic Development of a Norfolk Manor, 1086–1565. Cambridge, Eng., 1906.

Denholm-Young, Noel. "The Tournament in the Thirteenth Century," in R. W. Hunt, W. A. Pantin, and R. W. Southern, eds., Studies in Medieval History Presented to Frederick Maurice Powicke. Oxford, 1948.

DeWindt, E. B. Land and People in Holywell-cum-Needingworth: Structures of Tenure and Patterns of Social Organization in an East Anglian Midlands Village. Toronto, 1972.

Dictionary of National Biography. Ed. by Leslie Stephen and Sidney Lee. 66 vols. London, 1885–1901.

Diceto, Ralph de. Opera historica: The Historical Works of Master Ralph de Diceto, Dean of London. Ed. by William Stubbs. 2 vols. RS, London, 1876.

Dimier, A. "Violences, rixes et homicides chez les Cisterciens," Revue des sciences religieuses, 46 (1972): 38–57.

Dodwell, Barbara. "The Free Peasantry of East Anglia in Domesday," Norfolk Archaeology, 27 (1941): 145–57.

———. "The Free Tenantry of the Hundred Rolls," Economic History Review, 14 (1944): 163–71.

———. "Holdings and Inheritance in Medieval East Anglia," Economic History Review, 2d ser. 20 (1967): 53–66.

Dollard, John, Neal E. Miller, Leonard W. Doob, O. H. Mowrer, and Robert R. Sears, in collaboration with Cleelan S. Ford, Carl Iver Hovland, and Richard T. Sollenberger. Frustration and Aggression. New Haven, 1961.

Douglas, David C. The Social Structure of Medieval East Anglia. Oxford, 1927.

Drinkwater, C. H., ed. "Records of Proceedings Before the Coroners of Salop (A.D. 1295 to 1306, Temp. Edw. I)—A Fragment," Transactions of the Shropshire Archaeological and Natural History Society, 3d ser., 5 (1905): 148–87.

Driver, Edwin D. "Interaction and Criminal Homicide in India," Social Forces, 40 (1961–62): 153–58.

DuBoulay, F. R. H. The Lordship of Canterbury: An Essay on Medieval Society. London, 1966.

———. Medieval Bexley. Bexleyheath, 1961.

Ekwall, Eilert. Studies on the Population of Medieval London. Kungl. Vitterhets Historie och Antikvitets Adademiens Handlingar, Filologisk-Filosofiska Serien, 2. Stockholm, 1956.

Elwin, Verrier. Maria Murder and Suicide. 2d ed. Bombay, 1950.

Emmison, F. G. Elizabethan Life: Disorder. Chelmsford, 1970.

Faith, Rosamund Jane. "Peasant Families and Inheritance Customs in Medieval England," Agricultural History Review, 14 (1966): 77–95.

Farmer, D. L. "Some Grain Price Movements in Thirteenth-Century England," Economic History Review, 2d ser., 10 (1957–58): 207–20.

———. "Some Livestock Price Movements in Thirteenth-Century England," *Economic History Review*, 2d ser., 22 (1969): 1–16.
Farr, Brenda, ed. The Rolls of Highworth Hundred, 1257–1287. 2 vols. Wiltshire Archaeological and Natural History Society, Records Branch, 21, 22. Trowbridge, 1966–68.
FitzThedmar, Arnold. De antiquis legibus liber: cronica maiorum et vicecomitum Londoniarum et quedam que contingebant temporibus illis ab anno MCLXXVIII ad annum MCCLXXIV, cum appendice. Ed. by Thomas Stapleton. Camden Society, 34. London, 1846.
Florence of Worcester. Chronicon ex chronicis ab adventu Hengesti et Horsi in Britanniam usque ad annum MCXVII, cui acceserunt continuationes duae, quarum una ad annum MCXLI, altera, nunc primum typis vulgata, ad annum MCCXCV perducta. Ed. by Benjamin Thorpe. 2 vols. English Historical Society. London, 1848–49.
Fowler, G. Herbert. Bedfordshire in 1086: An Analysis and Synthesis of Domesday Book. Quarto Memoirs of the Bedfordshire Historical Record Society, 1. Aspley Guise, 1922.
Fowler, G. Herbert, ed. Calendar of the Roll of the Justices in Eyre, 1247. Bedfordshire Historical Record Society, 21. Aspley Guise, 1939.
———. Roll of the Justices in Eyre at Bedford, 1202. Bedfordshire Historical Record Society, 1. Aspley Guise, 1913.
———. Roll of the Justices in Eyre at Bedford, 1227. Bedfordshire Historical Record Society, 3. Aspley Guise, 1916.
Fransson, Gustav. Middle English Surnames of Occupation, 1100–1350, with an Excursus on Toponymical Surnames. Lund Studies in English, 3. Lund, 1935.
Fraser, C. M., and K. Emsley. "Justice in North East England, 1256–1356," *American Journal of Legal History*, 15 (1971): 163–85.
Friedrich, Paul. "Assumptions underlying Tarascan Political Homicide," *Psychiatry*, 25 (1962): 315–27.
———. "A Mexican Cacicazago," *Ethnology*, 4 (1965): 190–209.
Gauvard, Claude, and Altan Gokalp. "Les Conduites de bruit et leur signification à la fin du moyen âge," *Annales: Economies, Sociétés, Civilisations*, 29 (1974): 693–704.
Gegot, Jean-Claude. "Étude par sondage de la criminalité dans le bailliage de Falaise (xviie–xviiie siècle): criminalité diffuse ou société criminelle?," *Annales de Normandie*, 16 (1966): 103–64.
Gervase of Canterbury. The Historical Works of Gervase of Canterbury. Ed. by William Stubbs. 2 vols. RS, London, 1879–80.
Giraldus Cambrensis. Opera. Ed. by J. S. Brewer, James F. Dimock, and George F. Warner. 8 vols. RS, London, 1861–91.
Glasscock, R. E. "The Distribution of Lay Wealth in Kent, Surrey, and Sussex in the Early Fourteenth Century," *Archaeologia Cantiana*, 80 (1965): 61–68.
——— . The Distribution of Lay Wealth in South-East England in the

Early Fourteenth Century. 2 vols. Ph.D. thesis, University of London, 1963.

———. "The Distribution of Wealth in East Anglia in the Early Fourteenth Century," *Transactions of the Institute of British Geographers*, 32 (1963):113–23.

Gluckman, Max. Custom and Conflict in Africa. Oxford, 1965.

———. "The Peace in the Feud," *Past and Present*, 8 (1955): 1–14.

———. Politics, Law and Ritual in Tribal Society. Oxford, 1965.

Godber, Joyce. History of Bedfordshire, 1066–1888. Luton, 1969.

Godber, Joyce, ed. "Roll of Bedfordshire Supervisors of the Peace, 1314," in Harrold Priory, A Twelfth Century Dispute and other Articles. Bedfordshire Historical Record Society, 32. Streatley, 1952.

Gold, Martin. "Suicide, Homicide and the Socialization of Aggression," *American Journal of Sociology*, 63 (1957–58): 651–61.

Grand, Roger. "Justice criminelle, procédure et peines dans les villes aux xiiie et xive siècles," *Bibliothèque de l'Ecole des Chartes*, 102 (1941): 51–108.

Gransden, Antonia, ed. and trans. The Chronicle of Bury St. Edmunds, 1212–1301. London, 1964.

Gras, Norman Scott Brien, and Ethel Culbert Gras. The Economic and Social History of an English Village: Crawley, Hampshire, A.D. 909–1928. Cambridge, Mass., 1930.

Gray, Howard Levi. English Field Systems. Cambridge, Mass., 1915.

Great Britain, PRO. Calendar of the Close Rolls Preserved in the Public Record Office: Edward I. 5 vols. London, 1900–1908.

———. Calendar of Inquisitions Miscellaneous (Chancery) Preserved in the Public Record Office. Vol. 1, 1219–1307. London, 1916.

———. Calendar of the Patent Rolls Preserved in the Public Record Office: Edward I. 4 vols. London, 1898–1901.

———. Calendar of the Patent Rolls Preserved in the Public Record Office: Henry III. 6 vols. London, 1901–13.

———. Close Rolls of the Reign of Henry III Preserved in the Public Record Office. 14 vols. London, 1902–38.

———. Curia Regis Rolls Preserved in the Public Record Office. 15 vols. London, 1922–72.

———. Inquisitions and Assessments Relating to Feudal Aids, with Other Analogous Documents Preserved in the Public Record Office. 6 vols. London, 1899–1920.

———. Liber feodorum: The Book of Fees, Commonly Called Testa de Nevill. 3 vols. London, 1920–31.

Great Britain, Record Commission. Rotuli hundredorum temp. Henrici III & Edwardi I in turri Londiniensi et in curia receptae scaccarii Westmonasterri asservati. 2 vols. London, 1812–18.

———. The Statutes of the Realm. Vol. 1. London, 1810.

Green, Thomas A. "Societal Concepts of Criminal Liability for Homicide in Mediaeval England," *Speculum*, 47 (1972): 669–94.

Gross, Charles, ed. Select Cases from the Coroners' Rolls, A.D.

1265–1413, with a Brief Account of the Office of Coroner. Publications of the Selden Society, 9. London, 1896.

Grosseteste, Robert. Epistolae. Ed. by Henry Richards Luard. RS, London, 1861.

Hackney, Sheldon. "Southern Violence," *American Historical Review,* 74 (1968–69): 905–25.

Hair, P. E. H. "Accidental Death and Suicide in Shropshire, 1780–1809," *Transactions of the Shropshire Archaeological Society,* 59 (1969–70), 63–75.

———. "Deaths from Violence in Britain: A Tentative Secular Survey," *Population Studies: A Journal of Demography,* 25 (1971): 5–24.

———. "Homicide, Infanticide, and Child Assault in Late Tudor Middlesex," *Local Population Studies,* 9 (1972): 43–46.

Hall, G. D. G., ed. Tractatus de legibus et consuetudinibus regni Anglie qui Glanvilla vocatur. London, 1965.

Hallam, H. E. "Further Observations on the Spalding Serf Lists," *Economic History Review,* 2d ser., 16 (1963–64): 338–50.

———. "Some Thirteenth-Century Censuses," *Economic History Review,* 2d ser., 10 (1957–58): 340–61.

Hanawalt, Barbara. See Westman, Barbara Hanawalt.

Hanley, H. A., and C. W. Chalklin, eds. "The Kent Lay Subsidy Roll of 1334/5," in Kent Records: Documents Illustrative of Medieval Kentish Society, ed. by F. R. H. DuBoulay. Kent Archaeological Society, Records Publication Committee, 18. Ashford, 1964.

Harley, J. B. "Population Trends and Agricultural Developments from the Warwickshire Hundred Rolls of 1279," *Economic History Review,* 2d ser., 11 (1958–59): 8–18.

———. "The Settlement Geography of Early Medieval Warwickshire," *Transactions of the Institute of British Geographers,* 34 (1964): 115–30.

Harvey, P. D. A. A Medieval Oxfordshire Village: Cuxham, 1240 to 1400. Oxford, 1965.

Henry, Andrew F., and James F. Short, Jr. Suicide and Homicide: Some Economic, Sociological and Psychological Aspects of Aggression. Glencoe, Ill., 1954.

Hill, Rosalind M. T., ed. The Rolls and Register of Bishop Oliver de Sutton, 1280–1289. 6 vols. Publications of the Lincoln Record Society, 39, 43, 48, 52, 60, 64. Hereford, 1948–69.

Hilton, R. H. The English Peasantry in the Later Middle Ages. Oxford, 1975.

———. A Medieval Society: The West Midlands at the End of the Thirteenth Century. London, 1966.

———. "The Origins of Robin Hood," *Past and Present,* 14 (1958): 30–44.

———. Social Structure of Rural Warwickshire in the Middle Ages. Dugdale Society Occasional Papers, No. 9. Oxford, 1950.

Hilton, R. H., ed. The Stoneleigh Leger Book. Publications of the Dugdale Society, 24. Oxford, 1960.

Hobbs, A. H. "Criminality in Philadelphia: 1790–1810 Compared with 1937," *American Sociological Review,* 8 (1943): 198–202.

Hobsbawm, E. J. Bandits. Harmondsworth, 1972.

———. "Social Bandits: A Reply," *Comparative Studies in Society and History,* 14 (1972): 503–5.

Holt, J. C. "The Origins and Audience of the Ballads of Robin Hood," *Past and Present,* 18 (1960): 89–110.

———. "Robin Hood: Some Comments," *Past and Present,* 19 (1961): 16–18.

Homans, George E. English Villagers of the Thirteenth Century. Cambridge, Mass., 1941.

———. "Partible Inheritance of Villagers' Holdings," *Economic History Review,* 8 (1937–38): 48–56.

Hopkins, A., ed. Selected Rolls of the Chester City Courts: Late Thirteenth and Early Fourteenth Centuries. Chetham Society, Remains Historical and Literary Connected with the Palatine Counties of Lancaster and Chester, 3d ser., 2. Manchester, 1950.

Hoskins, W. G. The Midland Peasant: The Economic and Social History of a Leicestershire Village. London, 1957.

———. "Murder and Sudden Death in Medieval Wigston," *Transactions of the Leicestershire Archaeological Society,* 21 (1940–41): 175–86.

Howlett, Richard, ed. Chronicles of the Reigns of Stephen, Henry II, and Richard I. 4 vols. RS, London, 1884–89.

Hudson, William, ed. Leet Jurisdiction in the City of Norwich During the XIIIth and XIVth Centuries, with a Short Notice of Its Later History and Decline, from Rolls in the Possession of the Corporation. Publications of the Selden Society, 5. London, 1892.

Hudson, William, and John Cottingham Tingey, eds. The Records of the City of Norwich. 2 vols. Norwich, 1906–10.

Hunnisett, R. F. The Medieval Coroner. Cambridge, Eng., 1961.

———. "The Medieval Coroners' Rolls," *American Journal of Legal History,* 3 (1959): 95–124, 205–21, 324–59.

———. "The Origins of the Office of Coroner," *Transactions of the Royal Historical Society,* 5th ser., 8 (1958): 85–104.

———. "Pleas of the Crown and the Coroner," *Bulletin of the Institute of Historical Research,* 32 (1959): 117–37.

———. "The Reliability of Inquisitions as Historical Evidence," in D. A. Bullough and R. L. Storey, eds., The Study of Medieval Records: Essays in Honour of Kathleen Major. Oxford, 1971.

Hunnisett, R. F., ed. Bedfordshire Coroners' Rolls. Bedfordshire Historical Record Society, 41. Streatley, 1961.

———. "An Early Coroner's Roll," *Bulletin of the Institute of Historical Research,* 30 (1957): 225–31.

Hurnard, Naomi D. The King's Pardon for Homicide Before A.D. 1307. Oxford, 1969.

Jenkins, J. G., ed. Calendar of the Roll of the Justices on Eyre, 1227.

Publications of the Buckinghamshire Archaeological Society, Records Branch, 6. Bedford, 1945.

Jocelin de Brakelond. Cronica Jocelini de Brakelonda de rebus gestis Samsonis abbatis monasterii sancti Edmundi. Ed. and trans. by H. E. Butler. New York, 1949.

John de Oxenedes. Chronica. Ed. by Henry Ellis. RS, London, 1859.

Jolliffe, J. E. A. Pre-Feudal England: The Jutes. London, 1933.

Jones, G. I. Basutoland Medicine Murder: A Report on the Recent Outbreak of "Diretlo" Murders in Basutoland. London, 1951.

Jones, Schuyler. Men of Influence in Nuristan: A Study of Social Control and Dispute Settlement in Waigal Valley, Afghanistan. London, 1974.

Kaye, J. M., ed. Placita corone, or, La Corone pledee devant justices. Selden Society Supplementary Series, 4. London, 1966.

Keen, Maurice. "Robin Hood—Peasant or Gentleman?," *Past and Present*, 19 (1961): 7–15.

Kellum, Barbara A. "Infanticide in England in the Later Middle Ages," *History of Childhood Quarterly*, 1 (1974): 367–88.

Kimball, Elisabeth G., ed. Sessions of the Peace for Bedfordshire, 1355–1359, 1363–1364. Bedfordshire Historical Record Society, 48. London, 1969.

Kirke, Henry. "A Derbyshire Brawl in the 15th Century," *Journal of the Derbyshire Archaeological and Natural History Society*, 24 (1902): 78–81.

Knowles, David, ed. Decreta Lanfranci monachis Cantuariensibus transmissa. London, 1951.

Kopytoff, Igor. "Extension of Conflict as a Method of Conflict Resolution among the Suku of the Congo," *Journal of Conflict Resolution*, 5 (1961): 61–69.

Kosminsky, E. A. "The Evolution of Feudal Rent in England from the XIth to the XIVth Centuries," *Past and Present*, 7 (1955): 12–36.

———. "Services and Money Rents in the Thirteenth Century," *Economic History Review*, 5 no. 2 (1934–35): 24–45.

———. Studies in the Agrarian History of England in the Thirteenth Century. Oxford, 1956.

Lanhers, Yvonne. "Crimes et criminels au xive siècle," *Revue historique*, 240 (1968): 325–38.

Latham, R. E., and C. A. F. Meekings, eds. "The *Veredictum* of Chippenham Hundred," in N. J. Williams, ed., Collectanea. Wiltshire Archaeological and Natural History Society, Records Branch, 12. Devizes, 1956.

Levy, Robert I. "On Getting Angry in the Society Islands," in William Caudill and Tsung-yi Lin, eds., Mental Health Research in Asia and the Pacific. Honolulu, 1969.

Lipman, V. D. The Jews of Medieval Norwich. London, 1967.

Livett, Greville M. "Mediaeval Rochester," *Archaeologia Cantiana*, 21 (1895): 17–72.

Longrais, F. Joüon des. "Le Statut de la femme en Angleterre dans le droit commune médiéval," in La Femme, 2ᵉ partie. Recueils de la Société Jean Bodin, 12. Brussels, 1962.

Longstaffe, W. H., and J. Booth, eds. Halmota prioratus Dunelmensis: Containing Extracts from the Halmote or Manor Rolls of the Prior and Convent of Durham, A.D. 1296–A.D. 1384. Surtees Society, 82. Durham, 1889.

Lorcin, Marie-Thérèse. "Les Paysans et la justice dans la région lyonnaise aux xivᵉ et xvᵉ siècles," Le Moyen Age, 74 (1968): 269–300.

Luard, Henry Richards, ed. Annales monastici. 5 vols. RS, London, 1864–69.

Macray, William Dunn, ed. Chronicon abbatiae de Evesham, ad annum 1418. RS, London, 1863.

Maitland, Frederic William, ed. Pleas of the Crown for the County of Gloucester Before the Abbot of Reading and His Fellows, Justices Itinerant, in the Fifth Year of the Reign of King Henry III and the Year of Grace 1221. London, 1884.

———. Select Pleas of the Crown. Publications of the Selden Society, 1. London, 1888.

———. Three Rolls of the King's Court in the Reign of King Richard the First, A.D. 1194–1195. Publications of the Pipe Roll Society, 14. London, 1891.

Maitland, Frederic William, L. W. V. Harcourt, and W. C. Bolland, eds. Year Books of Edward II: The Eyre of Kent, 6&7 Edward II A.D. 1313–1314. 3 vols. Publications of the Selden Society, 24, 27, 29. London, 1910–13.

Malinowski, Bronislaw. Crime and Custom in Savage Society. Totowa, N.J., 1972.

Mandy, W. H., ed. "A Kentish Hundred: Pleas of the Crown for the Hundred of Ruxley," Journal of the British Archaeological Association, n.s. 22 (1916): 245–54.

Mannyng, Robert, of Brunne. "Handlyng Synne," A.D. 1303, with Those Parts of the Anglo-French Treatise on Which It Was Founded, William of Wadington's "Manuel des Pechiez." Ed. by Frederick J. Furnivall. 2 vols. Early English Text Society, Original Series, 119, 123. London, 1901–3.

Margot, Alain. "La Criminalité dans le bailliage de Mamers, 1695–1750," Annales de Normandie, 22 (1972): 185–224.

Martines, Lauro, ed. Violence and Civil Disorder in Italian Cities, 1200–1500. Berkeley, Calif., 1972.

Massingberd, William Oswald, ed. Court Rolls of the Manor of Ingoldmells in the County of Lincoln. London, 1902.

May, Alfred N. "An Index of Thirteenth Century Peasant Impoverishment? Manor Court Fines," Economic History Review, 2d ser., 26 (1973): 389–402.

Meekings, C. A. F., ed. Crown Pleas of the Wiltshire Eyre, 1249. Wiltshire Archaeological and Natural History Society, Records Branch, 16. Devizes, 1961.

Meyer, Paul, ed. L'Histoire de Guillaume le Maréchal, comte de Striguil et de Pembroke, régent d'Angleterre de 1216 à 1219: poème français. 3 vols. Société de l'Histoire de France. Paris, 1891–1903.

Michel, Dan. Ayenbite of Inwyt, or, Remorse of Conscience, in the Kentish Dialect, 1340 A.D. Ed. by Richard Morris. Early English Text Society, 23. London, 1864.

Middleton, Arthur E. Sir Gilbert de Middleton, and the Part He Took in the Rebellion in the North of England in 1317. Newcastle-upon-Tyne, 1918.

Morey, Adrian. Batholomew of Exeter: Bishop and Canonist. Cambridge, Eng., 1937.

Morris, Terence, and Louis Blom-Cooper. Murder in Microcosm. London, 1961.

Morris, William Alfred. The Frankpledge System. New York, 1910.

Murray, K. M. E. The Constitutional History of the Cinque Ports. Manchester, 1935.

Nash, June. "Death as a Way of Life: The Increasing Resort to Homicide in a Maya Indian Community," *American Anthropologist*, n.s., 69 (1967): 455–70.

Nicholas, David M. "Crime and Punishment in Fourteenth-Century Ghent," *Revue Belge de philologie et d'histoire*, 48 (1970): 289–334, 1141–76.

Oschinsky, Dorothea, ed. Walter of Henley and Other Treatises on Estate Management and Accounting. Oxford, 1971.

Page, Frances M. "The Customary Poor-Law of Three Cambridgeshire Manors," *Cambridge Historical Journal*, 3 (1929–30): 125–33.

Page, William, ed. Three Early Assize Rolls for the County of Northumberland, Saec. XIII. Surtees Society, 88. Durham, 1891.

Palmer, W. M., ed. The Assizes Held at Cambridge A.D. 1260, Being a Condensed Translation of Assize Roll 82 in the Public Record Office. Linton, 1930.

Paris, Matthew. Chronica majora. Ed. by Henry Richards Luard. 7 vols. RS, London, 1872–83.

Parker, John, ed. A Calendar of the Lancashire Assize Rolls Preserved in the Public Record Office, London. 2 vols. Lancashire and Cheshire Record Society, 47, 49. Manchester, 1904–5.

Pearson, F. S., ed. "Records of a Ruridecanal Court of 1300," in Collectanea, ed. by Sidney Graves Hamilton. Worcestershire Historical Society. London, 1912.

Pepitone, Albert, and George Reichling. "Group Cohesiveness and the Expression of Hostility," in Neil J. Smelser and William T. Smelser, eds., Personality and Social Systems. New York, 1963.

Pike, Luke Owen. A History of Crime in England. 2 vols. London, 1873–76.

Platelle, H. "Moeurs populaires dans la seigneurie de Saint-Amand d'après les documents judiciaires de la fin du moyen âge," *Revuè Mabillon*, 48 (1958): 20–39.

Pollak, Otto. The Criminality of Women. Philadelphia, 1950.

Pollock, Frederick, and F. W. Maitland. The History of English Law Before the Time of Edward I. 2 vols. 2d ed. reissued (first published 1923). Cambridge, Eng., 1968.

Power, Eileen. "The Position of Women," in C. G. Crump and E. F. Jacob, eds., The Legacy of the Middle Ages. Oxford, 1926.

Powicke, F. M., and C. R. Cheney, eds. Councils and Synods, with Other Documents Relating to the English Church, A.D. 1205–1313. Vol. 2. Oxford, 1964.

Pugh, Ralph B. Imprisonment in Medieval England. Cambridge, Eng., 1968.

———. Some Reflections of a Medieval Criminologist. London, 1973.

Pugh, Ralph B., ed. Court Rolls of the Wiltshire Manors of Adam de Stratton. Wiltshire Archaeological and Natural History Society, Records Branch, 24. Devizes, 1970.

Raftis, J. A. "The Concentration of Responsibility in Five Villages," *Mediaeval Studies*, 28 (1966): 92–118.

———. "Social Structures in Five East Midland Villages: A Study of Possibilities in the Use of Court Roll Data," *Economic History Review*, 2d ser., 18 (1965): 83–100.

———. Tenure and Mobility: Studies in the Social History of the Mediaeval English Village. Toronto, 1964.

Raine, James, ed. Historical Papers and Letters from the Northern Registers. RS, London, 1873.

Ratcliff, S. C., ed. Elton Manorial Records, 1279–1361. Trans. by D. M. Gregory. The Roxburghe Club, 208. Cambridge, Eng., 1946.

Raymond de Peñaforte. Summa Sancti Raymond de Peñaforte Barcinonensis . . . de poenitentia et matrimonio. Farnborough, 1967. Reprint of 1603 Rome edition.

Reynolds, Susan, ed. "Pleas in the Liberty of the Abbot of Battle at Bromham, 1289," in N. J. Williams, ed., Collectanea. Wiltshire Archaeological and Natural History Society, Records Branch, 12. Devizes, 1956.

Richardson, H. G. "The Parish Clergy of the Thirteenth and Fourteenth Centuries," *Transactions of the Royal Historical Society*, 3d ser., 6 (1912): 89–128.

Riley, Henry Thomas, ed. Liber albus: The White Book of the City of London, Compiled A.D. 1419 by John Carpenter, Common Clerk, and Richard Whittington, Mayor. London, 1861.

———. Memorials of London and London Life in the XIIIth, XIVth, and XVth Centuries, Being a Series of Abstracts, Local, Social, and Political, from the Early Archives of the City of London. A.D. 1270–1419. London, 1868.

————. Munimenta Gildhallae Londoniensis: Liber Albus, Liber Custumarum, et Liber Horn. 3 vols. RS, London, 1859–62.

Rishanger, William. Chronica et annales, regnantibus Henrico Tertio et Edwardo Primo, A.D. 1259–1307. Ed. by Henry Thomas Riley. RS, London, 1865.

Robert of Flamborough. Liber poenitentialis: A Critical Edition with Introduction and Notes. Ed. by J. J. Francis Firth. Toronto, 1971.

Roberts, B. K. "A Study of Medieval Colonization in the Forest of Arden, Warwickshire," *Agricultural History Review*, 16 (1968): 101–13.

Roden, David. "Demesne Farming in the Chiltern Hills," *Agricultural History Review*, 17 (1969): 9–23.

————. "Fragmentation of Farms and Fields in the Chiltern Hills: Thirteenth Century and Later," *Mediaeval Studies*, 31 (1969): 225–38.

Roden, David, and A. R. H. Baker. "Field Systems of the Chiltern Hills and of Parts of Kent from the Late Thirteenth to the Early Seventeenth Century," *Transactions of the Institute of British Geographers*, 38 (1966): 73–88.

Roger de Houedene. Chronica. Ed. by William Stubbs. 4 vols. RS, London, 1868–71.

Rogers, J. E. Thorold, ed. Oxford City Documents, Financial and Judicial, 1268–1665. Oxford Historical Society, 18. Oxford, 1891.

Russell, Josiah Cox. British Medieval Population. Albuquerque, N.M., 1948.

————. "Demographic Limitations of the Spalding Serf Lists," *Economic History Review*, 2d ser., 15 (1962–63): 138–44.

Rye, Walter. "The Riot Between the Monks and Citizens of Norwich in 1272," *Norfolk Antiquarian Miscellany*, 2 (1883): 17–89.

Salter, H. E., ed. Records of Mediaeval Oxford: Coroners' Inquests, the Walls of Oxford, Etc. Oxford, 1912.

————. Snappe's Formulary and Other Records. Oxford Historical Society, 80. Oxford, 1924.

Samaha, Joel. Law and Order in Historical Perspective: The Case of Elizabethan Essex. New York, 1974.

Searle, Eleanor. Lordship and Community: Battle Abbey and Its Banlieu, 1066–1538. Toronto, 1974.

Sharpe, Reginald R. London and the Kingdom. 3 vols. London, 1894–95.

Sharpe, Reginald R., ed. Calendar of Coroners' Rolls of the City of London, A.D. 1300–1378. London, 1913.

————. Calendar of Letter-Books: Letter-Book B. London, 1900.

Sheehan, Michael M. "The Formation and Stability of Marriage in Fourteenth-Century England: Evidence of an Ely Register," *Mediaeval Studies*, 33 (1971): 228–64.

Shirley, W. W., ed. Royal and Other Historical Letters Illustrative of the Reign of Henry III, from the Originals in the Public Record Office. 2 vols. RS, London, 1862–66.

Short, J. F., Jr., and Marvin E. Wolfgang, eds. Collective Violence. Chicago, 1972.

Stenton, Doris Mary, ed. The Earliest Lincolnshire Assize Rolls, A.D. 1202–1209. Publications of the Lincoln Record Society, 22. Lincoln, 1926.

————. The Earliest Northamptonshire Assize Rolls, A.D. 1202 and 1203. Publications of the Northamptonshire Record Society, 5. Lincoln, 1930.

————. Pleas Before the King or His Justices, 1198–1212. 4 vols. Publications of the Selden Society, 67, 68, 83, 84. London, 1952–67.

————. Rolls of the Justices in Eyre, Being the Rolls of Pleas and Assizes for Gloucestershire, Warwickshire and Staffordshire, 1221, 1222. Publications of the Selden Society, 59. London, 1940.

————. Rolls of the Justices in Eyre, Being the Rolls of Pleas and Assizes for Lincolnshire, 1218–9, and Worcestershire, 1221. Publications of the Selden Society, 53. London, 1934.

————. Rolls of the Justices in Eyre, Being the Rolls of Pleas and Assizes for Yorkshire in 3 Henry III, 1218–9. Publications of the Selden Society, 56. London, 1937.

Stevenson, Joseph, ed. Chronica de Mailros, e codice unico in bibliotheca Cottoniana servato, nunc iterum in lucem edita. Publications of the Bannatyne Club, 49. Edinburgh, 1835.

Stewart-Brown, Ronald, ed. Calendar of County Court, City Court, and Eyre Rolls of Chester, 1259–1297, with an Inquest of Military Service, 1288. Chetham Society, Remains Historical and Literary Connected with the Palatine Counties of Lancester and Chester, n.s., 84. Manchester, 1925.

Stones, E. L. G. "The Folvilles of Ashby-Folville, Leicestershire, and Their Associates in Crime, 1326–1347," *Transactions of the Royal Historical Society*, 5th ser. 7 (1957): 117–36.

Straus, Jacqueline H., and Murray A. Straus. "Suicide, Homicide, and Social Structure in Ceylon," *American Journal of Sociology*, 58 (1952–53): 461–69.

Stubbs, William, ed. Chronicles of the Reigns of Edward I and II. 2 vols. RS, London, 1882–83.

Svalastoga, Kaare. "Homicide and Social Contact in Denmark," *American Journal of Sociology*, 62 (1956–57): 37–41.

Tanner, R. E. S. Homicide in Uganda, 1964. Crime in East Africa, Vol. 1. Uppsala, 1970.

————. Three Studies in East African Criminology. Crime in East Africa. Vol. 2. Uppsala, 1970.

Taylor, Arnold J., ed. Records of the Barony and Honour of the Rape of Lewes. Sussex Record Society, 44. Lewes, 1940.

Taylor, Mary Margaret, ed. Some Sessions of the Peace in Cambridgeshire in the Fourteenth Century, 1340, 1380–1383. Cambridge Antiquarian Society. Cambridge, 1942.

Thirsk, Joan, ed. *The Agrarian History of England and Wales*. Vol. 4, *1500–1640*. Cambridge, Eng., 1967.

Thomas, A. H., ed. Calendar of the Early Mayor's Court Rolls Preserved Among the Archives of the Corporation of the City of London at the Guildhall A.D. 1298–1307. London, 1924.

Thomas of Chobham. Summa confessorum. Ed. by F. Broomfield. Analecta Mediaevalia Namurcensia, 25. Louvain, 1968.

Thompson, A. Hamilton, ed. Northumberland Pleas from the Curia Regis and Assize Rolls, 1198–1272. Publications of the Newcastle Upon Tyne Records Committee, 2. Newcstle upon Tyne, 1922.

Thompson, E. P. " 'Rough Music': le charivari anglais," *Annales: Economies, Sociétés, Civilisations*, 27 (1972): 285–312.

Thompson, Edward Maunde, ed. Customary of the Benedictine Monasteries of Saint Augustine, Canterbury, and Saint Peter, Westminster. 2 vols. Henry Bradshaw Society, 23, 24. London, 1902–4.

Thompson, I. A. A. "A Map of Crime in Sixteenth-Century Spain," *Economic History Review*, 2d ser., 21 (1968): 244–67.

Thompson, Walter Sinclair, ed. A Lincolnshire Assize Roll for 1298 (PRO Assize Roll No. 505). Publications of the Lincoln Record Society, 36. Hereford, 1949.

Thornley, Isabel D. "Sanctuary in Medieval London," *Journal of the British Archaeological Association*, n.s., 38 (1932): 293–315.

Thrupp, Sylvia. The Merchant Class of Medieval London, 1300–1500. Chicago, 1948.

Titow, J. Z. English Rural Society, 1200–1350. London, 1969.

———. "Some Differences Between Manors and Their Effects on the Condition of the Peasant in the Thirteenth Century," *Agricultural History Review*, 10 (1962): 1–13.

Tobias, John J. Crime and Industrial Society in the Nineteenth Century. Harmondsworth, 1972.

Tout, T. F. Mediaeval Forgers and Forgeries. Manchester, 1920.

Tout, T. F., and Hilda Johnstone, eds. State Trials of the Reign of Edward the First, 1289–1293. Royal Historical Society, Camden 3d ser., 9. London, 1906.

Trasselli, Carmelo. "Criminalité et moralité en Sicile au début de l'époque moderne," *Annales: Economies, Sociétés, Civilisations*, 28 (1973): 226–46.

Trivet, Nicholas. Annales sex regum Angliae, qui a comitibus Andegavensibus originem traxerunt, A.D. MCXXXVI–MCCCVII. Ed. by Thomas Hog. English Historical Society. London, 1845.

Vaultier, Roger. Le Folklore pendant la Guerre de Cent Ans d'après les lettres de rémission du Trésor des Chartes. Paris, 1965.

Veale, Elspeth M. "Craftsmen and the Economy of London in the Fourteenth Century," in A. E. J. Hollaender and William Kellaway, eds., Studies in London History Presented to Philip Edmund Jones. London, 1969.

Verkko, Veli. "Static and Dynamic 'Laws' of Sex and Homicide," in Studies in Homicide, ed. by Marvin E. Wolfgang. New York, 1967.

The Victoria History of the County of Bedford. Ed. by H. Arthur Doubleday and William Page. 3 vols. Westminster, 1904–12.

The Victoria History of the County of Kent. Ed. by William Page. 3 vols. London, 1908–32.

The Victoria History of the County of Norfolk. Ed. by H. Arthur Doubleday and William Page. 2 vols. Westminster, 1901–6.

The Victoria History of the County of Oxford. Ed. by L. F. Salzman, William Page, et al. 10 vols. London, 1907–72.

The Victoria History of the County of Warwick. Ed. by H. Arthur Doubleday, William Page, L. F. Salzman, and P. Styles. 8 vols. London, 1904–69.

The Victoria History of the County of York. Ed. by William Page. 3 vols. London, 1907–13.

Vincent of Beauvais. De eruditione filiorum nobilium. Ed. by Arpad Steiner. Mediaeval Academy of America. Cambridge, Mass., 1938.

Walsingham, Thomas. Gesta abbatum monasterii sancti Albani. Ed. by Henry Thomas Riley. 3 vols. RS, London, 1867–69.

Walter de Coventria. Memoriale fratris Walteri de Coventria: The Historical Collections of Walter of Coventry. Ed. by William Stubbs. 2 vols. RS, London, 1872–73.

Walter of Guisborough. Chronicle. Ed. by Harry Rothwell. Royal Historical Society. Camden Society 3d ser., 89. London, 1957.

Weinbaum, Martin, ed. The London Eyre of 1276. London Record Society, 12. Chatham, 1976.

Weinert, Richard S. "Violence in Pre-Modern Societies: Rural Colombia," *American Political Science Review*, 60 (1966): 340–47.

Westman, Barbara Hanawalt. "The Female Felon in Fourteenth Century England," *Viator*, 5 (1974): 253–68.

———. "The Peasant Family and Crime in Fourteenth Century England," *Journal of British Studies*, 13, No. 2 (1974): 1–18.

———. A Study of Crime in Norfolk, Yorkshire and Northamptonshire, 1300–1348. Ph.D. thesis, University of Michigan, 1970.

Williams, Gwyn A. Medieval London: From Commune to Capital. London, 1970.

Wolfgang, Marvin E. Patterns in Criminal Homicide. New York, 1966.

Wolfgang, Marvin E., and Franco Ferracuti. The Subculture of Violence: Towards an Integrated Theory in Criminology. London, 1967.

Wood, Arthur Lewis. "Crime and Aggression in Changing Ceylon: A Sociological Analysis of Homicide, Suicide, and Economic Crime," *Transactions of the American Philosophical Society*, n.s., 51, pt. 8 (1961).

Index

Index